The Unshaming Way

A Compassionate Guide to Dismantling Shame

Heal from trauma, unlearn self-blame, and reclaim your story

David Bedrick

North Atlantic Books

Huichin, unceded Ohlone land
Berkeley, California

Published by
North Atlantic Books
Huichin, unceded Ohlone land
Berkeley, California

Cover design by Jason Arias
Book design by Happenstance Type-O-Rama

Printed in Canada

The Unshaming Way: A Compassionate Guide to Dismantling Shame is sponsored and published by North Atlantic Books, an educational nonprofit based in the unceded Ohlone land Huichin (Berkeley, CA) that collaborates with partners to develop cross-cultural perspectives; nurture holistic views of art, science, the humanities, and healing; and seed personal and global transformation by publishing work on the relationship of body, spirit, and nature.

North Atlantic Books's publications are distributed to the US trade and internationally by Penguin Random House Publisher Services. For further information, visit our website at www.northatlanticbooks.com.

Library of Congress Cataloging-in-Publication Data

Names: Bedrick, David, author.
Title: The unshaming way : how radical witnessing can help us overcome shame, social stigma, / David Bedrick.
Description: Huichin, unceded Ohlone land Berkeley, California : North Atlantic Books, [2024] | Includes bibliographical references and index. | Summary: "A revolutionary 3-part model for dismantling shame: integrate trauma, unlearn self-blame, and reclaim your personal power"— Provided by publisher.
Identifiers: LCCN 2024007799 (print) | LCCN 2024007800 (ebook) | ISBN 9798889840756 (trade paperback) | ISBN 9798889840763 (epub)
Subjects: LCSH: Shame. | Psychic trauma.
Classification: LCC BF575.S45 B44 2024 (print) | LCC BF575.S45 (ebook) | DDC 152.4—dc23/eng/20240329
LC record available at https://lccn.loc.gov/2024007799
LC ebook record available at https://lccn.loc.gov/2024007800

1 2 3 4 5 6 7 8 9 FRIESENS 28 27 26 25 24

Contents

Acknowledgments

Let the beauty you love be what you do.

—JALAL AL-DIN RUMI

Doing beauty is different from doing it right, seeking perfection, or even performing heroic feats. It requires courage, the capacity of the heart, but that too is not enough. One must encounter beauty, allow it to weaken the knees, moisten the eyes. For me, raised as a child where school performance was the bullseye of worthiness, beauty lived in places that I was not. How does one do beauty as a teacher, a friend, a lover, a writer, a walker of this earth? Lisa showed me the beauty of my intelligence, the beauty of my gift, the beauty of my therapeutic practice, the beauty of my vulnerability, the beauty of my nose, eyes, and feet, and the beauty of my wounds. She saw the beauty of my unshaming way and how it compelled me to teach.

Walking by her side, I'm a humble learner who remembers, over and over, that I am not alone, that there's something far better than getting a good grade and any form of mainstream lucre or popularity. While some say one must love oneself before one can love another, I am not an example of this truism. I have learned to love myself because I have been shown a beautiful way, the way the woman I married guided me through (when I was open, not resistant). This book is about unshaming, but the seed of unshaming is loving, and loving for me is doing beauty's bidding. Lisa has incubated and gestated this knowledge with me and in me for the last twenty years.

When I was first approached by a publisher for *The Unshaming Way* (not North Atlantic Books, who is the publisher of this book), I was surprisingly unmoved, as if the wind of depression had breezed by. Lisa asked me, "Why are you not happy? Excited?"

"I don't want this coming year to have another project," I replied, "another weight in the backpack of my climb."

She said, "Why not have Candace Walsh help you?" Candace has been an ally before, is socially on point, is finishing her PhD in creative writing, and is a master craftswoman of essays, poems, and novels.

Due to my conditioned response to spending money, and my sense that I should do it by myself, I resisted. But beauty did her job, pointing me in the direction that Lisa clearly knew was best. Candace and I spoke for a couple of hours nearly every week for over a year. Drafts went back and forth, iterating to a form and language that did more beauty than I could have done alone—a beauty that transformed an interlocking weave of psychological information into a reader-centered journey. Along the way, the beauty of our friendship blossomed further.

For many years, I thought of my parents from the perspective of the abuse and trauma I suffered. I grieved and at times bemoaned my fate, and I crafted a fist ready for combat and eyes unblinded by the shame that blurs our clear vision of the violence we experience as children. It took many years for the love that was pregnant in our relationship to enter that space—a love that had been blotted out by brutality and terror. It wasn't through an intentional process of forgiveness that the love returned; it was through years of walking a path of self-inquiry, following my nighttime dreams for their direction, and being parented by others along the way. Today, I don't feel a conventional gratitude or the impulse to say, "thank you," but rather a simple recognition of the love inheritance hidden behind the generations of trauma that formed Martin and Louise Bedrick, both dead and gone, but who left love seeds for me to plant, nurture, and bring to flower.

I have always had a poet's soul, penning verse to express my feelings and experiences even as a young child. I remember my early intention to write, thinking: "How did my parents get to be this way, when it seems so obvious that their attitudes toward children, feelings, and our great social diversity were offensive to life itself? They must have forgotten what the eyes of the child so readily see. I will also forget; I better write it down." I wrote in verse.

Finding poetic voices along the way also taught me beauty. They were Maya Angelou, whose words made me weep deep; and James Baldwin, who never believed he was beautiful, wounded by his stepfather's ugly assaults, but who showed me America's ugliness and beauty hidden in this country's shadow. Another voice was Coleman Barks, translator of the thirteenth-century mystical poet Jalāl al-Dīn Muḥammad Rūmī. Coleman "unlocked these poems from their cages," as Robert Bly observed, by spending hours on the task daily without a thought of publishing. Lately, it has been Galway Kinnell's native wisdom about life and Mary Oliver's devotion to nature that have lit my way to doing more beauty. Perhaps one day I will live a pure poet's life, with beauty being all.

My life has been made more beautiful by the blessings that only elders can bestow. Thirty-four years ago, Dr. Arny Mindell heard my childhood story and said, "David, come see me." Arny's childlike dreaming eyes always saw who I was becoming. His understanding of the body's intelligence, what he called "the dreambody," is pivotal to my work. His unwavering belief in my nature seeded me with the essence of my vision of unshaming.

Salome Schwarz has been my spiritual friend for eighteen years. Her awareness cuts through the obfuscations of the mundane, guiding me reverently into the deep ocean where my spirit swims. She left her body one year ago; I'm still integrating her ways of knowing. For that and her unwavering love, I am compelled to give back. I prepared a luscious meal for her in my dream the other night. We have both arrived at the place we were meant to be: a place of greater beauty.

Tim McKee, from North Atlantic Books, was given a copy of my book proposal and immediately invited me to dialogue. I felt the high integrity of his publishing mission and alignment with my healing vision, one that cut deeper than the popular psychology of four or seven steps to healing, and one that intimately wove social consciousness into personal healing. Life brought me to the right publisher, and here the word "grateful" is fitting.

Perhaps my greatest teachings have come to me via the thousands of students and clients I've seen over the past thirty years. Step by step they woke me up to my errors and blind spots as well as the greatness of the work I was called to do when I was caught in a sense of self contracted by the trauma of my childhood story. Being a teacher simply does not flower without having students. Thank you; thank you all.

CHAPTER 1

Unshaming Orientation

I grew up in a family marked by violence. While my father's brutality was clear—belts, fists, and harsh words—my mother's denial, dismissal, and gaslighting of the violence had its own, more covert, power. These responses shamed me—led me to distrust my own experience, to ignore or dismiss my hurts later in life, and to think something was wrong with me and my suffering didn't matter, instead of asking myself the question: "What happened that caused me suffering?" As someone who was disbelieved by the person who was supposed to love me in the world, I came away from that situation convinced that people need to be truly witnessed, deeply believed. I didn't just think that we should believe that what a person says is matched by some objective observation. I believed that what a person experiences and how they behave, however irrational it might seem to an onlooker, are worthy and valid, and that the seeming irrationality is like a veil around sacred messages that will emerge, unfold, if you believe in people instead of shaming them.

Asserting this viewpoint at an early age provoked criticisms from both of my parents. My father called me a dreamer, which to him meant *out of touch* and *unrealistic*. My mother told me, "You can't change the world."

Ironically, their efforts to censure me drove me toward my life's purpose. I spent over thirty years studying Jungian psychology and nighttime dreams. (I don't think my father meant that kind of dreaming, but life has its own magic.) I pursued an education in conflict resolution focused on world problems—race, gender, wealth inequality, anti-Semitism—and eventually went to law school hoping to, yes, change the world. I focused on helping women and children navigate domestic conflict, divorce, and custody disputes.

My initial foray into understanding family and social dynamics led me to study organizational psychology at the University of Minnesota. That training formed the basis of a twelve-year effort to change the world by transforming institutions. I consulted with employees of 3M, Honeywell, the United Way, the US Navy, and dozens of other companies before furthering my studies by pursuing clinical training in working with individuals and large-scale conflict at the Process Work Institute, an offshoot of the Jung Institute. There, I became a teacher and adjunct faculty. In the following years, I opened a private practice, taught numerous classes, and wrote three well-received books on body shame, family violence, issues of addiction and power, and psychology's role in social activism. All of these experiences led me to this point: illuminating the ways shame operates—not just for my clients and social media audience, but also for you. Shame hides us both from others and from ourselves, preventing self-awareness as well as self-love.

Unshaming's Promise

In this book, you'll learn how shame is instilled in all of us, mostly at a young, tender age. How to recognize it instead of being run by it. How to *unshame* by dismantling existing internalized shame and preventing further shaming for ourselves and others. How to call shame out as what it is and rob it of its power. As you unshame, you'll also learn what shame has masked: your truths, your gifts, and the life path that was meant for you.

Shame enters us all through small cracks and crevices, sometimes unnoticed. Perhaps you don't like your body. That's bad enough, but then you think, "I'm such a loser, a failure." That's shame. Or maybe you have strong feelings you can't control: anger, grief, depression. That's difficult enough, but then you think, "What's wrong with me that I can't control this?" That's shame. Or perhaps you are a louder or quieter person than others, which people around you express in the form of criticism. That can lead to feeling bad or like an outsider, which is painful. But then you think, "Why can't I be different, be like other people?" That's shame. Shame is not criticism. It does more than hurt; it leads you to be disloyal to your basic nature, to turn against yourself. It's a self-attack, which means that without unshaming, you can't ever get away from the ongoing damage. Unchecked, as a worldview, shame annihilates. It's a unique form of violence. Unshaming is also a path of self-discovery. In a Jungian framework, unshaming is shadow work, shining a light on things that have been made invisible to us.

Shame is different from other assaults and violences, which injure our body or psyche without obscuring the fact that we're suffering because we were violated. Shame, on the other hand, twists and perverts this fundamental understanding, leading us to believe that we're not suffering because we were hurt; we're suffering because there's something wrong with us, and therefore we deserve to suffer. Conventional ideas of shame hold that you feel bad about something you've done or who you are. This aligns with a moralizing, Judeo-Christian view that sins should be punished. The greatest injury that shame creates is rendering ourselves invisible to ourselves. Thus, this fundamental belief system, when internalized, prevents all injuries and violations from actually being addressed. Instead, we spend our resources trying to "heal" what we believe is wrong with us instead of working to lift the veil of shame, which would allow us to see clearly and address the underlying wound. Too much of what people call "healing" banks on people believing the voice of shame, treating people as if something is wrong with them, robbing them not only of their money and time but also of their belief in themselves—their own authority.

You may be wondering, "Is there positive shame? Useful shame? Needed shame?" I've been asked this question many times. My research and study with people over the past thirty years indicates that there is no positive function of shame. That doesn't mean we shouldn't be furious about some people's behaviors, or that we shouldn't restrict or condemn those behaviors. It *does* mean that shame is not useful in bringing about sustainable change in such behaviors.

Thinkers and theorists who are aligned with a Judeo-Christian moral universe are more likely to hold the viewpoint that both shame and guilt are necessary to guide one's conscience, as if a conscience would be directionless without the whip of shame. However, researchers June Price Tangney and Ronda L. Dearing, authors of the 2003 book *Shame and Guilt*, discovered something different when they conducted a longitudinal study that followed four hundred children. They found that although guilt (as distinct from shame) did lead to some positive responses to harmful behavior, shame led to increased drug use, suicidality, and similar negative outcomes. Other studies have backed up these findings.

There are far more accurate words to address our moral concerns and outrage: *remorse, compassion, empathy, accountability, relatedness, amends, restoration, responsibility*, and yes, *guilt*. By responding this way, we can develop a clearer and cleaner understanding of shame's workings without a sloppy use of the word *shame* muddying the waters of our understanding. Using the word *shame* in a precise way is an important step toward growing less tolerant of its effects and clearer on unshaming's process.

People who continue to assert that shame is necessary, after being confronted with research and lived experience to the contrary, often argue that there are two kinds of shame: toxic shame and nontoxic shame. Yet dividing shame into two categories doesn't address the fundamental healing questions: What does healing shame actually look like? How can you heal yourself from a shamed state? How can healers, therapists, and facilitators address shame in a way that supports their clients?

To answer these questions, a clearer understanding is needed of the causes of shame and of what unshaming looks like. We also need an understanding of shame's relationship to early and intergenerational abuse and trauma (topics covered throughout the book and specifically in chapters 9 and 10) and what awareness and skills are needed to unshame.

Let's begin by taking a look at how shame is created and instilled in the first place.

Shame's Implantations

Some foundational experts in the field of shame, like Brené Brown, define shame as an emotion. In Brown's books, she provides examples of shame via stories that are almost always about people being criticized, internally or externally.

With gratitude and appreciation for Brown's contributions, I build on this definition to assert that shame goes beyond the experience of being criticized to encompass all kinds of assaults, including abuse. And criticism doesn't always lead to feeling shamed. Has someone ever accused you of something so ridiculous that it made you want to laugh? I'm guessing you didn't feel shamed at that moment.

What turns a moment of assault into shame? Many writers on shame talk about belonging, fear, power, and societal expectations. My research from over thirty years adds up to this: the way an assault lands in our psyche is due to the way others have witnessed us being assaulted—as shaming witnesses—whether they were present or we told them about it later on.

If they brushed off the assault and our injury through denial, dismissal, or gaslighting, or if they suggested that we deserved it, they were a shaming witness. And if this happened early or repetitively, we *internalize* that shaming witness. We believe that we can't be trusted to judge things accurately and that something must be wrong with our perceptions and feelings. We lose trust in ourselves and conclude that we don't matter. That denying, dismissing, or blaming voice relocates from outside ourselves—a shaming witness's viewpoint—to inside us. This has tremendous consequences because shame is a lens through which we see ourselves, distorting, corrupting, and blinding us to our true selves. As shame teacher Gershen Kaufman said, "Shame is a master variable," far more impactful than any single emotion.

Thus, when later assaults happen, including criticism, we don't respond from our natural reactions to being hurt. We don't trust ourselves because we believe that something is wrong with us. We don't have a self-loving, self-trusting layer around us that helps us process and respond with appropriate self-protection. We witness ourselves the way we were witnessed. This is internalized shame.

On the other hand, if other witnesses responded with compassion, belief, and protective responses, we internalize that way of seeing and witnessing ourselves. We are seen, felt, and believed. Therefore, when someone assaults or criticizes us later, we respond by caring for ourselves, protecting ourselves, and believing in ourselves. We are still potentially injured, but we don't internalize the unjust belief about ourselves. In this case, no shame is present.

Thus, shame is an internalized witness, not an emotion, although shame can produce emotions like guilt, embarrassment, and remorse. Shame as an internalized witness has certain characteristics:

- It denies, dismisses, or gaslights, rather than witnessing events and our actual experience.

- It objectifies. Its view is dehumanizing because it doesn't witness a feeling human being, a subject; it witnesses an object.

- It pathologizes. Shame "figures out" what's wrong with you that needs to change. It seeks to identify what is wrong with a person, not an injurious moment in that person's life.

- It is incurious. Shame doesn't inquire about what you experienced somatically, physically, or emotionally. Shaming witnesses never inquire about our actual experience. They come across as having everything all figured out.

We have all internalized a certain viewpoint from which we look upon ourselves. That viewpoint says growing, healing, and developing ourselves takes place by determining what's wrong with us—what our symptoms are, physically or emotionally—and fixing or removing them. It's an ever-present lens. Every time we do or feel something that creates discomfort, we are conditioned to think, "What's wrong with me? How do I fix this?" It's not a rare event; it's the sea we swim in. That view hides us from ourselves. It hides our real feelings, the stories we suffered from, hurts and injuries we underwent. It hides the truth of who we are and who we're meant to be. Shame leads us to normalize and socialize ourselves instead of unfolding the flower of who we are, connecting with our true selves, and bringing ourselves forward as gifts to the world. When we are filled with ideas and theories of ourselves, we can't help but neglect what our actual experience is. Why is experience so important? Because it is pregnant with gifts, medicine, and intelligence: by us, for us.

A Shame Scenario

Imagine this scene: A person stands up to give a talk to a group of people. In the middle of the talk, someone yells out, "You don't know what you're talking about!"

The speaker stops talking. They freeze. They don't know what to do or say. The audience also freezes, waiting to see what they will do.

The speaker thinks, *Why does he think that? How many other people here agree with him? Maybe I didn't prepare well enough. Why can't I figure out how to respond? Everyone's staring at me. I must look like a deer in headlights. I should be able to do something. What the hell is wrong with me? Do something!*

Three things are happening in this story. First, someone criticized the speaker in public. Being criticized in private doesn't feel good, but public criticism is even harder to deal with because one's injury is humiliatingly exposed to onlookers, and onlookers are witnesses who can shame or unshame. The criticism pierced right through the speaker. It hurt like hell.

Second, no one in the audience responded verbally, bearing com-
passionate witness to the speaker's pain. No one challenged the critic or
said, "Wow, how impolite," or, "Ouch, that must have hurt," Or "Are you
okay? That would be super difficult for me."

Third, the speaker's thoughts are overcome with questions, self-
doubt, and self-scolding. They're looking to identify what they did
wrong, and they're self-chastising about what they should be able to
do. They believe they must overcome their hurt, humiliation, and still-
ness. They believe they should be stronger, clearer, and able to respond
differently.

These three parts of the situation make up a scenario of shame. Let's
take them one at a time:

1. The Heckler's Assault

Everyone experiences criticism many times in their lives. Criticism is
often a verbal assault. It can hurt, knock you down, or put you down.
Public criticism can add humiliation to the pain.

However, criticism alone does not create shame. Sometimes crit-
icism bounces right off. The person may not feel hurt or injured at
all. The statement may be perceived as ludicrous or inaccurate. We
dismiss the critic, or we may be well aware of the issue and have made
peace with or even embraced it. Thus, it no longer affects us; we remain
detached.

Or one might say. "You just voiced a very strong criticism. I was feel-
ing stunned for a moment. I would love to hear your viewpoint, but I'm
not open to the way you shouted out at me. Let's have a dialogue." Or:
"Not only do I disagree with your statement, but I find your behavior
rude and unacceptable. I have something very important to say here, and
I won't be shouted at."

Why wouldn't these responses lead to shame? Because the person
is witnessing the criticism event, the public reaction to the event,
and their feelings. When this happens, the criticism may still feel
hurtful, but the person is much less likely to walk away feeling that
something is wrong with them or that they don't matter. These two

beliefs—"Something is wrong with me" and "I don't matter"—are the hallmarks of shame.

2. The Shaming Witness

The audience did not serve as a compassionate, unshaming witness. No one spoke up protectively or with concern for the speaker. No one bore witness to the occurrence. This silent crowd is an example of a shaming witness.

When someone is injured and no one responds with compassion, the person is vulnerable to thinking that their feelings are wrong and their response to the criticism is wrong, or even that they're not worth caring about. This heckled speaker would likely internalize the shaming witness, thinking that this attack was justified and they deserved it, and that they and their feelings don't matter. That's shame.

However, if the audience had responded with a demonstration of care, compassion, and empathy, or even anger at the heckler, the speaker would be less likely to feel shame. Or if they simply said, "Wow, that was a strong moment," shame would be less likely. I say *less likely* because if, due to previous shaming experiences, the speaker is vulnerable to feeling that something is wrong with them and they don't matter, the audience may not be able to fully protect the speaker from experiencing shame.

How we have been witnessed when criticized, or when we tell a story of being criticized, impacts whether we will experience and internalize shame.

3. The Internalized Shaming Witness

In our scenario, the speaker instantly went into a painful self-examination of what they did and how they were responding. They did not bear witness to the assault or its hurtfulness; nor did they reflexively summon a protective or self-defending response. The speaker's response—that of a shaming witness—joined forces with the heckler.

The speaker has not internalized an unshaming witness. Instead, he has internalized a shaming witness: one that analyzes to figure out what was wrong with them, one that doesn't take notice of their actual feeling experience and treats their hurt as if it is irrelevant. The speaker is blinded to their own integrity and authority.

If the speaker could have borne witness to their inner experience with protectiveness and compassion, as an unshaming witness, they may still have felt hurt; but their experience would not be shame and would not send them on a self-annihilating hunt for their flaws or into full-on denial of their experience.

It is no easy task to walk through the world with a self-awareness and presence that can withstand an attack without feeling deserving of that attack. Why don't we respond to all the criticism, inside and out, with an "Ouch" or a "Hey, back off"? Why is it so often difficult?

The reason: We have endured past experiences (usually during childhood) of being injured without trusted loved ones or peers coming to our defense or even acknowledging our experience. They may have been silent and cowed, like fellow schoolchildren when a cruel teacher ridiculed or mocked us. They may have joined in, like a parent who is humiliated that a church elder has found fault with their child and doesn't stop to find out more about the situation before reprimanding or punishing. No one acted as an unshaming witness for us—someone who dismantles the shaming event with their compassion. Instead, we were shamed. As shamed individuals, we accept the assault. When we have shame, we feel we deserve the assault. When we have shame, we simply believe the assault and proceed by trying to fix what's wrong with us. When we have shame, we suppress our experience, only to have physical and psychological symptoms later that we no longer connect to the earlier event; thus, we pathologize ourselves. In other words, we lack an inner protector and lover.

When shame is defined as criticism (or guilt, as discussed earlier) or as an emotion, we miss out on coming to recognize and navigate the complexity of shaming events. We also miss out on the chance to unshame ourselves. We unshame ourselves by using an internalized compassionate witness as an ally and force field. We unshame others by compassionately witnessing someone experiencing harm, defending them, and validating their experiences and their right to be treated with kindness. These actions add up to a shame-dismantling superpower.

Shame happens whenever we feel assaulted and are not free to make a boundary. It happens when we treat feelings as problems to resolve. When a group is marginalized and minoritized and nobody notices or bears witness to the injury being caused. When a person is abused and people deny or dismiss the violence. When we treat physical symptoms as weaknesses, a failure to measure up to social norms. When people view long-term consequences of trauma as pathologies instead of earlier experiences or intergenerational stories. Shame happens when we treat addictive tendencies as self-medicating, as if there's no valid hunger behind the hunger for a substance.

The Mycelium of Shame and Unshaming

Because shame is a lens through which we see ourselves, it can seem like a mycelium—the underground network that connects untold numbers of fungi—that feeds or starves different parts of us: our physical and mental health, our self-awareness, the way we subconsciously identify as marginalized, the way we subconsciously marginalize others; the way we hold memories of abuse and experience traumatic somatic responses; the way we care for our feelings. Unshaming transforms that mycelium into a nourishing, sustaining system that edifies you and others. Given the mycelial nature of unshaming, there is much interconnectedness among the themes of this book's chapters. When you read chapter 4, "The Role of Boundaries in Healing Shame," you'll notice that boundaries affect internalized oppression, abuse, and feelings. If you work on chapter 8, "Unshaming Disturbing Feelings," you'll notice its connections to social oppression, inner criticism, and abuse. All these topics are related. They're overlapping, inseparable.

You might be wondering: why parse out these foci into chapters? I do so because that taxonomy is the way we naturally think about ourselves and our healing. Each chapter is a different doorway into the house of healing shame.

Shame siloes us off from each other and from aspects of ourselves. Unshaming commences a reweaving and acknowledgment of the rightness of overlaps and wholeness. The categories also show how the lens of shame functions to illuminate aspects of our personal development and healing that were previously occluded or blurred. I've also structured the book so that each chapter builds on the next.

An Invitation to Self-Discovery

Given the numerous permutations of shame, it might be useful to focus on how shaming and criticism work together.

EXERCISE

Take out a pen and paper or a notebook and respond to the following questions.

1. Remember a time when someone criticized you. How did you respond? Did you take it in? Were you free to disagree and defend yourself directly (not lost in a fury, but clearly and forcefully)?

2. When you are criticized, are you aware of feeling hurt? Do you take your hurt seriously? Is there an inner voice that says something like, "Ouch, that hurts," so that you can then care for the injury?

3. Are you aware of how criticism lives inside of you—what people call our "inner critic"?

4. Do you speak back to that inner critic and defend yourself, at least some of the time? If so, describe what you tell yourself.

5. Do you default to thinking you need to change, correct, fix, or even "heal" yourself?

6. Where do you think you land? Do you have an internalized shaming witness, or an internalized unshaming witness?

An unshaming witness responds, can clearly defend and disagree, and notices an injury so time can be taken to care for it. An unshaming witness gets to know how you feel. What does a shaming witness do? It provides no boundary, meaning the criticism goes right in. We either believe the criticism ("It's true, I'm busted") or we feel victimized by it because we don't appropriately and directly defend ourselves, and perhaps we don't notice that this event was injurious. A shaming witness treats your feelings as something to fix.

You may be feeling despondent and perhaps even shamed about being shamed. The unshaming process might seem overwhelming. But it's worth it to replace your internalized shaming witness with a loving and compassionate one—to engage on this path of self-love and self-discovery and to reconnect with your path of heart. In the last chapter, you'll have the opportunity to combine everything you've learned to become an unshaming witness to the world.

An Introduction to Unshaming's Blessings

Some of the benefits of unshaming are developing the skills of seeing (respect), feeling (relating), and believing (radical belief). These skills can powerfully assist anyone who is feeling angry or depressed, or who is struggling with addictive tendencies or painful relationship patterns, which are all fueled by shame. Additionally, shame erodes self-trust, self-belief, and self-love. Unshaming's skills build self-trust, increase self-belief, and grow self-love.

You may, like most people, think of unshaming as a removal or abating of a painful feeling. But in fact, it's a restoration. We unshame to free parts of ourselves that were buried. As one of my Facebook followers put it, "Unshaming is redemption of our authentic selves. How hopeful and uplifting!"

How does this work? The act of unshaming witnesses a person's experiences with *respect*, which depathologizes. Instead of being diagnosed, the person's humanity and subjectivity are affirmed, not their objectification.

The act of unshaming *relates*; it witnesses with feeling. When a person experiences a listener's compassion, empathy, and heart, they internalize the sense that they matter, counteracting shame's message that they do not.

The act of unshaming witnesses with an absolute *radical belief* in the person. This kind of belief nourishes the person's trust in themselves, whereas shame leads to the internalization that they cannot trust themselves and they need outer authorities to tell them who they are, what they need, and how to feel and behave.

Let's go a little deeper with those concepts.

Respect (formed from the Latin *specere*, to look, and *re*, again) means inquiring further and more deeply into a person's actual experience. Often this looks like exploring a person's somatic experience, but it could be the experience of their body in motion, their posture (what we call body language), their visual experience (what they see and visually remember and imagine), and the dialogue that is going on inside their head (often inner criticism). In session, I make a detailed inquiry of these experiences. The person finds themself in the role of a subject, not an object, a pathology, or something to fix, which undermines shame's impact. In this book, readers will learn how to self-respect.

Relating is when we inquire deeply and compassionately into how a person feels. Especially when we inquire into how someone reacted to being hurt, neglected, or disrespected, they almost immediately experience themselves as mattering. When a person is hurt and no one responds with empathy, compassion, or a protective impulse, the person experiences themselves as not mattering. The feeling of mattering can be restored when another person inquires with compassion and empathy about one's feelings of being injured. If there isn't anyone at hand who can play this role for you, you can do it for yourself. When a person engages with self-inquiry while being a compassionate witness for oneself, this same restoration of mattering can occur.

Radical belief is when we believe a person and believe in them. Believing in a person means believing they have the answer to their difficulty and they know the kind of medicine they need for what ails them.

When we make our inquiry with this belief, people arrive at insights and momentary enlightenments. This tells us which direction their healing will take, and it restores their inner authority and their trust in themselves so they can stop projecting their authority outward on others, as shame has led them to do in the past.

In each of the following chapters, you'll witness me modeling these skills in action as I work to unshame people.

Remember when I said that we unshame to recover parts of ourselves that were buried? Another way to put that is that those shamed parts are in the shadow, as I touched on earlier. The *shadow*, a Jungian concept, is made up of all the qualities we don't want to own about ourselves. It's the part of a person that is split off from the person's dominant view of themselves because a dominant cultural view deems that part unworthy, unacceptable, impermissible, or immoral—and thus shameful. These qualities may be seen as negative, such as anger, hatred, or jealousy. Or they may appear as qualities that are seen as positive, such as feeling proud of oneself or believing in one's genius. Most people in our culture don't experience themselves as beautiful. Thus, beauty is in the shadow. Any extraordinary quality tends to be in the shadow.

Relegating these qualities to the shadow is always a form of suppression or oppression. And make no mistake: suppression and oppression are acts of violence. They violate. Shame enters when people, groups, or institutions deny the violence by agreeing with the suppression, or they gaslight you by telling you there's something wrong with you, and you need to fix or get rid of this quality, like a diseased limb.

Here's the deeper implication of connecting the shadow to shame: our healing task is to bring the shadow into the light. That means we need to own and integrate the shadow so it functions to deepen the person and make them more whole. Unshaming is shadow work.

Healing shame—which I call unshaming—is more than becoming resilient to shame or not feeling ashamed. Unshaming redeems the shamed qualities. If we don't own them and integrate them, we will remain cut off from our authentic selves, our powers, our gifts, and our life path.

I could spend the next hundred pages listing the benefits of an unshamed life, but the case is clear: shame hurts. It dismembers. It pathologizes what is beautiful and true. Unshaming is not just the absence of pain. It's spacious, free, and brave. When a formerly shamed part of yourself becomes unshamed, it doesn't just come into the light. It flowers.

Please take in this excerpt of Galway Kinnell's poem "St. Francis and the Sow":

The bud
stands for all things,
even for those things that don't flower,
for everything flowers, from within, of self-blessing;
though sometimes it is necessary
to reteach a thing its loveliness,
to put a hand on its brow
of the flower
and retell it in words and in touch
it is lovely
until it flowers again from within, of self-blessing.

When we unshame, we are reteaching precious, restored parts of ourselves that they are lovely. When we self-bless, we bloom.

CHAPTER 2

Becoming an Unshaming Witness to Yourself and Others

She sat eating dinner with her parents, refusing everything but broth and nonfat sorbet. She was malnourished and beyond thin. She had recently landed in the hospital twice from fainting while working out in the gym.

Her parents saw a pretty young woman, a beautiful daughter. They didn't even know that they were bearing witness to bodily violence. They didn't intentionally deny or dismiss the silent, painful story their daughter was telling; they were ignorantly blind, not mean-spirited.

Nonetheless, their witnessing communicated this message: "Everything is fine. We are not moved to compassion and concern as you sit there, weak and suffering. Please continue to hide your authentic self, your painful experience, your truth, behind 'thin and pretty.'"

They didn't intend to shame their daughter; they intended to wrap her in adoring eyes. Nonetheless, their "innocence" left her isolated,

believing it would be wrong for her to share the depths of her pain and
self-hatred—and worse, that something must be wrong with her for
having such depths within her.

We live in a world of witnesses, not just to violence and abuse but
to the ever-present flow of communication from body and psyche,
which continues for days, weeks, years, and generations after the
violence takes place. There are witnesses who align with a cruel
attacker, like my mother, who dismissed and denied the ways her
husband abused my brother and me. There are also witnesses whose
silence communicates complicity with a person's self-harm, as in the
story above.

Shame is created or deepened when someone shares intimate details
about their experience with a witness, and the witness offers unsolicited
advice, dismisses feelings, denies the experience happened, decenters
the speaker, tells the speaker their feelings are wrong, encourages the
speaker to feel sorry for the injurer, ignores the speaker, changes the
subject, or blames the speaker. This is a shaming witness.

There are also witnesses who can hold space for the speaker, in the
moment or later on, with curiosity, respect, and compassion. This is
a healing witness. Bearing loving witness means beginning with this
fundamental intention: *I want to know what it is like to be you.* This
requires making a genuine inquiry into what the other person actually
experienced. To make this inquiry, we need to explore what that person
feels, as a body experience; what they would do or say if they were free;
and what kind of inner dialogue goes on inside of them regarding what
they are sharing. This can happen at any time, which means healing can
also happen at any time. We can be free. We can be unshamed. And we
can unshame others.

A healing witness does four things:

- **Acknowledges.** "I see/feel/hear/perceive" the injuring, violat-
  ing event.
- **Empathizes.** "I feel empathy and compassion in response to
  your hurt."

- **Expresses** a protective response and/or supports the person's resistance. "You didn't deserve that. You're right to be angry."
- **Radically believes** the person's account, and radically believes in the natural healing directions and intelligence of the person's system. "I believe you; I believe in you."

The Essentials of Unshaming

Becoming an unshaming witness necessitates shifting your paradigm. American mainstream culture is permeated by an allopathic paradigm. That paradigm's message is: *When something bothers you, it's a symptom of an underlying illness that needs to be cured, and then you're better.* For example: "I have a headache." The allopathic paradigm's answer: take a pill. "I'm angry." The paradigm's answer: meditate and do deep-breathing exercises. How about "I'm depressed"? Think positive or take an antidepressant. All of those responses are fine. I support people getting the help they need. The radical part of this is that we overwhelmingly think that way. It's so fundamental to our beliefs about health and well-being that we default to that approach. Along with the medical industry, the alternative wellness industry treats people this way, too.

We need to divest from this default to absorb the main message needed to become an unshaming witness: symptoms are messengers that carry intelligence. Not about what's wrong, but about directions and steps your life wants to take to become more true and more you. In that case, instead of truncating yourself and taking pieces away from who you are, you're bringing more into yourself and your life, and becoming more you.

Conventional paradigms have a certain model of health. They say, "Your body temperature should fall within 97.6° and 99.6° Fahrenheit. Anything outside of that is not normal and needs to be treated." In reality, the fever response is an example of body wisdom: it's part of an immune response meant to kill germs. But this wise response is pathologized. There's no questioning of whether the norm is a good one or what the context is. We seek balance, harmony, ease, and comfort, often at the expense of our wholeness. We shoot the messenger who is invariably aiming to disrupt the status quo—our status quo. But, as we know, asserting and reestablishing the status quo is never sustainable for the long term, whether it's for an individual, a community, or the dominant culture of a nation. Over time, when we insist on the restoration of our status quo, we create a kind of inner totalitarian state and experience our symptoms as terroristic.

There's also a range of emotions considered by conventional paradigms to be normal, and emotions outside of that normal range of 97.6° and 99.6°, so to speak, are also pathologized. Such as anger.

For example, a client once said to me, "I'm afraid my anger is going to get me fired."

As he shared more, I realized that his boss was an asshole.

"Okay," I said, "what else can you do with that anger? You have to make it your own. It's already a part of you." I would never say *You have no right to feel that way*. His boss was an asshole, and he had a right to feel angry. The anger is like a fever trying to protect a body from an invasive germ.

I'm not saying that anyone has a right to be cruel or abusive because they're angry. If someone I care about is angry, I have a right to say, "I don't feel safe when you're angry. What are we going to do about it?"

An unshaming paradigm does not have a model of health. Let me be clear: if you're ill, you should still get medical care. I believe in and use medical care, too. We need to get help to relieve symptoms and suffering. Sometimes people can die without the support of antidepressants or chemotherapy. I'm also not expressing a lack of compassion. If you are experiencing physical suffering, I hope it diminishes or disappears.

And I believe the unshaming process can be part of the solution. I've noticed time and time again that a symptom is often also a messenger. Like a busy bike messenger, once you receive the message, they leave. If you don't answer the door or sign for the package, they're going to keep coming back. Thus, unshaming is worth pursuing, along with medical approaches. If the symptom is a messenger, then listening to the message and integrating its intelligence can not only relieve the symptoms *some of the time* but can also lead to more self-love, intimacy with others, and a life path that is truly yours.

It's hard to make that paradigm shift. I get it. It requires an ongoing commitment to noticing and reconceiving. But don't worry. If you decide to take it on, this book, along with your own efforts, will keep steering you toward that shift until it's part of how you see the world.

Let's look at how not having a model of health plays out in a therapeutic setting. When my client says, "I'm judgmental," how do I respond? To me, the state of being "judgmental" is not good or bad. Instead, I'm curious about it, because in an unshaming paradigm, I believe this manifestation of judgmental behavior is a messenger with an intelligent message. I want to hear that message! Unshaming is a process of investigation. For many who criticize their judgmental qualities, the symptom's message is: "Stand up clearly and directly for what you think and feel. Make strong and overt judgments. Own your powers to discern." It's not "If you can't say anything nice, don't say anything at all."

You might be wondering if unshaming means the freedom to do bad things without feeling bad about it. No, it doesn't. Yet I still apply the unshaming process to and with people who struggle with seriously harmful behavior, like child abuse. For instance, a client once told me they needed help because they hit their child. (If the child is in danger, outside enforcers must also be contacted.)

First I said, "If you want to hurt your child, keep your child away from you for now," because the unshaming process should never preempt taking steps to protect the vulnerable. At the same time, ignoring the client's plea for help would also be negligent, because the parent's anger would only fester and grow more severe in the darkness of shame.

Then I asked, "What's it like to hurt your child?"

"I get angry, and then I smack her," the client said.

"Can you show me the hand?" I asked, because the message often expresses itself somatically, in this case through bodily movement. "I want to know what you're doing. Right now, your child is safe. She's not in this room with us. What does the hand do?"

"I lose control!"

"Lose control a little right now."

As we continue the unshaming process, I learn that the person who loses control around their kids is controlled all day long at work. At home, that person feels set free.

I asked, "Tell me about the ways your job controls you." Maybe they're attached to a telemarketer station or they operate a crane, so they can't go to the bathroom or take lunch when their body needs it. This person needs to break free in their job instead of in harmful ways at home.

"We've got to help you find and claim moments of freedom all day long," I said. "The urge to break free is intelligent. In this safe space, we have to get to know the hand that hits your child. We aren't going to spend a lot of time on what you *wish* your hand was like; otherwise, we're never going to get to know your body's intelligent message."

My father spent his life as a broker selling insurance at his family business. He hated it. Whenever he came to a red light, he used to get apoplectically furious. When I told this to my therapist, he said, "Your father was sitting at a red light his whole life. He spent forty years at a red light. He should have run that light." My therapist was speaking metaphorically. My father should have created more movement and freedom in his life.

It was so true. In fact, sometimes when a fury rises up in me, I notice I have been unfree to follow my deeper impulses, needs, or life directions.

Next we'll discuss an example of unshaming that's related to how illness is shamed in our culture. People who are ill often need care, whether it's medicine, a device, or certain kinds of therapy. That legitimate need is often shamed. In this instance, a client of mine had asthma; she often took breaks during our sessions to go to the bathroom.

When I asked her about this, she said, "Well, I go to the bathroom to use my inhaler because I'm ashamed for people to see it."

I noticed that shame showed up when she mentioned the inhaler, so I expressed curiosity to begin the unshaming process.

"Can you take it out?" I asked. "Let's look at it together. Let's witness you doing it. How do you feel with the inhaler? When you put it in your mouth, what's happening? What's it like?"

Her eyes welled up with tears. "I also had asthma when I was a kid. My parents sent me to a mountain school where the air would be different. I was without my family for a while, and the inhaler was my only friend."

If I had said to her, *Let's look into medication changes that might help you to stop needing the inhaler*, that message about her loneliness and isolation would not have come to the surface. My intention was for her to feel more okay about having an inhaler, so I said, "It's your friend. It helps you breathe. Treat it like that. It's not a bad thing."

And yet so many people feel shamed by needing to take a pill or use an inhaler. If they have a negative, shamed belief about taking an antidepressant, every time they take the pill they're swallowing both a neurochemical medicine and a dose of self-shaming. It's like a harmful mantra. If you have to go get your tooth pulled or you need to engage in chemotherapy, it's important to recognize this act as a "yes" to life. It means "I want to survive this," not "I failed somehow" or "I'm worthy of punishment."

It's important to unshame the need.

My client having asthma as a child led to her being sent away from her family. "I thought I was sent away because I had done something wrong," she told me. As an adult, she sent herself away to use the inhaler, a continuation of that first isolation. The trauma happened again and again in small moments: *I have to go away from you in order to be myself.*

By cultivating conditions in which she could feel comfortable using her inhaler in front of me and eventually others, she experienced the use of her inhaler without an infliction of isolation. She could be herself and stay in the room.

Another one of my clients shared with me how her young son, who was slightly anemic, didn't want to take his iron pill.

I said, "Sit down with your child and the pill bottle and explain that this is to help him get stronger. Draw pictures together of what it means to be strong. Let him draw a picture of strength on the bottle with a

Sharpie. This time, every time he takes his medicine he'll be thinking 'I'm gonna be strong,' a positive association, instead of 'I have to take my medicine, I'm giving into something I don't want to give into.'" This set of associations creates a positive framework, which is what we should all have when it comes to doing things that support our health.

Another client might say, "I'm thinking about getting on antidepressants, but I have this idea that being on antidepressants is a bad thing." Their tone is saying *I need support to be okay with going on antidepressants*. Thus we pursue helping them make that decision freely. In my view, antidepressants are as much a part of nature as chamomile. Humans, who are part of nature, created antidepressants.

In contrast, someone else might say, "I've been on antidepressants for years, and people say I have to stay on them forever." Their tone is communicating that they need my support in communicating with their psychiatrist about safely reevaluating their prescriptions and dosages.

As unshaming witnesses, we need to put aside our personal biases. My responses are very different from social or political philosophies about pharmaceutical companies. I may have issues with the efficacy of some antidepressants (and other drugs) based on pharmaceutical companies' research claims. That's different from unshaming a person. Some people mix these things up. When it comes to working with yourself, those philosophical roadblocks should be removed. If you need it, you need it. If you want to be a vegetarian, but you need meat based on your body's ability to thrive, you can still have that philosophy while also being faithful to what your system needs.

Unshaming is a process. A person presents their concern, whether it's an asthma inhaler, their anger, or their cravings for ice cream, and I start to unshame it with them.

Unshaming Yourself

Before you can be an unshaming witness to those around you, you have to begin the process of unshaming yourself. Unshaming doesn't happen by learning a theory or observing a model. The key to your own unshaming is through experience. Experience is the sine qua non of unshaming. Objectivity is not the point.

A self-inquiry based on experience might ask these questions:

"What's it feel like to be me in that way?"

"What voices are in my head? Are they critical?"

What's your experience of being yourself? What it's like to eat ice cream? What's it like to love your sweetheart? It's a subjective experience. Subjective experience rules unshaming. People are subjects, not objects. Thus, unshaming is the opposite of being objectified.

When I work with a client, they are the subject. I have to get to know them. You might think you know all there is to know about yourself. Here's a happy surprise: you don't. Shame disconnects us from our experience and takes away our connections with ourselves. It disconnects us from our real intelligence and gifts. It disconnects us from believing in ourselves, which is the most loving act. When you unshame yourself through self-inquiry, you learn amazing things.

A lot of my students use the word *courageous* to refer to this process. It is! Unshaming is a courageous, curious inquiry into your actual experience. And this also means putting away labels, ideas, theories, and opinions you have about the issue you're about to examine. Otherwise, you're looking at it through a lens with opinions, which blocks your ability to follow the intelligence of the symptom or issue.

Consider the following two statements.

"I can see that I'm angry."

"My biggest problem is anger."

The second sentence is an opinion—a pathologizing one at that—which cuts us off from curiosity and self-belief. Somebody once wrote that the most dangerous person is one who trusts their own experience. Not dangerous in a bad way; they are dangerous to the success of other agendas because they can't be manipulated. They are strong because they trust themselves. The dominant paradigm of our society—treating symptoms instead of being curious about their messages—cuts us off from experience and banishes us to the quicksand of interpretations.

Before we move into accessing experience as a witness for ourselves, it's important that I share a lesson on self-consent. Just as a therapist has to be mindful of whether what they're doing in a session is right or wrong for their client, you need to discern whether what you're doing is right or wrong for you. It's a health question and an ethical question.

As you begin to access your experience and make a self-inquiry, imagine that you're floating down a river with many branches. The branches correspond to answers of *yes*, *no*, and *maybe* to each question or prompt you offer yourself. *No* doesn't mean you're bailing on the process; it means you're floating down a different branch of accessing experience. Follow the flow of *yes*, *no*, or *maybe* with every intervention you make. This is how we build a trusting relationship with ourselves, ensure that we are consenting to our own help, and avoid running over inner boundaries (which we will discuss more deeply in chapter 3).

You might be asking, "How do I know whether the answer is yes, no, or maybe?" I believe each of us has a place of inner knowing. The self-unshaming process refines and strengthens your relationship with your inner knowing. It's a big deal to start connecting to that, strengthening that, trusting yourself, becoming more dangerous.

Try to say this out loud: "I can feel this is not really right for me."

Does that make you feel anxious? If so, you're not alone. We've all been punished—in ways that range from subtle to severe—for breaking ranks with other people's and organizations' plans for us and their ideas about what we should be, how we should feel. Increasing allegiance to your inner knowing will support you in respecting your own boundaries and maintaining them with others.

Accessing Experience

Remember when I said the key to your own unshaming is through experience? I'm going to go deeper into that right now.

We access experience through different channels. Dr. Arny Mindell's Process Work taught me the concept of *experience channels*: the body's sensations, body movement, and inner dialogue. Being a witness to yourself requires developing consciousness of your own sensations and movements. This metaconsciousness will help you notice and track such questions as, "What does it feel like in my body?" "What movement did my hand just make?" In the discussion of experience channels below, I've added some channels that Arny doesn't use: voice/sound and facial expressions.

The Body's Sensations

One aspect of the body is what people call somatic experience, interoceptive experience, proprioceptive experience, or physical sensation. The language we use for this is important. When we need to name specific bodily sensations, often people will default to an emotion, mood, or feeling, such as anger, frustration, or tiredness. To describe bodily sensations, we need to use words like *tingling*, *heat*, *pressure*, *aching*, *numbness*, *vibration*, *sharpness*, *tightness*. It's sensory-grounded experience; it's direct experience. Direct experience is unshamed experience. It's not an idea, not an opinion filtered through a theory or judgment. It's not an illness or a pathology.

Body Movement

Bodies also communicate experiences in the form of movement: slumped shoulders, tapping foot, swirls of the wrists, grasping fingers. And bodies have impulses to move if you allow them to. Try standing and letting your *body move you*. If you keep supporting your body, you may find yourself swaying, rocking, punching . . . dancing. You can visually and proprioceptively notice yourself making these movements, and so can others. You can even start with somatic experience and allow it to be expressed even more deeply by moving with your feelings.

Voice/Sound

Sound is also a body expression. People's voices naturally change throughout the day—clipped when impatient, growling when frustrated, quieter when self-conscious. Often when we talk about other people, we change our voices as if to mimic them. People often whisper when they don't want someone else to hear, even when no one else is around. They're telling us there is an inner dialogue going on with someone who doesn't want to be overheard. Sound is a channel of witnessing your experience. Maybe you're working on having a voice in the world; speaking more loudly and clearly is a way for your own ears to witness this.

Maybe you're addressing your inner criticism. If you begin to say the inner criticism out loud, your ears will hear it; the little bones in your ears will shake and move. When you hear yourself say a mean thing to yourself, it might hurt. That's the point. If you can't hear it, it's like a silent poison. This simple intervention can cause you to stop a lot more quickly than trying to (silently) talk yourself out of feeling bad.

Facial Expression

Your face is a part of your body and its physical expressions of experience. Your facial expression will change when you're telling me certain things because it's a bodily expression of your experience. We sometimes forget how much our faces are communicating to the world about what we're feeling, thinking, and saying—or not saying. I recommend watching yourself in a mirror as you talk about your day.

People mostly identify with their faces. When I'm on Zoom and I see my face, I think, *That's me.* That's why it's a powerful channel. Changing my facial expression requires me to change, especially if I look at myself or show another person. There's a witness. If sadness flashes across my face when I mention a friend, I notice that I'm sad, and thus I can be curious about it. Go to the mirror and make an angry face, a pained face, a tender face. You may see how it starts to show up in your body as somatic experience. Tribal cultures often make literal masks—a manifestation of the power of the face we wear.

Inner Dialogue

Like the body's sensations, inner dialogue goes on inside of us. We can't see it, and sometimes we don't even hear it unless we tune in. Thus, in order to witness it, we need a way for the experience of that happening to be brought out. One of the best ways is to make that dialogue external by saying it out loud. External dialogue has experiential qualities. But how can you do this by yourself? It sounds silly, but it's powerful: Put two chairs close together, facing each other. Sit in one chair and say something. Then get up, sit in the other chair, and respond to the first statement. Moving the body helps us get out of our ideas and opinions. If we simply journal, we may not access the deeper intelligence of the body. When we move the body, it signals to our deeper selves, "I want to know you, experience you." When we move our bodies, we can more readily witness our own experience.

Amplifying Experience

You've chosen a channel to work with, and you're identifying your experience. Maybe you're noticing a tingling in your hip joint. Maybe you're seeing your hands make movements like wings. Maybe you're dialoguing out loud. Maybe you're noticing that your voice is getting squeaky when you talk about your boss. Maybe your nose crinkles when you mention exercise.

The next step is to *amplify* your experience. Shame suppresses and diminishes, so now go the opposite way: grow bigger, spread your fingers wider, wrinkle your nose really exaggeratedly. Imagine that the throbbing ache begins to pound; the burning in your tummy becomes even more fiery. We're trying to get your witness to notice it. Shame truncates and shrinks; unshaming amplifies. Sometimes it has to get big enough for our awareness to be jostled out of its trance and catch on. Imagine that all of you is tingling like your hip. Take that squeaky sound and make it even squeakier.

This is when people start to get insights, often in the form of answers to questions like these:

◆ How is this amplified experience something I would normally try *not* to express?

◆ Where in my life do I not feel free to express or show myself that way?

- How do I need to be more like that?
- How am I not noticing this is going on inside me?
- What if I were freer to express this?
- How would it be useful to bring this out more in my life?

Globalizing Experience

We've begun to connect with our experience in particular channels: somatic, movement, inner dialogue. That's a great beginning. We have left the world of theories, opinions, and judgments, which can go hand in hand with shame. We're making contact with facts: what's actually going on inside us, not facts about the world.

Now we can put our experiences together, especially if insight is not readily arising. It's like drawing a picture of a person and then adding eye color, facial expression, the way their arms hang, the way their back bends, even the energy that they exude. How do we do it? We add more channels to our experience. We begin to feel, then move our hands or arms or perhaps dance. We are more fully, more wholly expressing what lives inside us. Next we add some sound, maybe even a song that resonates with our body. Finally we make a facial expression, like wearing a mask.

What has happened when we add all these together? We begin to dance around the fire of our deepest experience, singing our song, wearing the face of our experience. We leave the identity we have grown accustomed to. We alter the shape of our being; we literally shape-shift. In this way unshaming is a shamanic intervention. Not in the sense that a shaman has been enlisted, channeling the medicine she acquired from another world. We ourselves are the channel; we become the shaman.

Shape-shifting in this way doesn't require that we heal our wounds in any traditional sense. We have not lessened our anxiety, cooled our anger, or developed our confidence. Instead, we have become someone else, have accessed a part of us that already has these qualities. For example, one part of us may be insecure, perhaps a remnant from a painful childhood story. We don't need to change that part or "heal" it; we simply gain access to other aspects of ourselves. The insecurity becomes one part of us in a body and psyche that are more whole. It becomes relativized—just one part of us in our inner multiplicity and diversity. This is so radically unshaming because we don't need to pathologize our difficulties. Instead, we need to let go of our identities enough to embody other aspects of ourselves—shadow parts.

Integrating the Intelligence

As you make deep and true contact with your actual experience, insights will arise, such as: "My anger is full of power, and I don't feel very powerful." "I really am quite scared. I didn't realize it, and I never show it." "When I drop down into my depression, I actually feel more at ease." "My stomachaches are telling me to complain and protest more. I'm too silent."

How do you know you're getting these insights? Sometimes it's obvious; the light goes on. But sometimes you'll find yourself smiling, giggling, or crying, or your energy will change from tense to relaxed or from relaxed to firm. At other times, it won't be obvious at all. In all cases, it can be really helpful to your development to take the unshamed messages and weave them into your daily life. I call this weaving *integration*.

Why make this intentional integration? Because through unshaming you will connect with parts of you that have been relegated to the shadows by shame's power to hide parts of you from yourself. Thus, you may try to be generous all the time, but shame has locked away your desire to take care of yourself. Or you may feel powerful and confident, but shame has hidden your vulnerability from you. You don't even realize you get hurt by people, though you may somatize that hurt and experience body pains that seem unrelated to your relationships.

The poet Robert Bly said that these parts get "thrown into the shadow bag," a heavy weight of things we carry or drag behind us. How do things get thrown into the shadow bag? Shame is a master at that!

To do this constant integration, we have to have more of a dialogue between our usual self and the part of ourselves in the shadow. The usual self is the identity (some think of this as our *ego*) we have grown accustomed to and prefer, and the shadow part is made up of all the qualities that are not accepted. They have been shamed at some point, or repeatedly at many points. The shadow part is the source of the message that arises out of the unshaming process. It's the voice of the shape-shifted you.

We may ask the shadow expression: Why are you here? Why do I need you? What can you do that I, the usual self, can't? How are you free in ways that I am not? Why don't I allow you to lead more in my life? These questions will produce further or deeper insights if they haven't already readily arisen, and we can use these questions even if we have already gotten the insight.

The point is this: you will want to weave the intelligence, beauty, power, and spirit/energy of the message into your usual life. Unshaming doesn't seek to simply give you more ease or help you release the energy of your difficulties. Instead, it helps you weave these ways of living into your life, making you more whole, animated with life energy, more authentic, and more able to express the gifts you were born with and live the life that was meant for you.

What's more, integrating these messages will often help ease your physical symptoms, make your relationships deeper and more intimate, reduce inner criticism, and foster a more loving relationship with yourself. We'll discuss these benefits more along the way. However, here's a caveat: unshaming does not mean all of your troubles, symptoms, and difficulties will go away. They may undergo significant change—and, yes, even relief—but as you become more you, you will likely come face to face with new difficulties. As an integrated person, you'll be stronger when you do.

EXERCISE

Opening to the Shadow

1. Think of a quality of yours that you dislike and that you would like to get rid of. Name the quality and your judgment about it.

2. Using the movement channel: put your criticism away and use your hand to express that quality. Allow it to make a gesture in movement.

3. Amplify: Allow your hand gesture to become freer. Exaggerate it, make it bigger. Whatever it is doing, do "more" of that. And then go even further, like a playful child being told to be really free to make that gesture. Continue the movement and allow yourself to enjoy it, without worrying about the initial dislike you had.

4. Integration: How is this different from the way you usually express yourself? Where could you use a little more of that form of expression? How might it help you solve a problem that's been bugging you for a while?

5. Reclaiming the shadow, shape-shifting: Imagine that you were the person who made that gesture. Forget about the rest of you for this moment, and say, "This is me. I'm like this." What kind of person are you? If you want to go further, stand up and walk around like that person would. Play. Embody. Enjoy.

CHAPTER 3

Shame, Physical Health, and Symptoms

One of my students, an Indigenous woman, wrestled with symptoms of lupus. This condition sometimes prevented her from keeping up with her responsibilities as a healer, an income earner, and a mother of two children. The word "responsibility" was very central to the way she felt about herself. In fact, this word comes up often for people who suffer from chronic illnesses that sap their energy.

As I began the unshaming process, we explored what it was like to be really tired, to give up. She closed her eyes, her body began to relax, and she said she was dissolving into the earth and felt a sense of being more like a river or an ocean, something fluid. She realized that these deep connections were part of what she called her medicine and that she had been relying on these gifts to do her work as a healer. Thus, what she had once viewed as a problem of responsibility management became a way for her to relate to her illness and symptoms as part of her gift. This changed relationship is what comes from the unshaming of physical symptoms.

She was heroic in her capacity to get up and take care of her responsibilities beneath the great weight of her pain and exhaustion. The wellness industry played into her desire to find more energy resources.

Sometimes that helped. But not being able to keep up at times added psychological suffering to the physical suffering. In fact, many who suffer from chronic illness sink into unbearable shame because they feel as if they can't keep up. They have internalized a viewpoint that says a person who is worthy of care and respect meets mainstream expectations about what a productive person and parent looks like. I have seen how relieving that shame alone brings healing tears for so many, even if they experience no relief from their physical symptoms.

How the Body Dreams

Arny Mindell's "dreambody" work states that just as the mind's dreaming expresses the psyche's shadow as we sleep, showing us parts of ourselves that our normal minds marginalize, the body also "dreams" by expressing deep experiences that interfere with our normal self or ego. In effect, the body's symptoms interfere with our normal identity, ego, or status quo. Thus the body's symptoms can be revolutionary challenges to our status quo. It is our marginalization and pathologization of these experiences that create the shadow. Essentially, shame veils these energies, intelligences, and ways of being. In this way, the body "dreams" in the form of physical symptoms that interrupt our normal life. The body says, "I'm a headache—a pounding energy that you try to not express." Or "I'm a migraine, pulling you out of your normal orientation, telling you to close your eyes and ears, to be still." The body—also called the *soma*—offers an unshamed viewpoint, but we need to learn the soma's language, which is a language of the senses, not opinions and notions.

An unshaming view of a stomachache goes beyond the sentiment "I need to get rid of this stomachache"; instead it views the stomach- ache as also being me. Getting rid of the stomachache without gleaning the body's intelligence is asking the body to get rid of a part of oneself, which is shaming and impossible. The intelligence could be, "I am 'bel- lyaching' and want to complain a lot more to the people who are upset- ting me." Or, there's burning acid in there, saying, "Learn to be more acidic and sharper when people are encroaching on your boundaries." It can be different for each person. Applying an unshaming viewpoint to physical illnesses and symptoms liberates people from shame and opens up a world of precious insights, which is a lifelong gift.

Where do these insights come from? One way is through a process of restoration. When a person identifies as a sick person (e.g., "I am sick") and proceeds with a dedicated healing path, after a certain amount of time this can erode the person's parallel wellness as a gifted being who has something to give to the world (i.e., they are not *only* sick). That's a big loss. Restoring awareness of our parallel wellness and reclaiming it yields powerful insights. In essence, we remember our wholeness.

This truth was powerfully communicated to me by my dear friend Marcus, who died of AIDS in 1995 when the medications for HIV were less effective than they are today. Before he died, Marcus said, "Everyone looks at me as if I have a skull and crossbones on my forehead. People only see me as a sick and dying person; that's [also] making me sick." Marcus was one of the most gifted therapists and healers I have ever met. Even as his illness progressed, his gifts deepened. He was not just "sick"; he was also more "well" than most.

Another aspect of a person that can become elided is their own nature. The more extreme the chronic symptom, the more difficult it can be to get along in the world. These symptoms affect relationships, work, financial status, and self-presentation as a good citizen. The more intense the symptoms are, the more difficult life is, and the more radical that person will have to be to live in this world, meaning there is a potential revolutionary spirit in that person who doesn't conform to a mainstream world's expectations.

Aisha's Story

I recently worked with a Black woman named Aisha who lives with chronic fatigue. (*Note*: all clients' names have been changed.) She told me, "I've been navigating chronic illness. I've had to go to a lot of doctors' appointments. I need to work and pay my mortgage, but there's a conflict between resting and fully engaging in my work to pay my bills and sustain myself. I'm in this tension spot. I need a new philosophy. I have tried to regulate my nervous system and still take care of my work. I'm frozen in fear. I can't commit to work appointments. I have to 'get better soon.' Culturally, we have only a few days to get better. I'm afraid I need more time than I can really get."

Aisha was familiar with the stress, the reasons for working and committing to her work. What was less known to her was the deeper experience of the symptom. I decided we needed to momentarily drop the outer question and dive deeper into the need for rest that was creating the fear. This fear, empowered by mainstream notions of productivity and timelines for getting over an illness, was marginalizing the actual intelligence inherent in her need to rest. This is how shame works: it pathologizes, decides that parts of us don't matter, and makes us hell-bent on getting rid of something that we don't even really know yet.

I said, "Let's take a moment to get to know your experience of rest. You only have to do that for a few minutes while we're together right now. It won't get in the way of your work tomorrow. We just want to get to know what the rest you are seeking is like. What is the deeper need?"

Most people would think that we all know what rest means, but people's experience is vastly different. Some imagine hiking up a mountain, some lounging on the beach, some spending hours in the kitchen cooking a meal, some sitting and reading, and some finally having time for conversations with friends. All of these are different needs, and we won't discover any of this if we don't unshame by connecting to the person's experience. Remember, shame hides experience, veiling it in ideas like "that's a pathology to get rid of" or "that doesn't matter, your experience doesn't really matter, you don't matter."

Aisha closed her eyes and got quiet for about a minute or two that seemed much longer than it was, because it was longer than the time people usually take to reflect when asked a question. This was already a good sign that we were unshaming; she was resting into getting in touch with herself. She might have never even done that before—taken two minutes to feel the need before she felt frozen, frightened, assaulted by cultural ideas telling her to get over the need as fast as possible.

Aisha went into her desire for rest, and she noticed her heart was beating fast. "I want to slow down," she said.

"Let's slow down together," I said in a slow, drawn-out voice, "sinking into resting and slowness."

"I feel my heart beating really fast," she said. Her mention of the heart again told me that the heart was the next step; the heart knew something that had been veiled by shame. The heart was saying *See me, witness me.*

"Let's go into that beating heart. Feel that beating heart. Don't try to slow it down or change it. Pay attention to it. Perhaps it can even get stronger." I say this in order to amplify the heart's experience, to welcome the forbidden, to unshame.

Aisha said, "Now my heart is slowing down."

"Ah, the heart was going fast, now it's slowing down." I said this just as an act of witnessing, with no other agenda. "Can you use your hands and show me how the heart is beating? Its speed and beating?"

She opened and closed her hands in rhythm with her heart. She smiled. "It reminds me of my ancestors drumming," she said.

This was so deep. We had entered territory that we can't learn about in books or theories. We were in her experiential world. She was moving out of the current cultural paradigm and into an ancestral paradigm. She continued to open and close her hands, lost in making the motions. It was as if she had been waiting a long time to do this, to have someone else witness it, to know it herself. I asked her if she could make the sound of the drum, to hang out with that and let that rhythm do whatever it was going to do.

She used her mouth and voice to make a drumming sound that matched the rhythm of her hands. She had shape-shifted from a culturalized (or externally and internally colonized, we could say) person into a woman with ancestral knowledge, wisdom, and rhythm. This was what her "rest" wanted; not sleeping, though there is nothing wrong with sleeping, but connection with her ancestors and how they lived in her. In a way, her illness was calling her back into more wholeness. In a way, her illness was a call to wellness, and her normal accommodated self was not a wellness to return to, but an illness that was disconnected from her depth, her soul.

I said to this new drumming person, "Dear drumming person: why are you coming to this person's life?"

Aisha said, "I am here to support her. I am here to give her energy to keep going."

"Keep going?" I replied, bringing in her earlier concerns. "How do I do it? I try and then get exhausted . . . then I worry about my mortgage . . . please give me your medicine."

The new drumming person said, "Follow the heartbeat."

"That's different," I said, speaking for Aisha's normal self. "I never thought about that. Say more. I usually try to rest or try to get to work."

"Your heartbeat keeps you present," the drummer said. "Listen to your body in every moment. Rest when you need to rest. Keep going when you want to keep going. You can't figure it out; just live moment to moment."

As she said this, her body changed, her energy shifted and lifted, her face opened into a smile. Something had been unshamed.

I said to Aisha, "Rest when you want to rest; work when you want to work; and stop trying to figure it out." Now that she had access to her newfound wisdom, I asked her, "What's so good about that answer?"

"It's easy—it has an easy, effervescent energy to it," she said, her face gleaming with light. "My heart cultivates its own energy. I don't need to."

She and I now witnessed that her illness knew something about staying close to the heartbeat, moment to moment. She was getting closer to her own rhythm, the rhythm of her heart, not the rhythm she had been conditioned to follow. This is true for many who suffer from chronic illness; their lives are moving toward following a different path, a different drummer, a new or ancestral song. When they don't follow that song, they get exhausted. In that way, the exhaustion is pushing or pulling a person closer to their nature, the natural or indigenous way. (Caveat: please don't read this as a disregard for or bypassing of illness or body symptoms. I am *not* saying that all illness is psychosomatic or that all illness is only in our heads, and that if we get our psychology together, all symptoms will disappear.)

The process involved being more indigenous to her nature or her ancestry. Mainstream American culture tells us, "Work really hard and then get your rest." "You can do that after you finish your work."

Aisha's heart was telling us, "No, I'm more moment by moment." Chronic illness defies mainstream beliefs about work and rest. Aisha's illness was teaching her that she had to find a rhythm that was hers amid the oppression internalized by her primary identity.

So many people wrestle with that. The internalized-oppression critic says, "I'm tired, I'm not productive, I'm not present for people, I'm inadequate because I'm tired," instead of "I have a different way of fulfilling my responsibilities because the way we're living is exhausting."

The workplace can be so shaming. For over a century, workers in the United States have fought for rights that are still unevenly granted, if at all, such as paid sick time; time off via the Family Medical Leave Act; pregnancy, maternity, and paternity leave; and bereavement leave.

Work Culture versus the Body's Intelligent Messages

The workplace in the United States and many other countries operates in accordance with the values of the marketplace. Those values hold high respect for toughness, productivity, pushing past limits, and being business-like (i.e., not taking things personally). This marginalizes other experiences, as well as people who identify as more sensitive, tender, or relationship oriented, which leads to potent internalized oppression—an issue we will delve more deeply into in chapter 6, "Social Issues and Shame."

This reminds me of a friend I met at a conflict resolution seminar I attended in 1990. Moses was raised in a tribal African village and later moved to the United States to go to school and work. He eventually got a job at a large company where he worked in a small cubicle. In his work review, his supervisor told him that he spent too much time talking to the other employees. In Moses's village, when work needed to be done, like plowing a field, a number of people would get together and work on one person's field and then they would move, all together, to the next person's field. On the way to the next field, they might meet someone and talk for hours, finding out how their relatives were and how they were all connected. "Connection, relationship, and community were the point; work simply set the need and context for us to be together," Moses said. "Why would I go to work if it were not to connect with other people?"

In his essay "The Moral Obligations of Living in a Democratic Society," Cornel West speaks of several nonmarket activities, i.e., activities that don't directly lead to production and commerce. These include parenting, which is based on service, care, mercy, and justice, qualities we need as a culture; and sweetness, kindness, and gentleness, qualities we need to build to sustain relationships. Even self-care and self-nurturance are nonmarket activities. In a market culture these are all seen as weaknesses to overcome, pathologies to heal, instead of qualities we need to create rich, whole, and sustainable relationships with ourselves, our bodies, and our communities.

Unshaming Inner Criticism and Body Symptoms

If you've ever suffered from physical symptoms (and who hasn't?), you have likely noticed that in addition to your symptoms, you feel bad about yourself—like a failure, unworthy, a loser. As we saw above, this arises in response to inner criticism, which is invariably tied to cultural ideas related to internalized oppression. Thus, when we work with body symptoms, we often have to bring the unshaming work to two different areas: unshaming the inner criticism (witnessing it in a way that allows the person to find their natural response to that criticism) and unshaming the actual body symptoms: the aches, fevers, limps, and tumors.

My work with my client Margot demonstrated the approach to these two processes.

"Thank you so much for having me," Margot said. "I'm excited, but I'm also nervous."

"I can be nervous for you if you want; then you don't have to be," I said, joking but also serious. Sharing feelings that often shame, like nervousness, helps create an unshamed atmosphere.

"Okay, great!" Margot replied.

I said, "I'm really nervous. What's going to happen?" I paused before continuing. "How would you help me if I were nervous?"

Margot said, "I would tell you everything's going to be okay, and maybe touch your hands. I would also say, 'It's going to be fine. You're perfect.'"

"Okay," I said. "That's good to know. We're perfect. See, you have the medicine to deal with these things. That's what I was wondering about. And I thought if you projected it onto me, then we'd find out what it is." Unshaming requires holding the belief that people, not the facilitator or healer, have the answer, the medicine, for their difficulties.

"Thank you," she said.

"What can we do?" I asked. "What kind of love can we bring to your life?"

"I have cerebral palsy," Margot said. "As I was growing up, there was a lot of physical abuse centered around my disability. If I fell, I was punished. If I didn't treat my legs, I was physically punished. Hard-core physical stuff. It was brutal. But I gained a lot of physical strength from it. I went from not being able to crawl to being able to walk independently by the time I was eighteen or nineteen. I internalized that the way to get better is to be really brutal.

"And then some things happened. I lost a lot of my mobility, and I gained weight. I'm trying to get back what I lost, but the old ways aren't working. My body's not reacting to the tough love. I have so much shame that I've gone so far backward, and it paralyzes me."

This is common with longer-term bodily symptoms. What once worked no longer works, and now the person may need to find other medical solutions as well as alternative, unshamed ways of relating to their symptoms.

To witness her experience, I asked, "How did you use the brutality to get stronger?"

"I would wake up at four a.m.," Margot said. "My uncle would make me walk two miles before school. I was always tired, and I was always hurting. But I somehow figured out how to override my own pain and body response. I would just push my body through it. Now, when I work with physical trainers, I tend to push myself the same way, yet I reach a point where my body just stops. There's so much resistance. I disassociate and have a hard time going on walks because I'm so depressed about how hard everything is."

I said, "I'm learning that being hard on yourself isn't working anymore. You're resisting that. Your resistance is important. I'm also wondering, 'What would Margot be like if she were just herself, if she weren't trying to overcome anything?'"

I saw Margot take that question in. This is my heart's question as well: What is Margot really like? Not the "sick" one or the one who is trying to heal; what would she be like if we didn't see her as having an illness at all, if there was no pathologizing view? That doesn't mean I wouldn't support her in getting physical therapy, as well as any medications that would relieve her symptoms. I simply want to help her build a more loving relationship with herself and out of that find out how she will live, what her gifts are, how she creates intimacy, and what her life path and purpose might be.

I continued. "To begin the unshaming process, it helps to know everything I can about your actual experiences. What does being brutal look and sound like to you? Let's pretend I'm you, and you're saying to me, 'Come on, walk two miles!' I would like to experience what's going on inside you. I have an idea, because you're telling me, but I'd like to feel it."

She didn't hesitate. "It's like, 'You're fucking up. You're pathetic. You disgust me. You're not doing it, you're not doing it! You're losing it. Harder! What are you doing?'"

I could feel the force of her internalized drill sergeant, but she was still holding back. "Can you exaggerate the tone of those words?" I asked. "Pretend you're the grossest human being on the planet."

Why would I ask Margot to do such a thing? Because when people first connect with an inner critic, they almost always express it as relatively neutral in tone, even if the words are harsh. Thus, the inner critic can sound pretty reasonable, even if its message is vicious. Perhaps the original people who said these things to Margot used a reasonable tone and seemed credible. But how could the impact of the phrase "You disgust me" ever be neutral?

Anyone trying to get in touch with that inner critic as part of the process of unshaming themselves needs to make the words more potent, to fully express the critic's tone. I want them to express that tone like they're auditioning for a play, not reading aloud from a book, i.e., with more amplification. Unshaming that critic will require Margot to witness it outside of herself, and for that she'll need to hear it as it really is. Amplifying the tone of these words awakens the witnessing function. Consider the contrast between "That dress doesn't fit you" and "You're disgusting!" The resonance of the second phrase wakes up the emotional body. Another reason why amplification is so important: inner criticism is invariably self-abuse that's not being witnessed. You need to witness it to know you're being abused, so you can make different choices.

When that early criticism happened to Margot, or to you, odds are nobody around you witnessed it in an unshaming way. They didn't express a compassionate and protective response. You also learned very early not to have a reaction to the inner critic. When inner criticism is not witnessed, we are hurt, and we believe it doesn't matter and we don't matter. We suffer painful feelings as a result of being put down, and we think we're having those feelings because something is wrong with us, instead of thinking it's because we're being injured. That is shame.

A story illustrates this principle. In 2005 Harvard University hosted a conference on the position of women and minorities in science and engineering. Lawrence Summers, Harvard's president at the time, gave an address at the conference, and in his remarks he said there were fewer women than men in the hard sciences because women may have less of a natural aptitude for those disciplines. Harvard got sued because of this comment, and Harvard had to put millions of dollars into diversity training.

Summers voiced the often internalized or unvoiced criticism. Yes, it was a sexist, ugly thing to say; but on a positive note, because he said it and it could be witnessed in the light of day, it could be addressed. This is why I encouraged Margot to emphasize it, not because I wanted to upset her.

Margot raised her voice, and her face became contorted and rageful. "You're fucking up. You disgust me. Keep going. No, that's not right. Keep going. Come on. You can do this. Why are you getting worse? Why did you lose it? You had it. Why did you lose it? You disgust me. What are you doing? This is pathetic. You can do better than this. I don't know why you stopped!"

"That's very helpful," I said. "Thank you for doing that. How are you doing? That's a strong thing to do." Often, it's good to slow down and pause for a moment. I've seen people start to cry because they never felt how painful it was before, or they become stunned by the utter violence that they have never truly heard before. Witnessing creates the space of hearing; witnessing unshames. But sometimes people are animated in a positive way by the insight they're getting.

"I feel it, but I'm okay," she said.

I explained to Margot that when people have a strong inner critic—that internalized voice that hurts them sometimes—it's important to externalize it so we can witness it. It's also important for her to hear it more consciously, and with a degree of separation. At that point we can realize, *Oh, this is what's going on inside of me.* This way we get to hear something we weren't quite hearing clearly.

I said, "Margot, the next step in unshaming is for *me* to use some of your internalized critic's words. The goal is for us to notice what it feels like when you hear them. What happens to you when I say these words? This is not a situation where you'll need to say anything in return. Your job is not to respond to me or figure out what to say. It's more like a meditation. Just see what happens to your body."

Now that I know about that voice inside of her, I want to know what her body does, what her deep truth is in response to that voice. But I'm going to prepare her for this step very carefully, to give her opportunities to protect herself. I do that by telling her what I'm about to do: "I'm going to say words like 'You're fucking up,' and 'You disgust me,' and 'Keep going.' I don't want to say those things until you feel ready, because just saying mean things to someone is abusive, and I don't want to be abusive. I want to find out what happens for you. Is that okay?"

This technique is so important because shame takes root when people are abused and there is no witness; but when they focus on their body response instead of on the words, shame doesn't enter. They don't lose touch with themselves; they don't become momentarily stunned, frozen, and traumatized. They are awake and can defend themselves.

"Yes," Margot said.

"Stay close to your body," I said. "If you can, get ready to feel things. Your eyes are closing. That's good. And you can be ready to feel them. And you tell me when you're ready."

She nodded.

"Okay. Here it comes. Remember, feel things. *You disgust me. Keep going. You had it once. What's going on? Get it back together again. You're fucking up.*" I stop. "I'm sorry, that was painful. I'm not going to do it again."

"That's okay, it was great."

"What happened in your body?"

"My right foot started tingling, my head got woozy, and there's a really strong fear in my stomach."

"Wow, that's excellent."

I believe we all have the medicine we need to heal ourselves; it just needs to be recognized and integrated. I echoed the criticism Margot had heard before so we could find out what her medicine for dealing with it might be. Her medicine seems to be related to her getting woozy, her feet getting tingly, and fear happening in her stomach.

I continued. "Margot, can you give your attention to those sensations again? Which one of those sensations is most powerful or interesting to you? Or are they all the same?"

"My right foot," she said.

"Take your time," I said, "feel that right foot, and what you're calling tingling, and imagine that tingling can grow just a bit. And tell me a little bit about what it's like." Unshaming leads us to stay close to her experience, in this case her sensory-grounded somatic experience. We are helping her learn not just about her illness beyond shame but also how to follow and trust herself—a powerful benefit of unshaming.

"My foot feels achy," Margot said. "It's sweating a lot. It's getting clammy. It's clenched. It's almost like I have a stomachache in my foot."

"I love the way you put that. You have a stomachache in your foot. If your hand were to do what your foot is doing, could one of your hands begin to show me what that stomachache in your foot is like?" Including additional ways of expressing the feeling by staying close to the body's experience helps the person and me to better witness what is happening; in that way, it continues the unshaming.

Margot clenched her hand and then opened it.

I said, "It clenches and then opens. So let's go slow. Clench it first as much as you would want your foot to clench. Don't hurt yourself. Tell me what that's like."

"It feels like it's *with* me," she said. "There's something positive about it."

"What's the positive part?"

"I feel like I'm holding myself."

"You're holding yourself. That's very touching to me. I'm so glad you shared that. Somebody else might think that the clenched hand is a fist, but in fact you're holding yourself."

"It feels protective."

Margot had gone through so much pain, had endured so much berating, and her body's medicine was to protectively hold her. That's beautiful, isn't it? I repeated and affirmed what she shared.

"It's protective," I said. "You're holding yourself. You've got yourself in your hand. *I got me.* Very good. And since your hand was closing and opening earlier, slowly open it now, and tell me: what happens then?"

"I feel a lot of grief. Other people might see me. I feel exposed."

"Do you think other people see you more as exposed or as protected and safe?"

"I think people see me as more exposed."

"Which way do you usually like to be?"

"I prefer to be protected," Margot said, closing her hand. "But I want to do *this* more," she said as she opened her hand.

Margot's system is showing us it has two reactions to criticism. One reaction is this "open, grieving" experience. And the other is a "closed, holding herself" experience. I trusted that as we got to know those two reactions, we would learn how she could deal with internalized criticism in a less brutalizing way.

I said, "If you were to hold yourself, Margot, not just with your hand, how would you do it?"

"Like with a hand on my tummy," she said. Her left hand moved up to her shoulder, and her right hand rested on her stomach. "I like to curl up, but I can't do that here."

"Let your left hand and your right hand continue to hold you," I said. "Imagine that those arms and hands are designed to hold you. Forget about what it feels like to be Margot. Imagine you are the hands holding you, almost like you're somebody else. You are just those hands and arms. Go ahead; hold yourself even more. Hand goes up, head goes down a little bit. Yeah, that's it. Beautiful. And you're rocking a little bit, forward and back. You're rocking her and holding her so perfectly. Imagine that you are that person rocking her. Not Margot, but the person rocking her. I want to talk to that one. If I were Margot, I'd say, 'Why are you holding me like this and rocking me like this?'"

Why was I helping Margot become the holder instead of the one held? Because this response was the one she knew the least. The part of her that self-nurtured had been hidden by shame. This shamed aspect had limited her response to either harshly overcoming her sense of weakness or feeling the pain of being put down.

"Should I tell you what I heard?" Margot asked.

"Yes. Tell me what you heard."

"'Because that's what you need,'" Margot said, quoting the voice she heard, and speaking in a tone of warmth, gentleness, and certainty.

"Tell me, how do you know that's what I need?" I responded, speaking as Margot. "Sometimes I think I need a more brutal, strong energy because at one point, it helped me." This was Margot's viewpoint at the beginning of the session.

"No, no, this is what you need," Margot said. Her certainty was powerful.

"How do you know?" I asked, continuing from her earlier point of view. "It helped me. I got stronger, remember? I walked two miles. It was terrible, but I got stronger."

"Yeah. But that's over now."

"Why is it over now? Why wasn't it over five years ago?" I asked.

One might wonder why I challenged Margot's new point of view. It might seem like we should teach this dawning understanding like a newborn, fragile thing. But it was necessary to put the two viewpoints in conversation. In this way she would integrate the unshamed intelligence.

In conventional talk therapy, therapists often work with the client's primary identity: the consciousness that they're already in. Therapists ask that consciousness to think about things differently—"What would a stronger David do at this moment?"—but our normal identity can only take us so far. Conventional talk therapy may not acknowledge that people can come up with their own medicines if nonprimary identities are brought into the experience. These medicines come out of their own flowering.

In an unshaming process, a different part of you is accessed: a shadow aspect, like the one we encountered when we found ourselves outside Margot's normal consciousness during the session I'm describing. Bringing Margot's presenting questions to this aspect would allow her medicine to flow into this usually present identity.

This brings me to an important unshaming insight: self-development is often related to decentering. What do I mean by that? Common presumptions of self-development include notions of becoming bigger (e.g., "I'm a pie that needs more pie pieces") or following a certain path (e.g., "I'm going this way, and when something gets in my way, I have to get through it or make a turn to continue forward"). In unshaming, I decenter the client's primary identity without making that identity wrong. Everyone has their own medicine inside them, waiting to flower. If the primary identity is centered to the extent that it crowds out other aspects and blocks their medicine, a change is needed.

Let's apply this to Margot's experience. We decentered her primary identity, the one with questions about why she can't "tough-love" herself into increased physical mobility. Outside of that limiting identity, she came into touch with the whole world. If you'll remember, I asked her, "Why is it over now? Why wasn't it over five years ago?"

"Because you've already learned," she replied.

"What did I learn from all that strong, brutal roughness?" I asked.

"What you are capable of."

"Okay," I said, continuing to speak from Margot's primary identity. "I'm capable of a lot. I can push through a lot of pain and a lot of difficulty and a lot of abuse. And I can even get strong doing that. Wow. That's good to know. And now it's time for something else."

I switched back to my own voice. "How are you doing, Margot?"

"Okay," she said.

"What's coming up inside you as we do this?" I asked, led by the feelings I could see in Margot's eyes and face.

"I'm feeling the energy of my mother. She's gone. She died when I was three and a half."

In these other aspects of Margot, her mother's healing energy and love were unblocked, released.

"Maybe your mother's arms and hands now live in you," I said. Margot nodded. She had connected her innate body wisdom, which led her to hold and rock herself, to her earlier story of losing her mother at a young age. Understanding oneself as a story that is unfolding, instead of a pathology that needs healing, moves a person from being objectified to becoming a subject. This is potent unshaming medicine.

I said, "Mothering includes holding and rocking, but it also shows up to say that you don't need certain things after a certain point. 'You don't need that anymore.' Mothers have a certainty children need. It guides and reassures them. When internalized criticism rises up, you need your internalized mother to rise up and protect you."

It was important for Margot to know that the medicine for that criticism is a certain kind of mothering. Some people have a medicine that says, *Screw you. Don't ever talk to me like that.* But that wasn't Margot's medicine. Her medicine invited her to hold herself. It might be your medicine, too.

This holding, embracing medicine had been released, and now it could be one of Margot's active resources. We also needed to address her sense of being exposed, symbolized by her open hand.

Now that we had found Margot's medicine in response to her old, more self-critical path, we could take the next step, which I touched on earlier: What if we didn't look at Margot's body as ill? What if we were looking at a person with a different way of walking, feeling, living?

"I'm interested in one more thing, Margot. What is your body like if nobody tries to fix it or change it at all? I think that's really important, because in the world we live in, having cerebral palsy means you need to work hard to overcome your difficulties so you can look a little bit more 'normal.'" For most people, their inner criticism is so powerful that the most important work is to unshame the criticism, as we had just done. In each symptom is also a way of being—wisdom and intelligence for life. That was the direction we were taking now.

"What does Margot's body do," I said, "and how does it move, if nobody is trying to fix or correct cerebral palsy? If it's just left to itself? That's what I want to know."

"I have so many different voices fighting to answer," Margot said.

"Let's leave the voices aside for a moment and hang out with your body. Let's say to your body, 'Thank you for learning to move and walk miles and overcome pain, but I want to get to know you as if we had never tried to get you to be different. I want to know you just as you would be without anybody trying to make you into anything. I'd like to meet you.' What would your body do if you never tried to change it?"

"I feel more energy," Margot said.

"More energy. That's good. Can you move your hands as if you're trying to seem quote-unquote normal? The way most people think one *should* be?"

Her hands moved in a linear, robotic, machinelike fashion.

"Nice! Can you put a little bit of a tune to that?"

She voiced a tune with a choppy, militaristic beat.

"Now let your hands be cerebral palsy hands. How would they move?"

Her hands made wavelike, round, circular shapes in the air. I noticed arcs and fluidity.

"Wow. Okay. Keep going," I said. "That's amazing. Let them be weird, strange, unique, perfect. That's who Margot is. That's what her nature is like. Keep going before we turn her into what we think people should look like. She looks like this! And what kind of tune goes with that?"

She voiced a fluid, light, playful tone.

"Keep going with that. Teach me the songs and keep going. How is this different than the other way?"

"It's fun!" she said animatedly. Her smiling face was childlike, lighthearted.

"It's fun?"

"I feel like I'm enjoying my life."

"Wow. Oh, that touches me. That makes me weepy. Fun and enjoying things." I go back to speaking from Margot's primary identity: "I think you're supposed to just get things done and overcome so I can march through life. And you're having fun and enjoying life. Tell me more about the importance of enjoying life."

"Why would you come here just to work?" Margot asked.

"Well, that's what everybody keeps telling me. Walk two miles a day, get over the pain, push through, get over my cerebral palsy so I can be normal like other people think I should be."

"I think that fun is freedom. There's more freedom when you're having fun."

"Wow. Having fun and enjoying life: that's what you came here for. I didn't know that. I thought you came here with an illness to overcome. You got strong. I didn't know your deeper reason to come here was enjoyment and the freedom and the fun of being alive. I didn't know that about you."

"Me neither," Margot said, laughing.

"You didn't know it either. Who would know? Everyone's convinced you that you've got an illness they should help you overcome. You're a lot of fun, aren't you?"

"Yes. Thank you."

"You're so welcome. What else could be useful to you before we conclude this work?"

"Just going through this process with you was a big deal because I don't talk about it publicly. I really, really appreciate you."

"I appreciate you also. I've learned two things. Pushing through things and getting strong can be helpful at times in life. Maybe it'll be helpful again at times. I'm not against that. Sometimes we have to be really strong, and I see that you have that in you. I've also learned it's important to hold yourself, mother yourself, as the mother and not the person being held and mothered. I was focusing on your hands, not on you being held, because that's what your body needed to get in touch with, that power, to protect you from that internalized critic with the attacking, hectoring tone and message."

I told Margot I was also fascinated by her claiming of life's fun, enjoyment, and freedom. When a child is told very early that they have an illness and they truly need certain kinds of help, like physical therapies and other medicines, they don't find out what they're really like. That process gets lost in identification with the illness. They never get to ask themselves, "Who would I be if I wasn't trying to make this illness go away?" We each deserve to know what we're really made of and what we're here for. Not as corrected or pathologized, but looked at as we looked at Margot: in the fullness and potential of her flowing, fluid, happy self.

Reclaiming Our Wholeness

When people suffer from physical illness and symptoms, they often also suffer from the shame of feeling unproductive, needing support, being more vulnerable than others, or feeling like losers or failures. Unshaming proceeds by outing these feelings and the viewpoints that create those feelings—viewpoints that people and the culture at large have almost always internalized. Closely following and unfolding the person's experience of these critical voices has an enormous unshaming impact, ridding people of the sense that there is something wrong with them, that their suffering doesn't matter, or, even worse, that their symptoms are a kind of punishment for being who they are. And unshaming physical symptoms and illness goes a step further. It challenges us all to pause, take a break from our usual pathologizing eyes, and see the person as part of nature's great diversity—as someone expressing a way of living and feeling that is outside the norm. Doing this requires viewing the symptoms as intelligent messengers. Witnessing those symptoms, unfolding the flower of their intelligence and message, allows their way to surface for the first time, allowing the person to achieve a life-changing insight: "Oh, that is who I am. I am like that. I am not just ill; I am also a unique part with special gifts and a powerful authenticity that my life will express."

Making Contact with the Healer You Are and the Medicine You Carry for Yourself and the World

1. Bring to mind a chronic symptom you experience. If you don't have any chronic symptoms, identify another symptom that you suffer from. It could be anything from a tumor or an immune issue to headaches or tiredness. Describe it.

2. Consider the history of that symptom. When do you first remember experiencing it? What was your life like then? Do that with a few other occurrences and notice if there are any patterns. We begin unshaming by connecting with the story of our symptoms.

3. Reflect on the suffering you experience. How does it affect you, your body, life, habits, freedoms?

4. Locate an area of your body where you experience this suffering readily in the moment. Feel the dis-ease in that part of your body.

5. As you bring your attention to that area of the body, notice the physical sensations—the sensory-grounded experience. Is it sharp, hot, achy, numb, tense, painful, heavy, pressured, tight, saggy . . . ?

6. Amplify that experience by imagining that those feelings could grow by becoming more intense or spreading out further. For example, if you are numb, you become more numb; if a pain is sharp, it becomes sharper. Take your time; amplification is very important, and most people want to figure this out in seconds. Two to three minutes will be plenty of time.

7. Now begin to let your body move that experience. Stand up and let your body begin to dance the way it feels. Start with your hands, if that helps. You can begin slowly and then amplify; exaggerate by making bigger and freer motions. Your body will know what to do. If there is anything strange about the movement, repeat it over and over. If there is already a pattern, repeat the pattern a few times.

8. Enjoy the dance. How is this different from the way you usually try to show up in the world? Talk out loud; imagine telling someone, "This is my dance. This is how I would go through life if I were free." You have now shape-shifted into the dancer.

9. While dancing, say out loud, "I carry a medicine that I and others need. This is how I need it. This is how others need it."

CHAPTER 4

The Role of Boundaries in Healing Shame

My client Max was a giver. He was compassionate toward his parents, even when they told him how to raise his own children. He was unfailingly kind to his children, even when they were rude and hurtful to him. He listened to his friends' troubles whenever they needed to vent. It never occurred to him to say "No." While he did his best to be positive and put on a smiling face each day, underneath his exterior he suffered from low self-worth.

Shame's Connection to Boundaries

What does this have to do with shame? Every boundary violation injures, at least a little, and shame enters whenever we're injured *and we don't notice*. We need a witness, and often the only witness to our injuries is us. Thus, each time Max didn't say no or didn't set a boundary— didn't tell his parents that they were insulting him with their condescension, or tell his kids that their behavior was rude and offensive, or tell his friends that he wasn't having a good time—Max was injured, yet he didn't notice it. He did not bear witness to the injuries, and this caused shame. In Max's case, he didn't understand where his low self-worth came from, so he thought, "What's wrong with me?" Shame drove Max to try to figure out what was wrong with him and to believe his needs didn't matter. Within this perspective, saying no seemed impossible.

"No" can be a dangerous word. It's dangerous because people who check in with their inner wisdom and say no are dangerous to the status quo. It can also engender strong responses in people like Max's family members, who are used to getting their way without resistance. Renegotiations will need to happen, but they're worth the conflict.

Boundaries and Relationships with Yourself and Others

Caribbean American poet June Jordan's poem "Taiko Dojo," which appears in her book *Haruko/Love Poetry: New and Selected Love Poems*, begins like this:

No! No!
No. No. No. No.
No! No!

It continues in the same vein. I love that this poem is called a love poem. We often associate love with always saying yes. Max tried to show his love by saying yes and dissolving his boundaries. Love is associated with merging, becoming "one" with someone else. However, ignoring your own needs to be agreeable or easygoing in a love relationship is not a loving act for yourself or for another. The person who loves you isn't getting to know the depths of who you are. You're not fully showing up. And constantly discounting your needs often creates a simmering resentment that may pop out to confuse and upset you both.

When I encounter something that is not congruent with my well-being, my system puts up a "No." It can feel like resistance, hardening, a protective instinct, a line, and a need to walk away.

If someone wanted to meet with me and they said, "How about ten p.m.?" and that was not a good time for me, I would feel a "No." Meeting that late would not be good for my system, and my body and mind know it. You, on the other hand, might be a night owl, so that example may not be helpful to you. What's a situation that elicits your easy "No"?

Max would easily agree to ten p.m., even if his bedtime was 8:30 p.m. He might hem and haw first, but if the person trampled over his subtle boundary by insisting or calling him a wimp, shame would lead Max to think, *Something's wrong with me for being so rigid. I don't matter. Might as well.*

Any boundary-crossing scene can become a mini-abuse scene if, rather than aligning with a compassionate, self-protective internalized witness, you are guided by an internalized shaming witness. Such a witness might say things like, *So what if it's uncomfortable? It doesn't really matter. My needs are not really that important. Why can't I be flexible?* We override the impulse to set a boundary by saying no. Women especially are socialized from childhood onward to respond politely with a smile no matter how they feel about the person and the context. If you have a compassionate internal witness, you trust yourself, which is a form of self-love, and therefore you feel more comfortable asserting a boundary.

When you can't assert a boundary, it's a lot harder to take care of yourself. When an injury happens, however small, it enters and is likely not registered as significant. With each injury that is not witnessed by a boundary, shame builds. It happens on a regular basis, so your system is living in a context where you're being injured, nobody's defending you, and you're not defending yourself. No witness to the injury and violation means more internalized shame, in the form of thoughts like *I don't really matter* and *What's wrong with me that I am suffering?*

There's no way to heal from shame without establishing boundaries. You don't have to get it right every time or turn into an Olympic medalist of boundaries overnight. You do have to become more free to set the boundary, even if you don't set it each time. If you can't set a boundary because you're not free to do so, shame enters. However, if you consciously decide not to set a boundary in a given situation, you've made a conscious decision to acknowledge your inner wisdom, and shame is not created.

Let's say you're invited to a birthday party on a night when you usually meditate. You feel the boundary come up inside you, but the friend who invited you is someone who puts a lot of stock in birthday celebrations. If you say to yourself, "I know this is not the best choice for me, but I'll bend," instead of "I'm such a pathetic introvert," that's a hugely different message to your system. If your ongoing conclusion is, "My needs don't matter; I don't matter," it's harder to pursue ambitious goals, like going to graduate school or writing a novel. People who think they don't matter will probably not take on Mary Oliver's question "What is it you plan to do with your one wild and precious life?" from her poem "The Summer Day." These small unboundaried injuries add up to one epic injury: you never find the life that's meant for you.

Boundaries are loving to people in relationships. Boundaries sustain love. They are natural, organic. Despite what many say, we don't have to learn to create boundaries so much as we have to heal from the events that first impaired their functioning.

When your boundaries were violated and:

no one showed you that they saw and heard what happened;

no one responded with empathy and compassion for your hurt;

and no one responded to protect you even if they weren't capable of doing so;

then you were not lovingly and fully witnessed. When our natural resistance to a violation is not affirmed at a young age, it often becomes hidden and suppressed, and shame enters.

When that happens to us, shame conditions us by wrapping around our natural instincts, convincing us that our resistance and impulse to make a boundary are arising because we are defective, inappropriate, confused, selfish, or even mean. Shame then disconnects us from instincts that allow us to create boundaries. It blunts our instinct to resist or to say "No" or "Get away." It pathologizes these instincts. If someone crosses a boundary, our ability to care for ourselves and resist injury is rendered powerless, made invisible even to ourselves.

This same wrapping and blunting can also interfere with us listening to the inner wisdom we all have that guides us on our life path. We can heal this disconnect through the unshaming process. Accessing the somatic experience is a great way of doing this, but it's not the only way. When someone leaves a comment on my Facebook post along the lines of, "How could you write this? You are so wrong," I register the person's style and tone and then I check my body. I might notice a tightening in my jaw and intensity in my eyes. I express this reaction with my hand, which rises in a "halt" gesture. My body says, "I am not open to dialoguing with you." It's a valid response.

Boundary-Setting Events and Responses

Because shame obscures, diminishes, and suppresses, when unshaming the holding of boundaries it's helpful to review a range of situations in which boundaries are needed, normal, and appropriate.

Resisting or Saying No to Assault

Assaults come in various forms, including sexual assault, physical and verbal assaults, and microaggressions. (For the record, I don't believe any aggression is "micro," but that's the term most people understand.) When someone is assaulted, shame is often present in the form of denial, dismissing, and gaslighting. In the event of sexual assault, first responders may deny and dismiss a violation by questioning either whether it happened or whether it was harmful. Family, friends, or coworkers may dismiss the abuse by calling the victim overly dramatic or sensitive. Law enforcement officers or others working in the justice system may blame the victim by pointing to the way they dress, behave, or look. All of these responses cause shame.

Of course, many assaults would be labeled as physical abuse, whether the assault is committed by a hostile stranger or by a parent delivering punishment. Being told we deserve these assaults is powerfully shaming; not having a loving witness afterward also shames. (We'll delve into unshaming assaults in chapter 9, "Shame and Abuse: Victims, Perpetrators, and the Witness.") In addition, many children are shamed into politely accepting touch from others, regardless of their discomfort and disagreement, in the form of hugs, squeezes, kisses, and even slaps called "love pats." This early shaming can manifest in adulthood as a lack of boundaries when people want to touch us; we don't feel free to say no to these physical assaults.

For example, a friend of mine does not like to be hugged in social situations. When people approach her with arms outstretched, she says, "I'm not a hugger" with a smile and backs up if she needs to. She feels comfortable maintaining her physical boundaries, and she does so pleasantly. She is not ashamed of this quality.

After I give a talk, sometimes a stranger will come up to me and say, "The story you told was so moving. Can I give you a hug?" If my boundary impulse is not shamed, I check my inner feedback by asking my body. If my body says no by tightening instead of relaxing into reception, I follow that intelligence. In those cases, I say, "Thank you for your kind intention. How about we shake hands?"

If the would-be hugger then challenges my boundary—if they say, "Why are you so sensitive? It's only a small gesture of comfort. I can't believe how closed you are. You must be triggered by an earlier event to act that way"—they are attempting to transgress my boundary by shaming me via denying or gaslighting my inner truth. The boundary violation creates an injury in the moment; the shaming can nurture the shaming witness that, over time, negates my needs, feelings, and instincts.

The disrespect and violation of our bodily integrity is almost epidemic, especially for children. Men are so accustomed to overriding these boundaries that shame leads them to lose touch with their feelings entirely. Women are so accustomed to being labeled as closed, unfeminine, or "bitchy" that they start to need homeopathic doses of these qualities to remain self-loving and unshamed.

It can be painful to recognize that we have these traits, but it's also liberating to detach from the impulse to justify or defend ourselves.

Resisting a verbal assault is unfortunately an ongoing act, as it takes the form of being faithful to one's experience while people try to deny, dismiss, and gaslight. In certain contexts it might require a level of privilege you don't have access to. It might put you in danger. That doesn't mean you're not courageous; being conscious of your boundary, even if you can't speak of it in a volatile situation, is still an unshaming response.

Assaults can also take the form of microaggressions. Psychologist Derald Wing Sue defines microaggressions as "the everyday verbal, nonverbal, and environmental slights, snubs, or insults, whether intentional or unintentional, which communicate hostile, derogatory, or negative messages to target persons based solely upon their marginalized group membership." A person who calls out a microaggression is often shamed because the dominant culture views microaggressions as insignificant and not an assault.

If you are the person being called out for committing a microaggression against someone with less privilege than you, you may feel shamed. The way to unshame the situation is also the right thing to do: apologize and be willing to listen without demanding to be educated. People from marginalized and minoritized groups are not free-range educators, especially given that they are often asked to justify their position only so someone can further debate and argue with them, which causes a secondary injury.

Saying No to Advice or Counsel

Many people reach out to others to share their difficulties and sufferings, only to be met with a firehose of suggestions, remedies, and advice. Although these attempts to help are often well-intended, when the recipient isn't asking for this kind of help, then their need to be witnessed is not met, and they don't feel seen, which can be shaming as well as frustrating. Their need has been overrun by the advice giver's need to feel helpful, intelligent, and caring. This is often a gendered response. Many of us were raised to believe that this is polite and caring behavior; women, especially, are socialized to form friendship bonds by exchanging confidences and advice.

If someone reaches out to you for help, here's a good question to
ask them: "Do you want to be helped, heard, or hugged?" If you're the
one asking for help, it can be useful to say, "I need to vent. Do you have
the bandwidth right now to hold space?" If the answer is yes, consider
defining what you're looking for: advice, witnessing, comfort, or some
combination thereof. That may not stop the person from giving you
advice, at which point it would be healthy to restate your boundary. It
can be difficult to tell a well-meaning person that we don't want their
suggestions, cures, or fixes, but it's easier when you've already shared
what you're seeking. To be clear, you don't need to prestate what you'd
like to hear in the listener's response. It's okay to let them know as it's
happening.

Saying No to Requests to Give

We are often asked to give of our time, energy, care, or other resources. If
this request is not congruent with your energy levels, available time, or
willingness, it would be injurious to go along with it. We need an inner,
unshamed witness who registers our inner "No" so we can say no out
loud. For example, when someone accepts an invitation to visit family
while knowing the visit will likely harm their mental health, they have
failed to set a boundary. Making matters worse, if the person comes to
believe that the suffering that results from their acceptance is caused by
their personal psychology—they're too stingy, they were trying to avoid
getting into unneeded conflicts, they don't speak up for themselves—
that infects the psyche with shame. Saying no, feeling free to change an
answer you've given, and even feeling free to change your mind are all
important unshaming skills.

Eliminating People from Our Inner Circle

Sometimes the only way to maintain a boundary with someone unsafe
is to eliminate them from your inner circle. This action inherently val-
idates your right to be safe, respected, and heard. If someone hurts
you and you respond by removing their access to you, you're rectify-
ing the situation by changing your outer life, instead of feeling like you

need to change your response as a way of "fixing" yourself, which is a shamed view. Setting this boundary may be met with powerful shaming responses, especially with family members or long-term relationships. Remember, a shaming internalized witness reliably leads you to two conclusions: you don't matter, and something's wrong with you. Those beliefs will stop you from taking this action or will cause you a nasty backlash in the form of an inner critic when you do.

Illness as a Boundary

Saying no is one of the main ways of asserting a boundary. In his book *When the Body Says No*, Gabor Maté writes: "When we have been prevented from learning how to say no . . . our bodies may end up saying it for us. . . . Almost none of my patients with serious disease had ever learned to say no." Thus, illnesses can play the role of boundary when people don't feel capable of saying no or otherwise holding a boundary. A person may agree to come in and work on their day off, even if they don't want to, because in the moment saying no seems impossible. Yet on the agreed-upon day, they may wake up too sick to work. The sickness is coming through in place of the unsaid verbal "No." To clarify, I don't think that being someone who struggles with saying no is making themselves sick, or that people with the illnesses have brought them upon themselves. As Mate observes, "If someone had been there to hear, see and understand . . . she could have learned to value herself, to express her feelings, to assert her anger when people invaded her boundaries physically or emotionally." He points out that being shamed sets us up to be violated, over and over, by hampering or immobilizing our ability to protect ourselves and assert our will over the will of others.

Unshaming the Holding of Boundaries

Many people who wrestle with boundaries dream at night of doors they cannot close or lock. On this journey, it may be useful to think of a boundary as a door. An open door, or a door with no lock, is a good metaphor for being unable to assert boundaries to protect yourself or affirm your needs.

When the act of setting a boundary is unshamed, you have the key on the inside and the freedom to open and close that door at your discretion. When that impulse has been shamed, often by someone who crossed that boundary in an abusive way (meaning your consent was not considered or respected), you may feel like that door opens automatically for anyone who approaches. Or you may not be able to find the key to lock it because someone else has it.

For example, when someone says, "Hey David, I hear you're often awake in the middle of the night. Can I give you some advice about that?" I consult my inner wisdom and decide whether to open that door or not. I check in with my body and its reactions: its feelings of openness and ease or tension, constriction, or dis-ease, to see if I have a yes, a no, or a maybe to hearing the advice.

If I say, "Well, I guess I should hear what you have to say," it's likely that I'm overriding my impulse to set a boundary. One part of me is open, but another is not so sure or is saying no. "I *guess* I should" indicates that I have an idea about how I should be that overrides my natural hesitation. But if I say, "Give me a moment," or "Not right now," I'm able to act in accordance with what is right for me. I have the key to my boundary door, and I'm using it.

If I don't have the key on the inside, then I bypass my own hesitancy, and perhaps I don't witness my "No." When this boundary is crossed, it will register to my psyche as injurious disrespect. My psyche will conclude that my needs don't matter, and/or that something is wrong with me for feeling sensitive, hurt, angry, or resentful after acting discordant with my deeper instincts and needs.

Often people will question and challenge a closed boundary. This can sound like any of the following questions or statements: "Why not? I just need a moment of your attention. Why are you being that way? Why are you so selfish?" And all I need to do is check my inner knowing and say to myself, "I notice I am not open at the moment." I don't have to entertain questions that disrespect my boundary, leaving me to conclude that I don't matter, or that pathologize me by suggesting it is my psychological problem that is stopping me from being open (leaving me thinking something's wrong with me). I can just speak clearly: "I see that there is not an openness at the moment," Or, "That is not right for me," or, "No thank you," or simply "No."

When you hold a boundary, you might hear, "Maybe you're just triggered, traumatized, following an old pattern." Don't let other people's use of psychological terms cause you to second-guess yourself, justify yourself, or override your experience. In those cases, I find the best response is, "Perhaps." I can decide, at a time of my choosing, to look into those issues and how they impact me. However, if I uncritically use psychological self-inquiry to override my boundary, it will invariably lead to shame.

Boundaries at Odds with Conventional Values

As we individuate, what is right for us becomes more specific, nuanced, and often discordant with conventional norms. For example, one day my client Samuel, who had gotten married a year prior, now wanted to take a trip to see old friends in another state. He'd been thinking about this trip for a few months, planning it and imagining it in his mind.

I said, "Why have you not scheduled the trip?"

"I can't tell my wife," he replied. "Every time I think of going, I feel so guilty. I think I should invite her, but I really want to see my friends by myself."

He was having trouble setting this boundary: *I want to be an individual on that weekend. I don't want to be in my married couple identity. We can be married and yet still do things on our own.*

I said, "Take a moment and get close to your feeling body, your soma. Are you there?"

"Yes."

"Imagine telling her, 'I've been thinking of visiting my friends for a three-day weekend. I would like to go alone, not together with you.'"

"Oh my god, I could never ever do that. I would feel so terrible."

"Okay. Now imagine I'm you, and your job is to make me feel terrible." I asked Samuel to do this so we could both bear witness to what lived inside him; I told him I called it the "guilt-maker." Once we learned about that voice, the voice that dismissed his needs and shamed him for wanting to say no by telling him he was a bad husband, then we could help him respond.

"Okay," he said, "I'll tell you what the guilt-maker sounds like. It says, 'You cannot go alone. You were just married. What kind of person are you? What kind of husband are you? And you say that you love this person. That's selfish. You can't go without her, it's just wrong.'"

After Samuel spoke those words to me, I froze. I thought I would easily speak back to his inner guilt-maker, but no words came up in me. That voice silenced me just as it silenced him. I looked at him and said with a jesting spirit and tone, "Dear friend, you can forget about going on that trip without your wife. There's no way." We both laughed hysterically. Sometimes humor is the best way of witnessing the power a voice and a belief system can have over us. While this moment hadn't yet freed him to take the trip alone, it allowed him to be free from the shame of wanting to go alone. He no longer saw it as a flaw, but as an inability to be free from an oppressive voice and belief.

I could have pushed him further to create that freedom, but I could see that he would only feel pressured and shameful around me because he wasn't ready to do that. So instead I asked him, "It's only been a year since you got married. Do you think there will come a time when you will feel free to set a boundary, to say no to your wife coming on a trip?"

"I do; maybe next year sometime."

A few months later he reached out to me via email: "Hey David, guess what? I went to visit my friends by myself. Who would have thought I could do it?"

The unshaming had done its work. His needs were clear to him, and he no longer pathologized his desire to create a boundary to meet those needs. He also wasn't shamed by me telling him to get over his guilt or not to let that stop him. He had his own process and timing. His sovereignty, his process, is what we followed when we unshamed; not an idea, protocol, or set of steps created by someone else.

Navigating Boundaries and Shame in Disempowered Situations

Being able to speak up whenever you feel a boundary violation can be more difficult if you're not in a privileged position. At this point in my career, I can speak up without fear of job loss because I don't have a boss. I work for myself. But many people are not in this situation.

How do you take care of yourself in a situation where you're disempowered? You may be living paycheck to paycheck. You may have a supervisor who can fire someone whenever they feel challenged or threatened. You may be financially dependent on family members due to illness or other circumstances. You may be a graduate student who needs a recommendation letter from your committee chair, so you can't rock the boat without fear of reprisal. You may be a person of color whose boss claims they're not racist, yet they come down harder on you than your white colleagues when you say no to working late.

These situations are all examples of unequal power relationships; many are oppressive. We need a social change, but unshaming does not require people to martyr themselves to this cause.

The unshaming answer to this conundrum has to do with the internalized loving witness. If the person can think, *This sucks and it's bad for me. There's a reason why I'm feeling injured and angry. I can't do anything about it right now, and it's painful for me to live in this situation,* that's an unshamed viewpoint. They know about the injustice, they know it's wrong, and they don't invalidate their own experiences, even if they aren't free to actually hold the boundary.

If that person has an internalized shaming witness, they'll think, *It doesn't matter. I have to do it anyway. The fact that this injures me doesn't matter.* That's a different description and self-concept. If their boss is sarcastic and nasty, and they react by thinking *I should put up with it* instead of *I don't deserve that,* shame is operating.

Other unshaming inner messages are:

"I get that this is a social issue. It's happening to me personally, but it's not a referendum on what I deserve."

"The stress of working two jobs makes it harder for me to be a good parent."

"My experience is true."

"Of course I'm upset, pissed off at times. Of course I get up at night feeling bad about these things."

"My dad visits every sibling on their birthday but me, not because I deserve to be ignored but because he's doing something wrong."

These statements are a form of self-embrace. They say, *I matter. It's happening because of the situation, not because of me.* The difference between these two internalized witness viewpoints is huge. The first person is self-annihilating, not in terms of taking their own life but in terms of being willing to be injured. People often resort to substances to deal with the pain of these inequalities.

In a racist society, individuals and systems treat people inhumanely. If a person of color internalizes that viewpoint, it devastates their life force, communication, and intimacy with self and others. It's very painful. Those things go in so deeply. We do not need to set a boundary to unshame; we only need to bear witness to the outer and inner messages.

As a Jewish person, it took me so many years of speaking up *more* to stop feeling like I shouldn't be listened to, that I should defer to certain people in non-Jewish spaces. I would try not to be too smart because I didn't want to awaken their animosity about striving Jewish immigrants. Then I went to a talk Nikki Giovanni gave in Portland, Oregon, I noticed how she was so free to be brilliant and creative. It blew me away. I didn't know how suppressed I was until then. She was acting as brilliant as she was. I thought, *When I'm in public I don't feel free to express myself so brilliantly.*

Giovanni said, "One day after I gave a talk, a person came up to me and said, 'You think you're so smart, don't you?' I told him, 'I won't criticize you for being ignorant if you don't criticize me for being intelligent.'"

Her response to this man changed my whole life. The medicine went in. I saw that message echoed recently by a T-shirt message: "If you think I'm too much, you should go look for less."

Years before I attended Giovanni's talk, when I moved to Minnesota from New York, people in Minnesota called me cocky. "You're trying to use $20 words," they would say to me. "You're always acting smart. You're making me look bad. You're making me feel inadequate."'

At the time, those messages went in without encountering a boundary. I interrogated myself. Was I acting? I guessed I was acting, especially because I didn't think I was all that smart. I told myself, "I really should stop doing this. It's obnoxious."

After I unshamed myself as an intelligent person *and* as a Jewish intelligent person, I was able to believe this statement: "I'm not acting. I am this way. I have a certain genius, and so do you."

If I'm in an unshamed universe, and someone says, "You're making me feel inadequate," that comment would bounce off my boundary. I would say with compassion, "Oh. I'm curious to know more about your feelings. Tell me about your feelings of inadequacy." Inside, that could feel like, *Umm. Something in me doesn't want to let that in. I'm not ready to entertain that. Something in me is not open to this statement.*

In a shamed universe, the comment would go in without hitting a boundary, and I'd think, *What am I doing wrong? How should I be myself differently to prevent this? I'm smart. That person feels inadequate. They're asking me to present a fake self so they can feel more comfortable. I guess that's part of my job description until I find a better one.*

What people call codependence (which I discuss more in chapter 11, "Patterns, Dependencies, and Codependencies") is complex, with several elements. One is a boundary issue. The organic "No" to what certain people call *enabling* is being defeated by the beliefs that "Something's wrong with me; I don't matter," which, as I've mentioned, are shaming beliefs.

Developing strong boundaries is a process. For instance, you may have vowed to check in with your body experience from now on, but then you realize hours after an encounter that someone crossed a boundary with a request or an unkind comment. If something like that happened to you recently, even if you didn't notice your body's response in the moment, recall that experience and notice your body's response now. Is it a tightening? A turning away? Does it have a sound—a growl, a rumble in your throat? Would your response move your hand up in a stopping motion?

Next, think of being asked for something that you fully, uncomplicatedly want to say yes to. How does that feel? Is it a blooming? Is it warmth? An opening, a nodding, a leaning toward the question? Does it have a color? If so, what is that color?

Nikki Giovanni, by being herself and sharing her strength, catalyzed change in me when I showed up to hear her wisdom. Being in the presence of people who model good boundaries as they move through the world nurtures our own unshaming process. How can you make this a part of your life? I do it by listening to the words of brilliant authors. I read bell hooks because she is brilliant and forceful. When beloved poet Etheridge Knight died, someone approached his mother and said, "Ms. Knight, you must be so proud of who your son became." "I'm proud of all my children," she responded, though only Etheridge won national recognition and book awards.

Having boundaries doesn't mean we don't feel pain when people say mean, hurtful, even vicious things. When I was in law school, I heard Maya Angelou tell the story of how a white woman came up to her after a talk Angelou gave. The woman said, "My daughter was suicidal. She went to hear you speak and it changed her life. I came to your talk because I wanted to see this woman who had such a powerful influence."

So far, so good. Angelou had just given a talk in front of thousands of people, one of many. She was a brilliant, critically acclaimed, award-winning, best-selling author and public figure who fully stood in her power.

The woman continued, "But I was shocked when I saw you, because you're Black."

As if a Black woman could not influence her daughter. As if a white woman was the only plausible identity of such a person.

Angelou told us, "I went home and I cried for two days."

Being unshamed doesn't mean that words don't hurt, especially when they carry the poison of systemic racism and other forms of oppression.

It just means that you don't internalize the message that you don't matter, and you don't think something is wrong with you for feeling angry, hurt, or "triggered."

Angelou taught me by her example that I could go home after a day at law school and cry—and still be strong, highly intelligent, and noble, after being told I was acting too smart, using fancy words, and showing off. I realized, "Oh, right! Things hurt! Hello." Being unshamed includes accepting our own reactions as a loving witness.

Inner Boundaries

We often think about boundaries in terms of saying no or resisting other people's wishes. But what about the boundaries we have with ourselves, when we need to say no to a part of ourselves? Often we don't notice when we cross our own boundaries. This is not a small thing. For example, if I treat my own needs as if they don't matter, I treat myself like I don't matter. It's a sacrifice that creates shame. An important part of maintaining inner boundaries is defining your needs and wants.

Let's say I'm up late preparing to teach a class, and my eyes are becoming sore and my vision is becoming blurry. My body is saying, "It's time to take a break. Get some rest." These are healthy expressions of a boundary. It says, "Stop working and rest!" But because my natural need to stop working when tired was shamed when I was a child, I have learned to dismiss those experiences and bypass the need for rest. Then later, when I'm irritable with a partner, I think I have irritability issues or problems in my relationship. That's how I begin to pathologize the backlash of having dismissed my needs. Instead of bearing witness to the need for rest earlier, and then seeing myself more clearly when I take out my tiredness on my partner, I conclude that I have "issues" that need resolving. This is how a shamed boundary around giving myself a break creates confusion, efforts to fix myself, and self-negation. Unshaming this boundary will restore its self-protective and self-nurturing powers.

Witnessing your inner boundaries can look like this: "I can't find my keys. Why am I such an idiot? Wait. I deserve kindness and patience. I am competent, but I have a lot on my mind. I will find the keys." Or, "I feel terrible every time I get on the scale. I'm going to stop getting on the scale."

When we develop and rely upon a compassionate inner witness, we stop treating ourselves in awful ways, as if we don't matter. We even learn to say no to inner criticism. Saying no to obsessive thoughts, especially when they're criticizing us, is one of the most difficult inner boundaries to set. (We'll explore this principle further in chapter 5, "Witnessing Inner Criticism and Self-Hatred.")

In training sessions with therapists and coaches, I teach them about what Arny Mindell calls *feedback*. In Arny's usage, the term refers to the flow of communication from the client that says yes, no, or maybe.

One's inner witness is a nonstop personal therapist, for better or worse. We give ourselves advice all the time, but it often contains harsh messages and doesn't feel good. It also gives us theories that we've heard about but that may be pathologizing. These theories can shut down curiosity and self-discovery. They can create a thousand and one action plans, none of which may be right for us. But that doesn't stop us from creating just one more.

Just as therapists must pay attention to their clients' cues, we need to pay attention to our own responses to requests, demands, and other people's agendas for ourselves. A wishy-washy yes is not a yes. We might notice in our body: "This doesn't feel good to me." That's an inner boundary.

Often we might realize that we're beginning to ruminate about something painful and unproductive. One person might think, "I don't think I like the direction I'm taking myself." Other times, it can go on for a while without redirection. Or it can cycle during the night, keeping us awake for that night, many nights, or months and even years. Or you might say to yourself, "I have no control over my thoughts." What seems like a lack of control is actually an overridden inner boundary. We don't witness our own feedback, the yes, no, or maybe to continue thinking, planning, or working on ourselves. I have had many clients who've said, "I've been working on myself for years and it still isn't helping." I instantly think, *What does working on yourself look like?* You can be assured that whatever they're doing, some part of them has not consented to it. They have bypassed their own "No," which creates suffering as well as shame from being treated like their resistance doesn't matter and there must be something wrong with them for not progressing.

Perhaps the most painful example of denying and dismissing our feedback to ourselves is when we've learned to punish ourselves for not acting in a way that we think is right. Then, instead of connecting to our natural "No" to being hurt as punishment, we think we deserve to suffer. This is perhaps the most insidious form of shaming. The notion that we deserve to be in pain always leads to shame. It's not that there aren't natural painful consequences for our actions; that's different from the belief that we deserve pain and suffering. The latter produces shame.

Mantras and meditation can help to develop an inner boundary. If I notice that I'm making myself feel bad, I can stop following my psyche by redirecting my attention to chanting. It doesn't have to be spiritual, although it often is. Catholic people may pray with rosaries; Hindu people may chant with a string of *japamala* prayer beads. You can also play music and sing along, engage in a task that requires your full attention, or watch a movie. These practices support your inner boundary against self-harm if they are performed consciously. When you commit to practices like these, you're saying to yourself, "I don't want to feel bad about this anymore. I'm going to say no to my own inner dialogue and the direction it's taking." That's a powerful thing to do.

Inner Boundaries, Privilege, and Eldership

When a person with more privilege is confronted by a person with less privilege, the person with more privilege may well need to bypass their immediate reactions by making an inner boundary. People with privilege often feel hurt if someone points out that their behavior is perpetuating inequality or oppression. If this happens to you, set an inner boundary by taking a breath. Feel your feelings, and then say no to burrowing into your own sensitive, vulnerable self. Spinning off into taking offense and centering one's own feelings prevents meaningful personal and social change. Hew to the boundary that is in accordance with your values. Stay available. Listen. Be curious. Reflect. Consider how you can do things differently going forward.

The most powerful people in the world often present, and experience themselves, as victims. Few people identify with their power, which means readily acknowledging the capacity to injure and abuse their power. They hold onto their power while simultaneously protecting themselves from criticism by presenting themselves as having been wronged. We often witness conflicts where all parties involved—whether they're individuals, communities, or nations—work to claim the moral authority of having been injured, wronged, or mistreated. When everyone identifies in this way, no one is responsible for the way they use power. In this way, we live in a culture with very few elders—people who can self-reflect when criticized for how they have injured others out of their meanness, manipulation, or lack of awareness. Once we have some degree of power, we need an inner boundary to separate the part of us that feels injured from the part of us that can injure. Revolutions can get started because of this tendency. When the powerful and privileged can't hear their defensiveness and self-protection and can't say no to it, accusations launched against them by those who are truly injured can escalate from words to shouts, from public call-outs to bullets and bombs.

Somebody must have the power; someone needs to be open to accusations.

We need elders—people who have worked on their story enough to hold another person's experience without collapsing, and to hold their own experience at bay while making space for another. People are standing for things that need to be heard. Political solutions won't work if there's no one to compassionately witness injustice.

Boundaries and Privilege in Action

If someone says, "David, you don't know what it's like to hold hands with my same-sex partner as I walk down the street; it doesn't feel good," part of me wants to say, "I have my own suffering; you're not seeing what I go through as a Jewish person who is living under the threat of anti-Semitism. Let me tell you about my difficulties."

If I say that, I have no ears to hear about my privilege, no ability to deepen my understanding and become closer to my friend by hearing about his experience. So instead I aim to put my pain aside and access my capacity to be an elder, a brother, a compassionate witness—someone who can accept my own privilege.

As a Jewish person, I belong to a marginalized group, but that doesn't mean I can't hurt someone else. I can be injured, but I am also someone who can cause hurt. To make this distinction and to choose the way I want to respond, I have to set a conscious boundary.

If a white retail store manager follows a person of color around a store because the manager is racially profiling the customer as a thief, the customer might turn around, call him out, and say, "That's fucked up."

The white manager might respond by saying, "You're out of line for talking to me like that. How dare you use profanity?"

That shuts down any possible social change.

If you find yourself in the store manager's role and you respond in this way, it is possible to repair the situation immediately by saying, "Wait. I never learned to roll with people speaking up like that. I'm sorry I wasn't able to meet you there. I'll do better going forward."

"Good manners" can so easily be weaponized and pass as a bid for civility. Often when someone does this they're unconscious of the white supremacist subtext. I used to participate in World Work, a large-scale conflict resolution summit where we'd work on world issues with people from over thirty countries. At one of these summits, a white participant said, "Black people are such good dancers." A Black participant responded forcefully by saying, "This is the kind of racism that hurts people."

The conflict became more heated when another white person said, "Calm down a little bit. If you're reasonable and peaceful, we can achieve our goals. We all want to learn."

A racist remark is assaultive. The Black participant spoke up to call it out, which was in support of the purpose of the event. He set a boundary.

Then a shaming witness entered in the form of a New Age viewpoint: "There's a better way to do this." The unspoken part of this message was, *The better way is our way. You people are too volatile and you don't know how to do conflict right.*

"Let's bring in the talking stick," said another participant. "This conversation is getting out of hand."

This speaker thinks they're being noble and spiritual, but they're acting superior, which ends up being more infuriating than the initial problematic comment. It's a shaming of a diverse communication style. WASP culture champions a "calm" communication style; yet it also champions never talking about politics, religion, and other areas of difference. Icing people out is common in WASP culture.

Other cultures have different communication styles. In Jewish and Black cultures, talking sticks don't tend to be the way. People speak up pretty strongly. They communicate strongly, fervently, fiercely. What looks like playing the peacemaker—"Let's all be nice"—is a shaming of a diverse style. Some nonviolent communication–type approaches are diversity-blind. People are different. Cultures are really different around how they process conflict.

In a different context that still relates to power and privilege, parents have to be able to say "I hurt you" to their children. They momentarily create an inner boundary, protecting their own feelings of hurt, guilt, or being misunderstood, so they can be there for a small, vulnerable person. They have to be able to say to themselves, "I'm a more powerful person in this person's eyes. I don't have to win the argument. I'm not just an injured person at the moment. I'm also the parent here." Being able to step out of a hurtful conflict, let go of being defended and aggressive, and hold space is a really special quality. If conflict triggers a posttraumatic response, that makes holding space exceedingly difficult. Thus, it's vital to prioritize trauma healing work so you can maintain inner and outer boundaries as a compassionate elder.

The poet Robert Bly once said, "It's the son's job to kill the father and the father's job not to take it personally."

How can the father do this? He has to draw an inner boundary by telling himself, "My son is individuating, which is healthy. It might feel like a metaphorical death, but growth and independence are leading him to the right path. It's not about me feeling victimized by his anger."

Most of what we learn about boundaries concerns itself with outer boundaries. And rightly so; when outer boundaries are unshamed and free, people protect their inherent sovereignty, and the path that becomes their authentic life unfolds more naturally and fruitfully. However, our inner work is also crucial because what happens in the outer world internalizes, and we learn to treat ourselves similarly, ignoring the ways we need to learn to say no to parts of ourselves—parts that are abusive, obsessive, or otherwise injurious. This leads to us stepping into elder roles, something the world needs more of: people who have developed the maturity to hear the voices of those who confront them, especially when those words come from people with less social or personal power and privilege. This is not the same as bypassing our feelings; it means using our awareness and inner boundaries to foster a more just world. (You'll be reading more about creating a just world in chapter 6, " Social Issues and Shame," and chapter 12, "Becoming a Witness to the World.")

Sustaining Strategies

When you become aware of your boundaries and begin to incorporate them in your responses, people in your life who are used to you acting a certain way will almost definitely resist. Some may be grumpy about not getting their usual way. Others may perceive your "No" as abandonment or another projection. You may choose to tell people you trust to be respectful and supportive of the process.

One way to address this resistance to your boundary is to say, "We could argue about it, but we don't have to. That doesn't feel good to me, and if you want to have a relationship with me, that's my response." My system doesn't have to stop holding its boundary. It's a genuine relating. We can also say, "If I override myself to make you comfortable, that won't build a deeper relationship between us."

At a training I was attending, one of my teachers, Jean-Claude Aud-ergon, was modeling conflict resolution by working on a conflict with a participant. Jean-Claude didn't agree with the participant's style of communication because he found it patronizing of others.

The person said, "Jean-Claude, let me explain what I was doing that you feel so offended by."

Jean-Claude took a moment to follow his body's intelligence and then put up his hands in a "halt" gesture. He saw that she wanted to jus-tify her style, as if his response to her was not valid. Instead, he trusted his body's response.

The person said, "You're misinterpreting me." She still thought Jean-Claude's response was misguided; she wanted to change his reac-tion to her.

Jean-Claude said to the student, "My hands aren't moving for some reason." His actions here modeled an honoring of his own boundar-ies. He was trusting his body, and his body experience was manifesting in a hand gesture. If he had been operating with a shamed system, he wouldn't have sustained his attention to his hands. He would have gone through an inner experience of self-dismissal and denial.

If you're staying close to yourself, your body will tell you import-ant things. You'll find boundaries in your own somatic expression that strengthen your assuredness, confidence, and ease.

EXERCISES

Self-Inventories on Boundary Setting

These journal prompts will bring your reflexive reactions into the light so you can have the awareness needed to make conscious choices.

1. What assault or hurt do you want to name—especially if you've felt pressured to deny or dismiss it?

2. When, if ever, have you taken other people's advice, help, sugges-tions, or coaching when you didn't actually want it? When is that most likely to happen?

3. In what ways are you giving when you are not honestly open to giving? Where could you stop giving?

4. What individual(s), if any, might you want to eliminate from your life as a form of boundary-setting?

Exploring Your Boundaries Around Unsolicited Advice

If you'd like to experience a deeper lesson in training yourself to pay attention to your body experience, take a minute to relax and settle into your body.

Then imagine someone who is not a close friend walks up to you and says, "Let me give you some advice."

What do you notice in your body when you imagine hearing those words?

Giving unasked-for advice is almost always a boundary violation. When I do this exercise in a group, people say things like, "I notice a pinch in my shoulder." "There's a tightness in my gut." "I feel an impulse to move." "I feel pushed."

Reader, now that you've noticed your own sensation, take one of your hands and express what's in your body. Maybe it's a tight or pinched hand, or a flexed, open hand.

If you could put words to what's in your body right now, what would they be?

People in my classes say things like, "Fuck you, get the hell out of my face." Yet if I hadn't asked them to track their body response, they might have just accepted the unsolicited advice out of what seems like politeness or habit. That's how strong people's inner reactions are, and yet they're often unnoticed. Our boundaries have been so shamed in the past, and that denial and gaslighting have been so internalized, that we need to make a commitment to identifying the boundary impulse and reweaving it back into our ongoing awareness.

CHAPTER 5

Witnessing Inner Criticism and Self-Hatred

Recently I worked with a writer and actor named Rob who hadn't been writing as much as he wishes he did. "I don't even want to write," Rob said. He thought of himself as a lazy loser.

We created a role play, allowing Rob first to play the role of the critic so I could get to hear its voice and witness it. This also allowed him to witness the voice of his inner critic. Most people don't witness their inner critic unless they hear it out loud or say it out loud to others. Saying it to others allows them to hear how ugly and violent their inner critic's messages are.

I then repeated the critic's words to Rob. He started to shut down at first, as he mostly agreed with what the critic had said. This is often the case; the person is not in touch with any other reaction to being criticized, in this case being criticized mercilessly and hurtfully. Where did we learn to just take it? It's a lesson we take away from the lack of witnessing of earlier abuse or other injuries that are denied, dismissed, gaslit, or unacknowledged.

As Rob went into the somatic experience of his response, he said he felt like a wall. I followed him, coaching him to stay close to the experience of the wall.

"The wall is unmovable and knows the truth," Rob said.

"What is the truth?"

"I do want to write. I've been trying to write so it sounds like other writers I respect, but that's not my way. I want to write in my own voice."

It's very common to walk around with a critic's hurtful interpretation of one's behavior or feelings. These put-downs and labelings hurt, and yet the person has no reaction to the pain. They don't even know they're getting hurt. It's an inner abuse scene with no witness. Once we support the person in unshaming the whole dynamic, they learn a deeper and more helpful and loving truth. This involves hearing the critic's words out loud, feeling their own responses, and having a witness present who believes in and sees the whole thing.

Rob's interpretation moved from "I don't want to write," to "I want to write," from thinking he should try harder to realizing he was under a pressure of expectations that were wrong for him, and realizing his resistance was not to writing, but writing in someone else's voice.

Inner criticism is rampant. The voices in our heads are often terrible: mean, harsh, condemning, belittling. Where do they come from? They appear to belong to us. But most people identify these voices as those of parents or teachers, implanted early and rooted firmly. However, when we examine these voices in many people, we find similarities in their values, beliefs, and styles. In the United States, they are often resonant with white supremacist, sexist, ableist, heteronormative, Christian-centered, capitalistic notions. The dominant culture's values show up in the media, textbooks, churches, and schools, and they're channeled by parents and teachers. What most people experience as self-dislike is first instilled by trusted adults and then reinforced by society in multiple, ongoing ways.

"I just feel bad." "I feel lousy." "I don't feel confident." When people say these things, there's something pressing down on them, knocking them down, and battering them. An internalized critical parent's messages are almost always intertwined with cultural voices. A mother's comment about her daughter's body is coming from the culture of fatphobia and patriarchal demands that women be small, light, girlish, and unthreatening. It's likely what the mother's mother told her, and so on. Body-policing comments have been instilled in girls for generations, if not centuries and millennia.

When we're up against a systemic story that reaches far back into history, it's likely not going to be resolved during an afternoon or a weekend workshop. The unshaming process is not about quick fixes. However, when the unshaming process is used, the next step in a person's unfolding or flowering of their life will surface. Even though the critic isn't totally gone, this step will be a meaningful one that will impact the person's life in significant ways. The next step might be to have new boundaries that include staying away from certain places and people.

Or perhaps the next step is not healthy avoidance but healthy resistance: calling out instances of the inner critic's abusive messages, talking back to it. It's a form of isometric resistance, and it gives the person practice at standing up for themselves. They're more easily able to renegotiate respectful communication and behavior with partners, friends, and family members. It's not a miracle cure, but these are sustainable steps toward a more compassionate and empowered life. Additionally, every person walking around with a harsh internalized critic also contains a sacred medicine designed to move them into healing and freedom. The unshaming process leads you to that medicine.

Witnessing the Inner Critic

Many people live in an internal abuse scene that goes unwitnessed and unnoticed. Witnessing these inner criticisms as oppression begins the unshaming process. It allows people to realize, "Oh, this is not just me. Others experience the same inner criticism." In other words, having an inner critic doesn't mean something is wrong with you; it's an unavoidable consequence of living in this world. But the unshaming process must go further. Inner criticism is an assault that can be abusive if the person hasn't learned to adequately defend themselves.

If inner criticism is happening unwitnessed, you're not noticing why you're feeling down or no good, which leads to the additional shaming of "What's wrong with me?" People often call feeling down or no good a confidence issue, but it's almost always an inner abuse issue. If a grade schooler is getting beaten up at school every day, you can't help them feel better without stopping the beatings. It's the same thing with inner abuse. Once you notice it, you can decide what to do about it. Witnessing it is part of the unshaming process, as my experience with Landon demonstrates.

Landon, from the Netherlands, was in a men's group I facilitated. I learned that he had been struggling with money. "Work has been a little slow lately," he said. "I am having a lot of stresses about money."

We could have given him a pep talk, but if he was being beaten up, then we needed to see and deal with that. Saying "I'm really being beaten up today" is very different from saying "I'm feeling low self-worth." If he says the latter, we can't witness the actual experience. Shame will hide the critic and prevent us from knowing how to help.

To create an unshaming atmosphere, I said to the group, "Money is such a big issue. Some have it and some don't, but not because some people are more worthy or work harder. It's not just a personal matter; we're all in the soup of how we measure ourselves and how we work out our relationship with money."

Landon said, "Money makes me question whether I've made the right choices with work and other things to be able to be financially sustaining. It makes me feel that I'm not good enough at what I'm doing. I'm not feeling successful in life."

"I see," I said. "Relative to money, there's a voice inside you that says maybe you haven't made the right choice, maybe you're not enough, maybe you haven't done it right. When you think about money, an inner critic comes up who questions you. But that inner voice wouldn't have to be critical. It could say, 'Let's think about money. What's going on?' But it doesn't. It's more challenging and creates a sense of 'not enough,' doing things wrong. How about if we get to know more about that voice?"

Landon nodded, and I continued. "If I were the critic, I would say, 'Maybe you're making wrong choices, maybe you're not good enough.'"

Landon smiled, indicating that he resonated with that voice; he felt seen. When someone accurately plays back the voices in their heads, even if there is no direct compassion shown, people feel understood. Unshaming breaks through the isolation, allowing a new witness to enter the system.

In order to deepen the experience, I asked Landon to play the critic so it could be outed even more. In this part of the unshaming process, we don't want to stop with just a few words; we want the person to express more fully what really goes on inside of them so we can witness their experience more completely.

Playing Landon, I said, "Go ahead, tell me how I've fucked things up."

He replied, "It makes me question my self-worth. If I'm not making enough money then I'm unworthy, I'm not good enough." Landon was still playing the role of himself. That was important, but we still needed to bring the critic out more. It would still be useful to hear him really explore, using his own voice, the breadth and depth of its viewpoints, attitudes, and tones toward him.

"Okay, Landon, now play that critic," I said. "I want to feel it, hear it. Really show it to me. Go ahead, give it to me straight, dear inner critic."

"You're not fucking good enough in life, you're not succeeding," Landon said. "You're not worthy. You could be making better choices in life. You're less of a man because you're not succeeding in life because you're not able to financially sustain, even in your relationship."

Now we could really hear it and feel it. The atmosphere in the room changed. The raw and honest violence of the words brought all of us into our feeling bodies.

Although Landon's critic voice began aggressively, it soon became sad and somber. He sighed, feeling how painful it was. When the voice was not directly witnessed—while it lived only in his inner world, creating unidentified experience—he simply believed what it said. Now he was beginning to feel what it was like to be on the other end of those voices. As we unshame, self-compassion enters.

Because I could now feel what it was like to have this voice speak to me, I could deeply empathize. "I'm listening to you voicing the critic as if those words are coming at me," I said. "I can hardly take it. I almost feel crushed, and it's not even being said directly to me. If someone said that to me, I would have a hard night and even many days. If it lived inside of me, that would have a big impact on my life."

Landon grins, smiles, even giggles. He closes his eyes, taking it in. Embodying the ruthlessness of the critic has done the opposite of having him identify more with it; instead, it has given him a direct experience of how hurtful it is. Before he did this, that voice stayed undercover, beneath shame's veil, leaving him to feel unworthy. Now it could be critically engaged and felt.

This voice didn't live only in Landon. Many of the men in the group acknowledged having a similar internal voice and experience. Their voices said things like, "This is how we size you up. This is how we compare you to other men. We're not going to lift you up; we're going to put you in your place." It's a cultural message. It may have been passed down through family or teachers, but it's also an internalized cultural oppression that injures many men.

The next step in working with Landon's inner critic, as in most inner critic work, involved me playing the role of the critic so he could more deeply feel and respond. When harsh criticism is present, a response is needed; otherwise it's actually an abuse scene.

I said, "Just sit and feel your body: your feet, abdomen, shoulders. Just be in your body. I'm going to say some of those critical words to you, and your job is to see what happens in your body. Don't try to respond or figure out if they're true. Keep your awareness on your body; witness what happens when these violent words are spoken to you. We need to 'see' what happens for you when these ideas come at you regularly. Tell me when you're ready."

I never want to speak hurtfully to another unless their witness is present. The fact that there hasn't been a witness is what locks in the shame and disallows healing. That's how shame germinates.

"I'm ready."

"Okay. Stay with your body. 'I don't think you've made the right choices. Your worth as a man is sized up by how much money you make. You're not doing well.'"

Landon said, "I instantly notice that my eyes start to water, get moist, and a tightness in my throat."

I didn't say more at the moment, because I didn't want to injure him. As soon as his body reacted, we had all we needed. No one should say that to him unless he's ready to be in himself.

"Stay with the watery eyes," I said. "Someone says these things, and you get teary. And if those tears in your eyes were to spread out, moist eye feelings all through your body. What do those moist eye feelings say?"

"Everything is going to be okay," Landon said. "You are worthy."

Landon has become a compassionate witness, leading me to be on the other side so that we can keep unfolding, unshaming.

I said, as Landon, "But I don't feel okay. I'm not doing so well. I feel my worthiness as a man sinking. Your moist eyes are needed to help me. I'm out of touch with how much it hurts. I don't even know I have tears when those words are said to me. I don't stop and notice the tears in my eyes; I just feel bad and think I need to do things differently. I don't stop and feel."

Landon's eyes were teary. My eyes were teary too, as were many of the men's eyes.

I asked, "How many of you men measure your worth, in part, by how much money you make?"

Many men, including me, raised our hands.

At another moment Landon might have experienced some push-back, some resistance to the oppression. But for many men, getting to know the tears is big.

Landon's relationship with money showed us an inner relationship that many people have, that many men have. And one thing we usually don't see is the feelings, the tears, that are around when money is around. More men need to be in touch with their tears when compared to how others are around money.

Men need to communicate with other men and say, "This is how it feels to be compared, sized up in terms of money. Let me show you my tears. It hurts."

Unshaming Inner Criticism

There are two paths to unshaming inner criticism. One is by outing the inner critic and supporting the person's response to it. The other is by working directly with the shamed aspect of the person.

Let's start with the first: outing the inner critic and supporting the person's response to it in words, tone, movement, and sound. Supporting the person's response includes identifying the person's suppressed reaction to being criticized.

Words

When I work with a client to out their inner critic, I ask them what messages they hear from this critical voice, and to say the statements out loud. I want to hear the exact words. Those words need to be witnessed for the person to become aware of what is actually happening. When the words are said out loud, we both become witnesses; in fact, this may be the first time the person truly hears what is going on in their heads. One example might be, "You are lazy and careless."

Tone

The next thing I focus on is tone, which I believe is the most important element. When I hear people make these kinds of statements, I often notice that they're said with a mild or reasonable tone of voice. The person who first said these things, such as a parent or a teacher, may have used a reasonable, even neutral tone of voice. And this tone might have given a destructive statement like this more credibility back in that moment. In a culture that doesn't value emotional intelligence, people are less aware of the *tones* of their inner voices. Inside the body, the tone is often a lot more potent and vicious, carrying energies that include contempt, disgust, fury, hatred, or jealousy. Thus, I'll ask the client to say it with more vehemence. Why? Because shame mutes experience, including inner criticism, but unshaming amplifies, allowing us to witness the experience as it really is. Sneaky attacks are much harder to take on and banish than loud, obnoxious ones, which allow us to clearly witness how uncalled for, even clownish, these statements are. The criticism, once a sly, intimate whisper, becomes outed as a malicious, abusive attack. Until criticisms are outed for their tone, they operate like microaggressions: easier to bypass and dismiss. When we don't notice the actual violence in these inner critics, people make shaming assumptions: "What the fuck is wrong with me?" or "It doesn't really matter that I'm being abused; I don't matter."

Sound

Making sound is also an important access to a person's response to inner criticism. What is the tune that goes along with living in response to an internalized criticism, versus a tune that goes along with the person's authenticity? The first might be a stentorian, military rhythm; the second is often a swooping, joyful tune reminiscent of birdsong.

Words, tone, movement, sound: in the unshaming process, everything belongs to the scene. Nature has put those things together, along with the intelligence and medicine of the shamed behavior or quality, to guide us. They all belong to the story of the person. It's naive to believe you can talk yourself out of shame without engaging with the complexity of the story of you. This process is not about amputating or erasing a "problem," but ultimately of unfolding, petal by petal, in the warmth of the unshaming sun.

Bearing Witness

Next, we need to bear witness to the person's response to the inner criticism. People have two general categories of responses to criticism: one is pain, and the other is their natural resistance, wanting to defend, flee, or fight back. When criticism is strong, whether internal or external, we often fall into a kind of traumatic response: we feel hurt, freeze, and lose touch with our responses. If you ask a person how they feel immediately after being strongly criticized, many will say "I don't know." We become slightly or extremely dissociated. Where does the response live, if not in their conscious mind? It may show up in dreams and in their projections, but the place to locate and engage with those responses most effectively is in the soma. Thus, when people speak their inner criticisms aloud, I also track body expressions in the form of movements or postures that go along with the spoken inner criticism. That expression is a piece of important information. Perhaps it's a clenching of the hands, or arms extending out to the sides. It might also be a somatic sensation: a pain in one's chest, a tightness in the throat, tingling legs. I don't interpret these gestures; rather, I ask the person to exaggerate the movement or sensation and tell *me* what it expresses. Exaggerating rather than interpreting supports the person's authority and natural intelligence. That's the unshaming way.

Once we out the inner critic and acknowledge tone, movement, and sound, I find out what response the person has to this externalized criticism. I don't *figure* it out; I notice what the person is revealing in their responses to the criticism. That response contains the unique, intelligent medicine we each carry inside of us.

An Example of Outing the Inner Critic

Consider the client who said to me, "The help I need is around the regrets in my life. There are so many things I didn't do."

I wondered if the issue was mainly about regrets, or whether instead there might be an inner critic telling him he should have done something he didn't do. A person's conscious understanding of their difficulty is often not informed by their deeper truth when it's veiled by shame, which focuses on one viewpoint and denies, gaslights, and ignores all other truths. Instead, it's informed by social and psychological ideas and how the person was criticized as a child. Those misinterpretations are almost always shaming. Their message is, *You're screwed up in a certain way.*

"I'd like to know more about what you mean by 'regret,'" I said.

"There are a lot of things I haven't done."

"Let's hear about them."

"There are things I didn't complete. They're valid regrets."

"I hear you," I said. "Let's try something. Pretend that I'm you. Please share these valid regrets with me so I can hear what's actually going on inside. Otherwise, it may just be a feeling or opinion. Feelings and opinions often have shame in them, whereas experiences don't." I'm asking him to put it into words.

He said, "You can't do anything. You don't have the ability or capacity to do things."

Whoa. That was really fascinating. I noticed that what he called "regrets" was actually an ongoing voice inside him, telling him he was unable and lacked capacity. There was no upset, no compassion or any mention of what he hadn't done. This internalized critic was disguised by the gentle, almost sentimental term *regrets*. It's like a parent hurting their child and telling them it's for their own good. When that happens, the person disconnects from their responses, somatizes their suffering and resistance, and treats those unconscious responses—pain, anger, depression—as pathological traits. Rather than going to the root of the issue, these responses become the focus. The person might be diagnosed as having chronic pain, rage issues, or depression. They might be gaslit. This often results in more shaming.

Now I understood why Landon hadn't completed certain things. How could he, when he was constantly being told, "You can't do anything" and "You have no abilities, no capacities"? The inner criticism is an incantation, a potent curse. Wrestling with a curse is very different from feeling regret. He was putting himself down in a very heavy way.

I said, "I'm going to say those words back to you, and I want you to tell me what happens in your body when I say them. Don't think about the words, just focus on your body. Ready? 'You can't do anything. You have no ability or capacity to do things.'"

"I feel a lot of pain in my chest," he said.

That pain in his chest wasn't from regret, which is a form of grief. He was feeling pain from being verbally assaulted.

"Can you turn this pain in your chest into an expression you show me with your hands?" I asked.

He made two fists. "Yeah."

"What do the fists want to say?"

"Get away from me or I'll make you sorry."

He reminded me of a bouncer standing outside a doorway, protective and confident. He possessed the ability to turn away the destructive statements that had been torturing him for most of his life.

"Look at that strength," I said. "You can do so many things with that strength."

"Whenever I feel these feelings, I just try to run away from them," he said. "It's like they're a predator."

Part of what kept him the prey of this inner critic was his unawareness of it. When he externalized this voice, he noticed it and could talk back to it. It was no longer a slow, invisible drip of poison. When he claimed his power, he could defend himself from a position of authority, not victimhood. His strength was his medicine.

I said, "I see you rising above this inner critic, claiming your righteously ferocious birthright. When you claim your strength, you turn the predator, the inner critic, into prey. Every day you should spend some time finding those voices. Say them out loud. 'You, inner critic, can't do anything to me. You don't have the ability or the capacity.'"

Working Directly with the Person's Shamed Aspect

Another approach to addressing internalized criticism is to work directly with a person's shamed aspect. This is especially fitting when a person is hung up on what they perceive as a specific shamed personality trait. For instance, they might say that they're lazy, too angry, or a procrastinator. The person who thinks they're lazy may think they have failed at being more productive or active. The person who thinks they're too angry might find that meditating or counting to ten is not taking the anger away. And thinking one is a procrastinator rarely promotes change.

When someone comes to me with their self-shaming label, I treat the critic's eye as a high beam pointing to an area that needs unshaming. I see the identified focal point, even though it's shamed, as a spot where the person's intelligence or superpower is.

I say, "Let's study [the shamed aspect] with an unshaming eye." I ask the person to go to that place in themselves and unfold it. I do this by asking them to share about the *experience* of being lazy or too angry or a procrastinator. Not an idea or even a feeling word, but an experience of it. An event. What's it like when you're procrastinating? What does it look like? What are you doing instead of the task you feel you should be doing? Witnessing experience is the unshaming way.

For instance, the procrastinator might say, "I watch TV." They're finding a place where they get a taste of the energy of something they love. I ask a lot of questions, because just like outing the critic, the story of this procrastination scene has intelligence and medicine in it that is revealed by curiosity. I'm tracking the intelligence of their system. The premise of my interest is this: *What you're doing is intelligent.* That's how we unshame: instead of labeling a behavior as a pathology to be removed, we find the deeper intelligence in it.

"I watch *Love Boat* reruns," the procrastinator says.

"Okay, *Love Boat*. What's it like to watch *Love Boat*?"

"It's mindless and interesting."

Though their idea of mindlessness comes from a place of criticism, I think it's an important aspect of what they need. "Tell me more about that."

"I need a space where I don't have to think about politics," they say.

They're not choosing to watch *King Lear*. They're watching *Love Boat* because they need something they're not getting in other areas of their life. They need time to go by, time in which nothing matters. They need to be suspended above their life. It's an altered state, a meditation. Mindlessness is a kind of meditation. How profound! Yes, watching *Love Boat* in this context is actually profound. Perceptions of time and space change. Calendar time goes away. Einstein said time and space are relative, and people use interventions to change their experiences of time and space. Dancing, singing, falling in love, watching TV, cannabis; yet people tell themselves, "I'm procrastinating, I'm not getting anything done." Unshaming takes the veil of shame away, allowing the deeper intelligence to be heard, witnessed, and appreciated.

I say, "What's it like in your body to be there?"

I notice the client's hands float back and forth gently. People's bodies start saying things so quickly. I'm getting that they need to float more.

I'm unshaming the activity of watching *Love Boat* or the Food Network or whatever it is because I'm taking everything they say as having an innate intelligence. For instance, another client, a writer who felt she was procrastinating instead of writing her book, said, "I like to watch the Food Network because it inspires me to cook new things in the kitchen. A creative flourish comes up. I'm making things. It's pleasure."

I noticed that this activity was pointing her toward creativity that felt pleasurable. I said, "I hear you saying that watching the Food Network instead of writing your book is giving you pleasure. You're seeking pleasure because your body's intelligence knows that you need it. You've lost the pleasure of writing, the way it used to be sheer fun. How about if you focus on the pleasure of creating the book, and not concerns of how it will be received?"

Their conflicted desire to watch the Food Network contained their own sacred medicine: a prescription for more pleasure.

Destiny's Shamed Aspect

Inner criticism came up during a recent session with a client named Destiny. I started the session by saying, "Tell me what's on your mind and heart."

"Well," Destiny said, "the last ten or so years I've been through a really tough time. I went from the person that I knew myself to be to being kind of underground. I've begun to really notice that I'm missing my own energy. I'm the type of person who, when I see something that I want to do, I go and do it. But I feel disconnected from that part of me."

"So you used to be a 'go and do it' person. What have you been like instead?"

"I've been doing nothing," she said. "I've just been kind of floating, and hiding, and just ignoring anything that doesn't feel soft and fuzzy."

Notice that Destiny has a shaming viewpoint of floating and of needing more "soft and fuzzy" in her life. Her inner shaming witness labels it "doing nothing, hiding, ignoring." This kind of communication points to the problem of shame: the person no longer explores and wants to learn about their impulse toward aspects of themselves, which are often disavowed needs. Instead, they label those aspects as problems or pathologies to eliminate.

"I hear you describing two ways of being," I said. "One of them is a 'go do it' person that you said was more like you ten years ago. And then there's another person, or a 'part,' as somebody would say if they were doing family systems work. It's another part of you. This part doesn't do anything. She floats, hides, and ignores things unless they're soft and fuzzy."

By saying this, my intention is to frame Destiny's communication in ways that bring deeper awareness to the shaming aspect of her self-perception. This allows us to explore the shaming dynamic and begin the unshaming process.

"Yes, exactly," Destiny said.

"Okay. Unshaming involves understanding and getting to know each part of you for its essential truth, need, or value. I look at the 'go do it' person in a positive way; you already do that too. And then I also look at the 'doing nothing' person in a positive way. I have to see what she's about, without judgment. I'm going to look at her to understand her."

Destiny had been shaming her "doing nothing" part, which shuts down curiosity and discovery.

Destiny continued, "I used to think about phases of my life in chapter titles. One chapter used to be 'The Rock Star.' Another was 'The Worm.' I am both. I'm getting a little tired of the Worm."

"I understand," I said. "The Worm is the 'doing nothing' aspect. I have to learn a little bit about that worm before we throw it overboard, so it's not thrown away out of a sense that something's bad about it. Not that the Rock Star shouldn't take over your life more; but we have to make sure we're not doing that by thinking, 'I've been screwing up for the last ten years, doing nothing.' When we try to cast a part of yourself away like trash, it tends to come back and demand to be seen and loved like the rest of you. And I don't want that to happen to you."

"Me neither," Destiny said. Thus begins the deeper unshaming inquiry.

"The 'doing nothing' person says, 'I don't want to do anything unless it's warm and fuzzy,'" I said. "What's it like when you're treated other than warm and fuzzy? What does the Worm do?"

"It goes underground. That's my introvert side. It needs the solitude, it needs the cocoon, to be safe for a little while."

"That's beautiful, Destiny. And right now, can you imagine that you're literally underground? You can breathe down there, because you're a worm. Feel it in your body. What's your sensory experience down in the earth, underground?"

"It's like a kind of insulation where I don't have to feel anything."

Feeling nothing is a very special kind of feeling. I knew that because Destiny had been going there for years. It must have been a really important and special place that I wanted to get to know, so shame wouldn't enter if she decided to leave. Many people shame "not feeling," but here I don't treat that as a problem; instead, I treat those words as pointing to an experience that needs to be more deeply known. Some folks, at some moments, need to be more in their feelings, and some are quite the opposite.

I said, "What's good, Destiny, about feeling nothing?" When you're participating in an unshaming process with yourself or others, remember that these dialogues require us to remove our own biases so that we don't collude with the person's shaming biases.

Destiny said, "There's protection. My body just relaxes. There's this image of my mind starting to move around inside of a library."

As Destiny was supported to deepen her experience, new information arose. That indicated the unshaming process was working. We now knew that where once there had been a label of doing nothing, there was now a potential need for relaxation. And, a new image—the library—was introduced. This mysterious image signaled that it was worthy of deeper exploration.

"Fascinating," I said. "Your body relaxes, and then your mind moves around in a library. Incredible. I imagined the relaxing might happen, but the library . . . that's a mystery to me. That's marvelous. Look around at the library inside your mind. Are you in a certain section? Is it a big library? Are the shelves tall?" I offer these details as a way of prompting her to get closer to what the library signifies to her.

"Yes, old books, and the kind of books that a lot of people might find boring," she replied. "Reference books, and textbooks, and ancient knowledge." Destiny's clear answer indicated that the inquiry into the library was important. If it hadn't been an important inquiry, she might have mentioned something unrelated to the library or might have simply not known how to answer. If that had been the case, I might have to let go of the library inquiry because following Destiny's impulses was critical to the unshaming process.

Destiny had been thinking of herself as doing nothing, ignoring life, and hiding. That's a shamed view. The unshamed view is "I've been in a library down below the earth, reading texts and studying ancient knowledge."

I didn't want to stop there, though. There was more to be gleaned. "Tell me about this ancient knowledge that lives inside of you, Destiny."

She said, "Maybe it's more timeless, outside of all the noise and the negativity, the things that people fight about. It's really important for me to be able to communicate outside of conflict. Conflict is important, but there seems to be so much conflict for its own sake in today's world. And I just don't feel safe there."

"Wow. Some part of you could live in the 'doing' world as a Rock Star. But you don't feel safe there, and so a part of you lives in time-less knowledge." This framed the initial conflict without shame, as both aspects were worthy and important to Destiny's life. Many therapists and other well-meaning people might say to Destiny, "You don't feel safe in conflict; let's help you feel safer in conflict." I teach conflict resolution, and I appreciate that intention, but the part of Destiny that conceptualizes doing nothing as time spent in a library is saying, "No, David. There's a timeless wisdom that doesn't involve conflict. Don't forget that."

I wanted Destiny to teach me more about this because I wasn't in this session to tell her what to do. I was there to facilitate the unearthing of her intelligence and integration of her own medicine, her way, not my way or pop psychology's way. The unshaming way. But I was also eager to learn because I sensed she was about to share some amazing insights, wrought from ten years of her study. Her internalized shaming witness did not value these insights—yet.

Destiny said, "I think I'm trying to understand love when it's all wrapped up and intertwined with all of the noise and conflict of engaging with myself, and with the people I love, who have their issues too."

"Yes," I replied. "My partner and I have conflicts at times, and we've got to work out our differences. But the glue that holds us together has nothing to do with those conflicts. It's beneath all that. It's down in the earth. Beneath all that stuff, there's something we can call love." Here I offered a bit of my own experience to create an unshamed atmosphere together, where she could feel less marginalized because others were similar to her.

"I think I'm struggling with trying to find how to be at peace with the love that I'm given, even though it's not a love that I understand," Destiny said. She was trying to integrate two aspects of herself. One was a noisy, conflictual part. The other experienced not just a safer world, which was already important, but a world of timeless wisdom, something more profound and needed when Destiny entered the noisy conflictual world.

I said, "Can you close your eyes for a moment and go back underground? You want to connect these two worlds so that when you decide you're tired of being down there, you don't lose touch with it. That's the unshaming way." I spoke to her as her Rock Star self, asking her to connect with the worm, the wise librarian. "Dear worm woman under the ground, can you please teach me? Give me a message. Help me out.

I don't want to lose touch with you." Because both parts of Destiny were important and because Destiny's initial request was to come out into the world more, I wanted to help her build more of a relationship between the two. Initially, shame defines the relationship as a good-bad binary. Now this process was lifting both parts into the light of an unshamed awareness. Jungian analysts would call this integration, or shadow work. The Rock Star has been in the spotlight. The Worm has been in the dark underground library while being disavowed by the primary identity or ego.

"You have to keep the roots in place," Destiny said. "That will allow things to flow up into the flowering side." Destiny's response showed her the way to have a more sustainable relationship between these parts.

That's so beautiful, and you might be thinking that this is a perfect last line. It could be! But it's not enough to know what we need to do; we have to know how to do it.

"How do we keep connection with our roots?" I asked.

"I have to learn to close my ears to outside voices that tell me that the buried part of me is somehow not a good thing."

The unshaming was complete. Destiny now had free access to both parts of herself. She had the power of a person who was not at war with themself, but instead had woven together the parts. She now had the power and depth of someone who was whole.

Destiny's wisdom is telling us that accepting the messages of shaming voices cuts us off from our roots, our timeless knowledge, and our ability to stay grounded amid all the noise and conflict. Looking to others to check that we're doing the right thing is not a rooted action. When we do that, we drift wherever the wind takes us. We have no inner authority rooting us to the earth.

Our culture tells us that we should be doing and getting and going. We should be rock stars, influencers, popular, elected, winners. But our capitalistic American culture should not impose itself on our wisdom and knowledge. In fact, the values and people who shame Destiny in her underground library of timeless knowledge could be seen as the ones with the problems: superficiality, distractions, noise, unnecessary conflict. In this way, we could say that the worm woman is the healthy one. She's got the medicine.

The medicine she discovers for herself will also become the medicine she offers the world. Over time she will learn to bring people into the underground library of wisdom, their own wisdom, and the collective ancestral wisdom. The unshaming work flowers into Destiny's path in the world: Destiny is a medicine woman, and now she knows what her medicine is, what she's been alchemically cooking in those ten years. If we didn't walk the unshaming path, Destiny might come out of her ten years underground, but who would she be? She would come out without the wisdom. She would get into conflicts and then turn against herself when retreating back into her safer underground wisdom. She would label her time underground as a waste, coming up as if she wasn't weaving mythical threads into gold. And most important, she would not know what her path of heart is, what her gifts are.

EXERCISE

Feeling and Expressing Hurt and Resistance in Response to Inner Criticism

1. What criticisms do you regularly have of yourself? If you're not sure, what do you most dislike about yourself?

2. Rise to your feet, facing a chair or another part of your room. Imagine someone there that you will criticize. Tell them what you, as the critic, think. For example: "You are so lazy. You procrastinate all the time. You're a loser. You're so stupid, sensitive, loud, hard to get along with." Say these criticisms out loud at least three times, each time making the words and tones more powerful, intense, even ruthless.

3. Step over to that other side of the room or that chair (the place where you were directing your criticism) and imagine those words being said to you.

4. Feel the hurt in your body. Where do you feel it? Bring your awareness to that physical, somatic experience, and make a sound. Amplify the sound, expressing the hurt.

5. Now feel your resistance to these words being said to you by imagining the words being said to you again, but this time notice if your body wants to turn away, stiffen, curl up, or become more tense. Feel that experience somatically. Take your time.

6. Amplify that experience by turning further away, adding more tension and stiffness. And then amplify further by allowing your whole body to express itself. Do this by supporting it to become tense everywhere, or really curl all the way up. Speak some words of resistance—think of a phrase or sentence and say it out loud.

Feeling and expressing hurt and resistance is a powerful healing experience, allowing you to get to know and love yourself more deeply.

CHAPTER 6

Social Issues and Shame

In an appearance on the *Today* show, Michelle Obama told a story about her experience in an ice cream store with her daughters when her husband was president and her daughters were children. She had asked the Secret Service staff to stay back so she could share this everyday moment with her kids without drawing a lot of attention. Just as it was their turn to order, a white woman cut in front of them and gave the employee her order.

She said, "So I stepped up, and I said, 'Excuse me?' I was like, 'You don't see us four people standing right here? You just jumped in line.' She didn't apologize, she never looked me in my eye, she didn't know it was me. All she saw was a Black person, or a group of Black people, or maybe she didn't even see that because we were that invisible." In a separate public appearance she talked about the incident as an example of Black people being "treated like we don't exist. . . . And when we do exist, we exist as a threat. And that's exhausting." She noted that most white people didn't understand the "daily slights . . . in our workplaces, where people talk over you, or people don't even see you."

She provided some unshaming medicine by sharing her experience publicly. Through speaking about this form of microaggression, she witnessed the racism behind it, making it visible. Sharing stories about microaggressions renders people less likely to dismiss their feelings, less likely to internalize shame.

Although the literature and teachings on the issue of social injustice and bigotry are wide, deep, and plentiful—especially by educators who can speak from the authority of their own experience within their social identity—the lens of shame and the power of unshaming offer a unique and illuminating vantage point, turning our focus from the perpetrators and victims of assaultive behavior and policies to how all of us witness these transgressions. Let's begin our discussion by examining how understanding shame highlights the distinction between direct assaults and microaggressions.

Direct Assaults, Microaggressions, and Internalized Oppression

Direct assaults on our social identity need to be witnessed and named, of course. These are blatant, overt, and often institutionalized assaults: racial profiling by police, sexual harassment and rape compounded by the court system's secondary assaults, bullying of queer youth, the US government's refusal to comply with Native American treaties, and the resulting physical assault of Native protestors at Standing Rock. When such assaults go unwitnessed, their impact on people is shame, leading people to be pathologized or treated as if they don't matter.

Assaults can also take the form of microaggressions (like Michelle Obama's example above), which fly under the radar of mainstream awareness, making them less likely to be witnessed and more likely to lead to shame: wait staff giving the restaurant check to a man, not a woman; a cashier waiting for a person of color to put money on the counter so they won't have to make physical contact; assuming gender pronouns; or treating a person with a stutter as if they are not intelligent.

Dr. Kevin Nadal, author of *Microaggression Theory: Influence and Implications*, made the following observation on NPR's *Life Kit*: "The difference between microaggressions and overt discrimination or macroaggressions is that people who commit microaggressions might not even be aware of them." Because microaggressions are not as easily seen or witnessed, those who are injured by them are more likely to be seen as problems or as if their feelings don't matter. In other words, shame is more likely.

In chapter 5, "Witnessing Inner Criticism and Self-Hatred," I talked about how inner criticism is not just an individual issue; it almost always channels social and institutional biases and viewpoints too. In this chapter we'll apply that principle by examining shame in the context of social issues. I'm also going to share how being a compassionate witness to people from marginalized and minoritized groups is necessary, grievously rare, and an act of unshaming.

Direct Assaults

In the book *The Luminous Darkness*, theologian Howard Thurman, one of Martin Luther King Jr.'s greatest influences, tells the story of being a young boy living under segregation, raking leaves for a white family after school in order to earn some money. The family's young daughter followed him around as he did his task, scattering the leaves as he raked them. Thurman asked her to stop scattering the leaves because it was making more work for him. She refused to stop, so he threatened to tell her father.

She became angry, took a pin out of her pinafore, and stuck him in the back of his hand.

"Ouch!" he said. "Have you lost your mind?"

"That did not hurt you—you can't feel," she said, echoing a belief that many white children were taught at the time. What a clear example of denial, dismissing, and gaslighting—finding a way to believe that a group of people does not feel pain, even in the presence of their truthful reactions to mistreatment and severe abuse. We could readily say that the girl didn't "mean" any harm; we needn't attribute conscious mean-spirited intent to her action. Treating a person as if they have no feeling, as if they don't feel pain, or even as if they are too sensitive is the basis of shaming them. Jabbing Thurman with a pin was an assault;

treating him as if his pain wasn't real was a shaming act. Something similar happens today in medical offices and hospitals where people of color are treated as if they don't hurt or as if their symptoms and pain don't warrant treatment or medication—a form of systemic shaming.

"Something is wrong with you" and "You don't matter" are messages of shame. Failure to witness racism has a shaming effect. Unshaming difference by being a compassionate witness is a powerful form of activism that anyone can practice.

How people dialogue about social violence, forms of social oppression, and marginalization is a window into the stories we tell ourselves about our nation, illuminating how we shame or unshame the oppressed. These narratives either help us to face ourselves and bring about change, or they chain us to the unjust systems and dehumanizing practices of the past.

Healing narratives create a container for our collective understanding and healing by affirming the social causes of our hurts and the natural reactions of those affected. Dehumanizing and inflaming narratives shame by denying and dismissing the social causes, and they gaslight those who express their anger, grief, or other feelings that disturb the dominant culture.

Let's look at a particularly challenging example of this behavior: the murder of Tyre Nichols, a Black man, by five Black police officers. (Of course, a similar analysis of how shaming narratives operate could be applied to any social oppression.) Many narratives about this incident denied and dismissed the role played by America's racial caste system and institutions. They concluded that race was not a factor in the murder. They suggested that the grief and rage of Black people have nothing to do with their racial identity and history. Research published by the American Psychological Association showed that "the denial of structural racism appears to be a big barrier to racial equity because it allows for more victim-blaming explanations of systemic inequality." These narratives gaslight people's reactions to racial violence, suggesting that the reactions are inappropriate, caused by psychological dysfunction. Professor Angelique Davis and Dr. Rose Ernst define racial gaslighting as a process that relies on "racial spectacles," as we are all currently witnessing. Their research has found that acts of gaslighting "contribute to white supremacy at large."

Narratives of denial, dismissal, and gaslighting are weaponized to relieve dominant cultures of responsibility and accountability at the expense of oppressed subgroups. How does this happen? Here are some examples of narratives around this incident that illuminate the problem, drawn from comments on my social media posts about Tyre Nichols's murder:

"I find the event excruciatingly, heartbreakingly horrific ... whatever the patterns that created this inhumanity."

The denial and dismissal in this comment enter here: "whatever the patterns that created this inhumanity." That comment specifically omits race and the racial caste system. This kind of response decenters the issue of race, blurring the focus and the central issue.

"Memphis is peacefully protesting (much to the dismay of those who want to see us burn or tear each other apart). We're here to honor Tyre and create change."

This person engaged in the gaslighting of people who responded to the murder with anger and outrage by focusing specifically on those who "burn and tear." Instead of affirming the pain and rage people experienced, this comment censored and morally policed people's outrage. This not only gaslights people's reactions but also further inflames people. In fact, when people say, "I can readily see why people would want to tear and burn," that validates and calms the people who are outraged.

"This is a horrific incident, but justice is being served here. It is so unfortunate the evil that fuels these occurrences, but God will always prevail. His death will not be without purpose or meaning and it will spark goodness out of darkness!"

This narrative is a particularly insidious form of gaslighting, suggesting that people should focus on the "goodness," even godliness, that can come out of horrific suffering. Offered only days after the brutal murder, it dismissed the agony people felt, inflamed their suffering, and encouraged people to judge forms of feeling and expression that are more connected to the "darkness."

"You do realize all the officers were Black. These were five men on a power trip. Not everything is about race. I'm sick of people fueling the divide when it's about personal responsibility."

This narrative denies and dismisses the issue of race entirely. This is perhaps the most dangerous type of narrative because it invalidates the daily experience of people of color while suggesting that there is no reason to respond to the event by addressing systemic racism. This particular narrative caused the most confusion for my white community. People asked, "How can the murder of a Black man be a racist act when the murderers were five Black police officers?" Because racism is systemic, an institutionalized caste system. I use the word *caste* here in the context of Isabel Wilkerson's masterwork *Caste: The Origins of Our Discontents*, which meticulously delineates the underlying systems that unevenly distribute power to groups based on social identity and have profound impact beyond status, to affect our protection, health, and emotional well-being. The law enforcement system has been a central cog enforcing the caste system in the United States for centuries. Therefore, witnessing unwarranted and unreasonable violence perpetrated upon a person of color, regardless of the race of the officer, must make clear that such murder is not just the result of the actions of one or more officers; it's also the result of living in a marginalizing and dehumanizing system.

This understanding was echoed by the Center for Police Equity, which said that their "concern has never been with the hearts and minds of individual officers or chiefs. . . . Any officer working in such a system risks finding themselves engaged in behavior that is racist in nature, even if they do not personally hold racist beliefs or are themselves Black."

In a *Harvard Law Review* article about James Forman Jr.'s book *The Black Police: Policing Our Own*, Devon W. Carbado and L. Song Richardson write, "African American police officers have to negotiate and reconcile two historically distinct strivings—the strivings to be 'blue' and the strivings to be 'Black'—in one 'dark body.'. . . How they perform that negotiation and reconciliation is not simply a matter of individual choice, individual agency, and individual commitment. Structural factors are at play as well."

Healing racism requires more than identifying "bad" police officers and prosecuting them, just as healing social oppression must go beyond an analysis of perpetrators and victims of the violence. It also means interrogating the narratives we receive and carry as a culture, especially those that deny structural racism and gaslight responses to extremely avoidable tragedies. It means being a compassionate witness by listening to validate and unshame rather than to argue, deny, and dissemble, which reinforces internalized oppression.

Microaggressions

As we saw above in Michelle Obama's story, not all assaults are as overt and easy to see. Microaggressions are less blatant, less likely to be compassionately witnessed, and thus more likely to be dismissed and gaslit. The result: people who are being mistreated often second-guess themselves, pathologize themselves, or hide their wounds, even from themselves—all of which are aspects of shame.

Over the past few years, more people have been raising awareness of microaggressions. As trans people often use pronouns that align with their own gender identity (rather than their pronouns assigned at birth), it's important to address them with the pronouns they use and request, such as *she/they*, *he/they*, or just *they*. Refusing to do so is injurious, and acting like it doesn't matter creates shame.

When such unconsciousness prevails, it carries the belief that marginalized communities' difficulties and barriers to conventional measures of success result from either psychological or moral inferiority of the individuals. That's pathologizing, dehumanizing, and implying that people don't matter. That's shaming. In Brené Brown's book *Imperfect*, she writes, "Dehumanization—the core of racism, sexism, homophobia, transphobia and all systemic forms of oppression and/or bias—is a form of daily trauma."

Assaults on our identity can also be perpetrated by people who cri-
tique the way we communicate and express ourselves. For example,
some of us hold our bodies more still, while others wave their hands and
arms when they speak; some readily reach out with warm touch, while
others retreat from physical contact; some are more likely to engage in
fierce debate, while others are more likely to be quiet and listen. Forms
of expression that align with mainstream culture are supported. But
when this cultural pattern goes unrecognized, people in that culture
assume that other forms arise because people are psychologically or
morally less fit. That's how shame enters.

When I was at a conflict resolution seminar with about three hun-
dred people, a conflict arose about racism in the United States. A Black
woman confronted a white man, accusing him of racist language and
treatment. As the debate became heated, another white person spoke
up and said, "Everyone, let's calm down. We can speak one at a time,
not over each other." The initial assault was direct, but the assumption
that speaking calmly was the right way is an unconscious microaggres-
sion, carrying the idea that white mainstream ways of communicating
are superior, and shaming heated reactions to injury. One Black man
witnessed the shaming and said, "I'd rather people make direct racial
insults than assume my style of relating is inferior."

When we are told and come to believe that our authentic form of
expression is wrong, or when it is judged without a witness, shame
enters. Societal oppression enters us in the form of shame. I first became
aware of this when working as a consultant at a Fortune 500 company.
I got feedback from the managers that they thought my partner in the
consulting firm would be a better fit for the company as a consultant.

"Why?" I asked.

"You move your hands, get emotional, and use academic words,"
they said.

I took it in and laid a whole trip on myself. Why couldn't I be relaxed
and poised? Then I talked to my mentor, Len Hirsch, about it.

He said, "That company is notoriously anti-Semitic. Your partner
is a classic unemotional, reserved WASP. They're having an issue with
your cultural difference. There is nothing wrong with you."

When he witnessed me compassionately, noting the hurtful feedback, it instantly unshamed me. It still hurt, but I no longer assumed something was wrong with me.

When it comes to the problem of shame, microaggressions need focus and conscious witnessing so the people who encounter microaggressions don't internalize the sense that something is wrong with them or that they don't matter. As an ally, it's important to speak up, to be an "upstander rather than a bystander," says Dr. Jess Zonana, psychiatrist and medical director at the Weill Cornell Medicine Wellness Clinic, which offers mental health care to LGBTQ+ individuals. "As hard as that might feel to do, it's even harder to do when you're the object of the microaggression," she says.

Internalized Oppression

It's easy and common to internalize oppressive biases against oneself and not notice, to treat ourselves the way dominant systems of oppression treat us, but this makes the need for witnessing—and healing—essential. In fact, because we rarely discuss how oppression lives inside of us, a level of self-pathologizing and not mattering forms for almost all of us. In one workshop I led, a woman said, "I've been working in therapy for many years, and I'm still angry." The word "still" is invariably a sign that shame is present. "Still" indicates that someone thinks they should have solved an issue already or that something is wrong with them. Further, the agenda of removing all of her anger aligns with sexist biases, which often indicates the presence of internalized oppression. Many women resonate with this story because one of the ways patriarchy works is by dismissing, denying, and gaslighting women who express a healthy resistance to submitting to conventional gender norms by feeling anger.

Many women have learned that "healing" means to get over or be rid of their anger, before they actually connect to their experience at a somatic level. Once I was working in a session with a woman who was well-versed in feminism and activism and who worked to promote voices of women in the world; but when I asked her to share what it was like to be angry, she didn't seem to have access to her own voice and creativity. After I witnessed her difficulty, she saw this lack of access to expressing anger as a form of society-inflicted blindness to her internalized oppression. Shame, rather than self-appreciation and self-worth, wrapped itself around her anger, leading her to believe something was wrong with her. Instead of noticing the ways her anger was a healthy response to encountering micro- and macroaggressions, she pathologized herself and this anger, and thus saw it as something to eliminate from herself. But that's like trying to remove a limb. Her anger was a sacred, just, intelligent, and protective part of her being.

Blindness to internalized oppression is so common because it is so rarely witnessed. Even in the literature, there is much greater focus on examples and personal stories of external oppression. I find that people often focus either on an external issue or on their inner selves in the form of psychological work, but not both. Yet it's important to do both because they flow together and offer complementary support. Some will become more clear about the outer world when they work on their inner selves. Some need to learn more about the outer world to realize it's not just about them.

Unshaming work with regard to social oppression and injustice must highlight how these phenomena live inside of us as individuals, creating marginalizations, priority systems, and unjust allocations of resources within us. When this recognition does not happen, people shame their suffering, concluding something is wrong with them or that their suffering doesn't matter.

About ten years ago, I worked with a Jewish man in his seventies who has now since passed on. He stood about 5′1″ and was very self-conscious about his height. He saw it as the major issue of his life. I asked him when he started to feel self-conscious about his size, and he said, "When I was a child." He talked about being bullied by other kids.

"Tell me more about the bullying," I said.

He thought for a while, then exclaimed, "Oh my God, they were beating on me because I was Jewish." He was blind to this part of his story and to his internalized oppression, and it took being asked to remember the details of the bullying for this aspect to surface in his memory and be witnessed. He had pathologized himself, thinking he only had low esteem because of his height. He never made the connection to his social identity. His actual story had to do with being short and Jewish, because the other kids picked on him and beat him up because of those qualities. This is an insidious form of self-negation and shaming for most of us who have internalized hurtful views of ourselves and are blind to the social lens. We often think our inner criticism arose from family members alone or simply because there is truly something wrong with us. Witnessing the social dynamics unshames.

Here's a different example of how blindness to internalized oppression creates shame. A client of mine said, "I grew up evangelical, but I'm not anymore." But what people experience inside—how to be, what's right and wrong—that doesn't change because one day you decide you're not going to do that anymore. If a person grew up in a strict religion, their inner life functions like brick structures that are as hard to move as the foundations of a building. This is another form of internalized oppression. Before this client could grow toward having a harmonious outer and inner experience of being postevangelical, he needed to unshame by outing the evangelical voice and its messages, not denying or dismissing them. Otherwise, when he suffered, he would conclude that there was something wrong with him.

Similarly, many immigrants changed their names when they came to this country. My family changed their name from Bedrickoversky to Bedrick. Along with wanting to assimilate, they hoped this would give them a freer life disconnected from their history. But a name change doesn't change a person's inner experiences and stories; in fact, it can serve to render those experiences and stories invisible, making the pains and sufferings appear like pathologies (Why am I like this?) instead of stories (What happened that gave rise to my suffering?).

In my session with a client named Moriah, we'll see how powerful internalized oppression can be, and how the unshaming process empowered her to shift it. We'll also observe the power of being attentive to both the inner self and the outer world.

"I've been reflecting on visibility and why sometimes I don't feel seen," Moriah began. "As an Indigenous child [in Canada], I felt that I was ugly.

I'm just now realizing how long I've carried that feeling. Then yesterday, someone made a racist comment about my eldest child's appearance. It's generational; it's personal. I wonder whether shame makes me hide. Is there a part of me that feels like it's not safe to be seen?"

"Thank you for bringing that forward: a childhood issue, your child, and then an issue of being an Indigenous person," I said. "If I ever say that in a way that is not right for you, I won't feel criticized. Sometimes psychological and healing ideas refer to a person in a one-size-fits-all way, neglectful of how a person is a representative of a group with a shared identity and set of experiences."

Moriah's experience brought to mind an instance when I'd worked with a Black woman who shared the pain of a doctor denying her account of being in physical pain, and I shared that story with Moriah. "We had to deal with her individual injury and also engage with it in the context of medical racism," I said. "It's not an either/or situation. The conventional approach can bring shame because then one might think, 'What is wrong with *me*, that I felt ugly as a child?' rather than seeing it in context of dominant American ideas about beauty, especially decades ago, when white, blond-haired, blue-eyed women represented the one and only ideal of female beauty in popular culture. I'm going back to what you were saying about visibility and being seen in a certain way. Let's try to enter that experience and unshame it, Moriah. I want to bring forth the eyes and the consciousness behind them that looks at someone and says, 'That's an ugly person.' For us to unshame, we have to reveal those eyes. They have to show up and be accountable for what they're seeing. Otherwise, they will remain internalized. You're nodding. What are you thinking?"

"I see the eyes," Moriah said, "but they're shape-shifting and hiding in the floor. I can't quite get hold of them. They keep dancing around, and they take on different shapes. Now they're appearing in a forest."

"Fascinating," I said. "I didn't know that you were going to see it that way. Do you see a person, a head, a body? Or just the eyes?" Here I asked her to amplify and add detail to her visual experience to deepen it and allow it to be more fully witnessed.

"The eyes are so clear. The other part's a shadow," she said.

"Is there a way you could enter or shape-shift into those eyes?" I asked. "They're also inside you, because they look at you from the inside. It's internalized oppression." Having a person channel internalized oppression brings it to life, a rare and powerful act of witnessing and unshaming.

"I see them as missionaries, priests, nuns," Moriah said. "They move me to a residential school classroom. I see this image often. They're standing tall. I'm sitting down like a child, and they're standing taller than me." As in the United States, the Canadian residential school system removed Indigenous children from their families; its policies forbade their ancestral languages and dress. Teachers and staff were responsible for untold deaths of Indigenous youth, in addition to physical and sexual abuse.

I said, "Would you be able to pick one of those people, who is channeling something that many people channel? Maybe entering one of them might help us get to know it. In the unshaming process we have to out everything. I'm not going to shame those eyes. I may disagree with them fiercely, but that's different than shaming. I may tell that person, 'I won't let you look at my friends in that way.' That's not shaming. It has to be brought forward, because it's very hard to address a perpetration that's not outed. If it never comes forward all the way, we don't know what's actually happening. Shame hides the whole damn thing. See if one of those people in the residential schools has those eyes, even a little bit of them. Let's pretend that I'm you, and you're looking at me through those eyes. What are you seeing?"

Moriah said, "You have the wrong hair, you have the wrong color skin, you have the wrong eye shape. You are less than me. I'm more powerful than you. You are not enough, so we have to change you." Moriah's channeling of the eyes' message allows us all to bear witness to its malice, its deadliness. We have taken the helmet off Darth Vader to see its misshapen and insidious intent.

To keep bringing consciousness to her suffering, I asked, "Where did you get the idea that my hair, skin, and eyes are less than beautiful?"

We counter oppressive assaults by standing against them; we counter shame by making it more visible.

"Everybody knows this," Moriah said.

"Oh, I see. You think, 'It's just true. It's just obvious.'"

"I look around, and all the people around me look the same, and you look different."

"And where did you get the idea that different means less beautiful, less powerful, less worthy?" I asked. I am not asking these questions in an accusatory way; I don't want to "win" an argument. Unshaming arises organically as awareness enters the cracks and hidden recesses.

"Different is dangerous," she said.

"You feel like you're in danger around me and people who look like me. Is that what leads you to attack and insult me?" I said.

"Yes, there's something that scares me," she said. "That's why I have to put you down."

"Tell me about your fear."

"It feels like anything that's not assimilated causes me to shake and to judge it. It's not safe to be around," she said.

"I'm hearing you," I replied. "You're not safe, you're in danger. You're shaking. And then somehow, rather than being scared like a child might be, something else happens in you. You decide to look down on *me* and think *I'm* ugly. That's an interesting shift that you make from that place." Outing the nuances and layers of detail is a powerful unshaming technique, increasing the person's inner witnessing framework.

"Now, be in your own self, in your own body, in your own spirit," I said. Now that we knew much more about the eyes that lived in the world, the eyes that she had internalized, the next step was to learn about how Moriah responded to these eyes. That would require more than intellectual discussion or critique of those eyes, which are the approaches many would use to disabuse her of these hurtful notions. Unshaming requires that she come to know her experience in response to these eyes. That way she is not relying on another's authority about the issue, but her own body and truth.

"Got it," she said.

I said, "I'm going to represent this. This is not David's voice. I'm channeling something because it has to show up so that we know what to do with it. It lives in the world, and it's internal to many people. I can't make it go away, but I can find out what cooks in you when it's offered to you directly now, not hidden behind the trees in the forest, as just eyes."

"Okay, I'm ready," Moriah said.

Speaking as the eyes, I said, "I'm scared of you. You are different and I get scared. And when I get scared, I look at you and I see hair that's not right, and skin that's not right, and eyes that aren't right. And I need to feel big and strong, and more powerful and better than you. That's how I deal with it."

"And when I stay with myself, the first thing that comes is compassion," Moriah said. "Compassion for the fear."

"Trust that," I said, as me this time.

"I understand that fear," she said. "I have compassion for the way that you are handling it, and it still causes harm."

"It doesn't really matter to me that I'm causing harm," I said, returning to the oppressive role in the conversation. "This is the way I am. That's the way I deal with it." I remained unmoved by Moriah's compassion. Why? Because I knew that she had applied compassion in the past, and it didn't often help; because I know that these kinds of beliefs can be powerfully resistant to change; because I didn't want to trivialize the problem by having it go away easier than it actually does in the world. I wanted to see if Moriah had other needed medicine, beyond compassion.

"You're hurting me," she said. "You're hurting my future children. You're hurting their children and their children by treating me this way." Moriah is discovering more of how she really feels and thinks, and as she does, she implores these eyes to respond to her hurt. That's what she would naturally do in life.

"Over here I feel for you a little bit," I said, "but something in me is not willing to take it in. I can't allow myself to feel for you. I'm sorry. This is what I've learned to do to take care of myself. I think I'm going to continue to do it. I might even teach my children the same."

"Then I just feel something in my body goes like that," she said, raising her hand in what looked like a shield, "and I turn and then I walk away." This was new; a next step. In addition to her great compassion, which didn't stop the abuse, her body brought in another medicine.

Now I spoke as David again. "Sorry, Moriah, to stay with the ugliness of this attitude, but I don't want to make it artificial and make it all nice when it's as ugly as it is. This is the ugliness we're looking at. I'm calling this 'ugly' because we're talking about beauty. You put your hand up and then you want to turn away."

"I've tried to understand you, and there's no communicating with you," she said.

"Moriah, imagine in your depths that you've turned around and walked away. And let's trust you all the way—because that's what unshaming does—and let's imagine that there is nothing you can do to change this consciousness. This thing stays this way. It will continue to injure you, and your children, and your children's children. Imagine that you know that. And you're walking away. What happens now? Stay with that."

"I just saw myself walking toward that forest that I saw the eyes in," she said, "and it looks dark, but then it says, 'Walk towards the beauty.' I'm not sure what that means, but that's what I heard." I knew we were in the right place for Moriah because she was connecting to beauty, which is where the social wounding landed.

I said, "Something says, 'Walk toward the beauty.' Stay with that. Keep listening to that voice. Unshame everything; everything belongs. Stay with that voice, keep listening to it. Its tone, its words. What do you mean, walk toward the beauty? There are ugly eyes in there."

"But I have a boundary now," Moriah said. "It feels like an actual energetic boundary or vortex that I'm walking through. I actually even start to run."

"Tell me more. Go toward the beauty. What you're saying is important, but I don't quite get it. 'I feel safer. There's a boundary around me, a protection around me, but I'm in an area where there's ugliness, there's eyes that would injure.'" I'm restating her words to help her focus on the unfolding moment, to keep alchemically cooking the vision and feelings she is having.

"I'm just seeing my hand go up," she said. "That was the boundary, and that's going to bring the beauty. When you believe yourself, it seals something up. The eyes are still there, but they can't get in."

"Wow. The boundary creates beauty. I love that. Let's take one more moment with that sealed place. What's it like for you?"

"As soon as you said that, these ancestors came with drums and it became just this beautiful harmonic drumming," Moriah said. "The drumming is so powerful and pulsating and alive. There's a massive amount of protection there."

"That's incredible," I said. "And then with the boundary and the connection to your ancestors, shame won't enter. Your compassion is beautiful. but not sufficient to fully witness how lethal the assault is. Now the words are still hurtful, but you know they are not true. They are seen clearly; they don't enter the psyche and body. That makes a world of difference. Moriah, thank you so much. I am touched by the depth that you brought and where it took us."

As I reflected on her words, I saw how the whole unshaming session began with her not feeling beautiful, only to later discover a profound kind of beauty in her clarity, boundaries, and ancestral connection.

Sometimes understanding and compassion don't change outer bigotry or the internalization of that violence. People don't always say, "Oh, good, I want to go work on that and learn. I'm going to read books. I'm going to study Indigenous poetry. I'm going to go to therapy. I'm going to do something to heal my consciousness.' Often, we need to go further to unshame the person, not only allowing them to find more powerful protection from social violence but also giving them access to something they didn't know was there—in this case, the beauty, the drumming, the ancestors in addition to the hurt. Shame can steal our connection to our deepest gifts and medicine.

Moriah said, "I was thinking about my response to someone making a racist comment toward my son yesterday."

I said, "Moriah, if the world won't change enough this year or next year, your son is going to keep on encountering racism. How will you help him?"

"He spoke up about it," she said. "He told somebody. His generation is shifting, and it's been ongoing. It connects to having a boundary. He's able to speak up right away and set a boundary."

After having this experience with Moriah, I saw the deep importance of creating and strengthening an inner boundary, as we discussed in chapter 4. It can protect you and usher you into a nurturing space of beauty and resources.

Unshaming Is Believing

I believed Moriah when she told me that white people's reactions to her instilled the belief that she was ugly. But too many people deny, dismiss, and gaslight people's firsthand accounts of racialized oppression and even genocide. For example, I was recently watching a documentary about the Holocaust. It presented interviews with people from all around the world, and the most common thing people would say about the Holocaust is, "I just couldn't believe it was true. I just couldn't believe it was happening." It's hard to perceive the prevalence of this response in our fellow humans. Instead of pursuing changes to reduce suffering, they say they don't believe it. This resistance to belief is so rarely addressed directly. We need compassionate witnesses to step forward during acts of social bigotry, hatred, phobia, and marginalization. These acts are assaultive and often lethal, just like other crimes.

As with all assaults, two types of injury follow. In the case of police brutality against Black people, the first type of injury is literal: police beating and killing innocent Black people. The second injury, shame, enters when the first injury is not witnessed. This happened when a queer friend of mine went out to dinner with her wife and put her arm around her wife at a restaurant. Another diner stared at them, shook her head in disgust, and whispered to her husband. They both looked at the queer couple and smirked; then the woman glared at the couple until their meal was over.

When my friend told an acquaintance about it, they said, "It wouldn't have happened if you were more discreet." The gaslighting messages were that my friend had suffered because of her actions, and that her suffering didn't matter; she didn't matter. These messages imply a third message: "I don't believe you were actually assaulted." This second type of injury can also be deadly because it can imprison people in a self-concept that prevents the flowering of their gifts, their love. This identity-based shaming exists as a problem for all marginalized and minoritized groups, including people of color, women, Jewish people, Muslims, immigrants, and people with disabilities, among others.

Social media discourse provides perhaps the most powerful space for connecting and educating today, but it also reveals how assaults on social identity and shame operate, and how shaming witnesses undermine the belief that there was an assault. For example, I posted on social media about how many states outlawed the teaching of advanced placement African American history, citing it as an example of the US racial caste system. I received over two thousand comments in response, so I studied them. I noticed in the comments a pattern of misunderstandings, defenses, and blindness that served to uphold the racial caste system, fomenting a lack of belief in systemic oppression. Outing these patterns can be useful to examine in the context of unshaming social harm.

I also observed that some white commenters spoke of having been attacked by a Black person, saying that this was also racism. They aimed to make this experience equivalent to the racism that Black people experience. This claim denied and dismissed the systems of the caste. One Black person injuring one white person is not the same as a systemic set of practices, beliefs, and policies that permeate our systems of employment, health care, law enforcement, justice, housing, education, and banking, among others. The injury spoken about by these white commenters is not an injury experienced by all white people systematically, even if the Black person they encountered happened to hate that white person or even all white people. They did not suffer from a *system* of oppression. Positioning one event as proof of an equivalency aims to dismiss the racist injury, which is a shaming move.

Many commenters argued for a critical examination of how African American history is taught in high schools, wanting it to be unbiased. However, these same commenters did not argue for a critical examination of how conventional US history is taught, a history known to be centered on white people and men. This misunderstanding is important because it speaks to the essence of white privilege: to have an assumed and presumed right of entitlement, space, and voice while being unconscious of that privilege. In other words, "My right is unquestionable; your rights must pass through *my* evaluation." Witnessing privilege is fundamental to unshaming because it represents the often unconscious and unseen manifestation of a caste system.

The commenters on my post offered argument after argument to prohibit the teaching of advanced placement African American history. What does this have to do with shame? Outlawing this education reveals the way the culture witnesses Black experience, and it delivers shame's message: "Your history, suffering, and injustice don't matter. You don't matter." The lens of shame highlights the depth, clarity, and need to declare "Black Lives Matter." Mattering unshames.

Unshaming Complicity with an Oppressor

When a person's social identity is connected to what we see as an oppressive culture, they also may need some unshaming. Otherwise guilt, apologies, and hiding will veil the experience of actual empathy, pain, and remorse.

I once went to a conference with attendees from many different nations in Europe. As we introduced ourselves, I heard, "I'm Josef from Switzerland," "I'm Anna from Italy," and then came "I'm Karl from Europe." Karl was a German man. Later, when I asked him about his choice of words, he said, "I was thinking, 'everyone's going to see me as a Nazi.'" There's nothing wrong with his suffering, but when shame enters, hiding his suffering, healing becomes blocked for him and for others.

I witnessed this from another angle when I was teaching a course on the connection between body symptoms and psychology in Poland. A young German man came to see me for an individual session during the course.

"What do you need help with?" I asked.

"Nothing," he said.

"Why did you come see me?"

"My grandfather was in Hitler's army, and I needed to tell you, a Jewish person."

We both cried. When I told Arny Mindell about this, he said, "We're all in prisons."

I'm not saying that what this German man carries is the same as what I carry, or that anyone from a marginalized group owes a representative of a historically oppressive group forgiveness, a hug, reassurance, or to be present with their shame and sadness. Still, I believe he and I both got freer that day. Before that, I could not fully see him in his pain and suffering, and he might have not seen mine. Bearing intimate witness doesn't change his feelings; it simply unshames them, allowing us both to show up with our authentic experience and create a healing space.

During the same course, a Polish woman came to a private session with me. She said, "I live on a cobblestone street made of headstones from a Jewish cemetery. I drive on this street every day, and I needed to tell a Jewish person." She needed a witness so she could feel and share the pain instead of thinking her pain did not matter. Her raw pain, unshamed, again opened the door to deep healing.

The outing of experiences between groups is really incredible. It's not a sharing of equivalencies, but it is a kind of sharing that gets at inner experience, and that's where unshaming happens. It has a medicine power in it that political discourse doesn't have. Sharing experiences allows your humanity to be present in that story. It allows a witnessing. Recall how we discussed in chapter 1 that shame is not the same as guilt, accountability, remorse, or the need to make amends. When one carries shame, it doesn't foster greater compassion or moral behavior; instead, it disconnects a person from these qualities, leading their moral actions to be performative at best, instead of authentic.

I remember being at a town hall meeting in Oregon during an ongoing political debate about whether to allow school libraries to carry books that depicted same-sex couples as parents. Evangelicals opposed this, and they put forward a political measure to ban the books. Queer folks were rightfully upset about this, and a group of conflict facilitators organized a town hall to give both sides a chance to be heard and to hear each other. During the meeting, evangelical folks stood up and read from their Bibles.

Someone said, "That's not how you should interpret the Bible."

Another person asked, "Would you be willing to not read from the Bible and just tell us what you think?" Humanization can happen when people speak from their own viewpoints rather than arguing principles or acting as a mouthpiece for a text.

One facilitator asked the evangelical people, "What would your life be like if you hadn't been saved?" The evangelical people told horrific stories: "Without Jesus my life would be lost," and other things like that. Many of their stories were trauma stories.

This questioner then asked the group of queer people, "Where would you be without your solidarity with other queer people?"

"I'd be suicidal without people beside me," one person said, and others expanded on that.

Maybe nobody changed their politics that night, but people walked out talking to each other. That was really touching to me. Human beings showed up. Not all of them present at the meeting that night showed up, but some did.

"What's it like being you?" is a humanizing question. It needs to accompany—but not replace—critical thinking and debates, which highlight injustices and suffering, and give people a chance to use their voices. Answering the question "What's it like being you?" names experience and can unshame. Dialogues that drop into personal experience, beyond ideas, opinions, and judgements, dissolve the veil of shame, allowing healing to take place at a deeper level. Dialogues about experience can name abuse, and that's important. Human experience and dialogue can be a huge social intervention if they're given a forum in which to happen.

It's important to distinguish between shame and inner criticism. Inner criticism functions as an assault; it injures: "You're ugly, stupid, immoral." Shame enters when injury of a systemic nature is not witnessed. When it is witnessed, as we saw with Moriah, the person becomes aware of the assaultive nature of the criticism instead of believing it or thinking their hurt doesn't matter. When confronting social injury, we must witness the systemic aspects of an injury, not just the individual hurt. We need to witness the systemic bias. When this happens in a group, it often strengthens the group's immune system against shame and replaces loneliness and isolation with solidarity, connection, and support. Our antishame immune systems are always strengthened in the presence of a loving witness to social, cultural, and systemic forms of oppression.

James Baldwin's "A Letter to My Nephew" is an act of compassionate witnessing intended to strengthen the immune system of a vulnerable young person, as in the following passage: "This is the crime of which I accuse my country and my countrymen and for which neither I nor time nor history will ever forgive them, that they have destroyed and are destroying hundreds of thousands of lives and do not know it and do not want to know it.. . . It is the innocence which constitutes the crime." This innocence, as I discussed above when I talked about unconscious privilege, is one of denial, dismissal, and gaslighting.

Baldwin is doing the witnessing for his nephew: "Here you were, to be loved. To be loved, baby, hard at once and forever to strengthen you against the loveless world. Remember that." He knew his nephew would need a certain kind of love that would give him an immune system against shame, against internalizing bigots' opinions of him and his potential, his glorious gifts.

What does a strong immune system look like? When someone criticizes my communication style as being too animated, too "New

York"—a coded way of saying "too Jewish"—I can now respond in unshamed ways:

"Communication is a diversity issue."

"Your way of communicating is perhaps a bit muted, suppressed, lacking passion."

"Did you know that your preferences for communication styles includes a subtle bias against people who are different from you, like Jews and Latinx people, for instance?"

I don't walk away thinking "What's wrong with me?" or "My way is not good and needs to be corrected and fixed" or "The hurt I feel doesn't matter—I don't matter." In other words, I don't internalize the shame of the gaslighting culture. I may feel hurt, but I don't think something is wrong with me.

Assaults on our worth, dignity, beauty, power, and intelligence are perhaps most insidious and far-reaching when these attacks are on our social identity. Often, as Wilkerson demonstrates in *Caste*, these attacks are built into our systems, creating and enforcing castes not unlike those we see in India or those that existed in Nazi Germany.

But our analysis of social injustice and injury must not stop with our efforts to prevent these assaults. It must also educate us all about the impact of how these assaults are witnessed, something we are all tasked with, whether we are the perpetrators, victims, or neither. Witnessing assaults has a dramatic effect on the perpetuation and healing of these wounds. That is why understanding shame in this context is imperative. In addition, shame, as a lens, specifically highlights the distinction between direct assaults and microaggressions, allows us to perform narrative analyses of social commentary, and offers a powerful tool for understanding and healing internalized oppression.

EXERCISE

Restoring Your Identity's Immunity to Pathogens

1. What identity, social category, diagnosis, or subculture do you identify with?

2. What are some of the hurtful attitudes, behaviors, or beliefs about that?

3. If those attitudes, behaviors, or beliefs were to be put into unfiltered words and stated completely bluntly, what would people say? Don't hold back; say what many people never dare to say to your face.

4. Now imagine saying those same words to a big rock, a piece of wood, the sky, or a mountain—something in nature that cannot be harmed by those words. As we did with our work on inner criticism, say these words out loud three times, each time making the tone and words stronger. It's important to hear the words with your ears, even though many people never say the actual words to you directly.

5. Next, use a hand gesture to express the energy of these words. For example, make a slicing motion, a jabbing motion, a punch, or hold up a hand as if to say "stop." Get to know the attitude and energy of what you face regularly.

6. What would it feel like if these words and this energy came at you? If you're not sure, imagine someone saying these words to you, and feel it in the body—somatically. Would it cut you, smack you, knock the wind out of you?

7. If you were free to say whatever you wanted in reply, what would you say? If you're not sure, go back to the energy you expressed in step 5 with your hand gesture. But this time, allow yourself to use this energy. Make the hand gesture and add words of defense or counterargument. Say the words out loud at least three times. Get to know what it's like to be injured and to stand against social bigotry.

If social oppression is a significant part of the pain you experience in life, let me suggest that you do this exercise once a day for thirty days. That will help you build your immune system against this kind of toxicity, helping you refrain from somatizing people's attitudes toward you.

CHAPTER 7

Body Shame

"Every body has a story and a history," writes Roxane Gay in her powerful memoir *Hunger*. She "ate and ate and ate," hoping to make herself bigger, so that her body would be "safe." Gay doesn't offer her story as motivation or to show us a path to being smaller or managing our eating habits. She doesn't even write about loving herself the way she is. Instead, she shares her story, her truth, her subjective experience. That's a strong example of unshaming.

When we apply the unshaming concept of being curious about experience to the topic of body shame, so much intelligence, self-advocacy, and medicine comes forth, as it does in the story of my client Isabella.

Isabella began our session by sharing her concerns about her self-described need to lose weight and change her eating habits. She didn't want people to see her "looking like this."

"I don't like myself," she said. "I need to be healthier. I'm eating too many carbs nowadays."

Improving one's health is a worthy goal, but when they don't like themselves—when they feel a need to be invisible, unseen—I know shame is likely to be intricately woven into their system. When the impulse to lose weight is motivated by body shame, the results are almost never sustainable and are invariably hurtful.

I asked, "What would you say is the main focus of your hunger?"

"Potatoes," she replied. At this point a lot of people would offer Isabella strategies to diminish or regulate her carb intake. But offering that solution before listening to her body's story and experience would imply agreement with a shaming view, instead of looking for the intelligent message behind the craving, the hunger behind the hunger.

First I wanted to learn more about the timing of her change in eating and weight because some people change their eating patterns in response to stressors or abuse. When that happens, there's a story that needs to be witnessed.

"At what point did your eating habits change?" I asked.

"About five years ago."

"Was anything difficult going on in your life at that time?"

"Yes, that's when I had an online acquaintance who went from being friendly to writing me invasive and vile sexual messages, against my stated wishes and consent. After I blocked him, he found my address somehow and began stalking me. He mailed me letters and left flowers and perfume at my door."

I asked Isabella if she had ever realized that her eating habits had changed around that same time, and she hadn't. It's interesting that she, like so many people in similar situations, didn't notice this change. But when a person doesn't relate to themselves with compassionate, unshaming self-inquiry, it's often because there was no compassionate witness to one or more violations in their earlier life who would have asked thoughtful questions about their experience. This is important because compassionate witnessing has healing power. In addition, it would have modeled this process for Isabella so she could internalize it. Instead, when Isabella's pastor violated her when she was fourteen, the community blamed her instead. At an early, vulnerable time in her life, they criticized her and told her there was something wrong with her. When this happens, people internalize that way of seeing themselves from then on, criticizing and pathologizing themselves and looking for ways to fix themselves enough to be acceptable.

Isabella's self-criticism, which echoes the criticism leveled at her by her mother and other people in her life, also echoes misogynistic, capitalist, fat-shaming societal beliefs. Why misogynistic? Because when women monitor their body and don't feel worthy unless they're a specific size, their confidence and self-actualization are undermined. Why capitalistic? Because weight-loss programs are a big business; the net worth of the diet industry in the United States alone is $76 billion, according to the *Wall Street Journal.*

Internalized shame precludes compassionate self-reflection, the act of noticing and of being curious. "What's going on with me? Why did my eating patterns just change in an odd way?" Opinions and theories show up: "I need to be thinner and healthier." "I'm undisciplined." "I'm making myself unhealthy with bad choices." "I'm self-medicating with food." These opinions and theories interfere with getting to know oneself.

I engaged Isabella by expressing curiosity about her experience. "What happens when you think of this man, this stalker?" I asked.

"I want to go away," she answered. "I imagine going into my bedroom and putting on a sweatshirt and pair of sweatpants. Then I put on another sweatshirt and pair of sweatpants on top of those. I layer on more and more. Then I get into bed, under all my blankets."

"And what does it feel like in your sweatshirts and under the blankets? What's so good about that?"

"I feel safe, comforted; no one can see me."

The intelligence of Isabella making her body bigger is clear. She was seeking a suit of armor made of soft layers. She was also seeking to camouflage her body's form. This was a protective response to this predator's invasive acts, giving her the feeling of comfort and safety, because for women in US culture, gaining weight fends off a great deal of unwanted, preying attention from men. This unshaming view of Isabella's behavior shuts out the world of "What's wrong with me and how can I get fixed?" and ushers us into the world of "What's right about me and what am I doing?" With that heart and understanding, Isabella and I could begin to work on actions she could take to feel safer in every aspect of her life, instead of focusing on where the protective impulse landed: in the realm of eating and weight.

If I had taken the approach of strategizing with Isabella to decrease her carb intake and lose weight, we would have missed out on treasure chests of information, insight, and intelligence. We wouldn't know Isabella as a subject, a woman with a story instead of a pathology. We wouldn't have discovered the intelligence behind her response. In a world in which men prey on and violate women and other disempowered individuals—within oppressive, patriarchal systems like law enforcement and religions that ignore, gaslight, dismiss, punish, and humiliate them for seeking protection and justice—the intelligence of Isabella's body would never have been acknowledged. This intelligence knows that her own need for protection and safety against a stalker is more of a priority than her looks or her body mass index (BMI). Unshaming her means trusting her, not giving her a program that indirectly feeds her shame. She needs support in designing an approach that addresses her comprehensive need for safety. If I as a well-intentioned man tried to help her lose weight, I'd be representing a societal blindness to her story and to sexism. Her psyche would register that I was an instrument of this shaming structure.

This is why conventional diet programs almost always fail, because they inflict harm on their clients by prescribing external fixes without granting the person dignity as a subject with a story and a body attempting to deliver intelligent messages. They are allies not of their clients, but of body shame and their bottom line.

If you do an online search on the term "weight loss," you'll need to wade through pages of links before you read about a woman who was raped as a girl and who now feels safer in her big body, or about how people address their deeper hungers by eating certain foods. Only 10 percent of women who lose weight keep it off. Eighty-one percent of ten-year-old girls are dieting, regardless of their BMI. Ninety-seven percent of women have violent voices in their heads that talk about their bodies. Being overweight or even mildly obese is not a health risk, while gaining and losing lots of weight *is* risky.

The best studies in this field are meta-analyses, meaning they review multiple studies and build a data set that is much more powerful than any individual study. Perhaps the best study on this topic ever done (Katherine M. Flegal, PhD; Brian K. Kit, MD; Heather Orpana, PhD;

and Barry I. Graubard, PhD, "Association of All-Cause Mortality with Overweight and Obesity Using Standard Body Mass Index Categories: A Systematic Review and Meta-analysis," *JAMA* 2013, 309 (1): 71–82) found that "overweight is associated with significantly *lower* [emphasis mine] mortality overall relative to the normal weight category." In addition, "We did not find significant excess mortality associated with grade 1 obesity, suggesting that the main contribution to excess mortality in obesity comes from higher levels of BMI."

A patriarchal culture that objectifies women's bodies and circumscribes the expression of their power is inextricably woven into weight-loss efforts. Most pertinent to unshaming: women do not stick to or comply with these programs because their body's intelligence resists the self-hating and body-shaming attitudes that informed their initial motivation to lose weight. All the while, the diet industry profits by banking on women's body shame and perceived failure around weight.

I dream of a world in which all diet programs would have an intake process that asks, "Have you experienced abuse?" The body expresses intelligent messages through eating patterns and habits as well as how its shape shifts with life experiences and aging. These messages are often, but not always, directly related to abuse people have survived. They're also related to having perfectly legitimate needs that women are forbidden to embrace and express. These needs seek alternate modes of expression through eating habits and preferences. (We'll be discussing abuse in more detail in chapter 9.) If eating programs were informed by unshaming practices, clients would have a chance to receive the messages from their bodies' intelligence. As it stands, people's cravings and eating practices are shamed, which doubles down on existing internalized shame and serves as an obstacle to sustainable change and healing.

Another way bodies are shamed is in medical settings. For instance, I'm afraid of needles due to a traumatic childhood experience. And I've interviewed many people, men and women, who don't get medical help because it involves stepping on a scale. They have grown to expect a shaming statement, such as "Looks like you've been eating too many French fries," or "Putting on a few extra pounds, I see," or, "You know this is unhealthy, don't you?" A lot of people don't tell anyone about these humiliating exchanges. They want to avoid being shamed by someone who says, "Get over it, don't be so sensitive," or who smirks and says nothing.

Regarding needles, I've learned that it helps me manage my fear to ask the practitioner to get the shot ready, and then to give me the chance to say, "Now." Being able to request when I get the shot makes it much more bearable. I think my fear may be more about feeling powerless than an actual needle penetrating my skin. With regard to body size and weight, people have options. You can ask not to be weighed. You can request to not be told what you weigh. You can also make it clear that you're not there to talk about weight. One example: "I always appreciate when a doctor is sensitive to body shaming and body positivity." It can be helpful to role-play with a trusted person beforehand. Some people feel safer having an ally come with them to their doctor, or working with a doctor who is more aware of body shaming.

If you relate to this, consider saying to your doctors or dentists, "I've had some trauma related to medical care." Using the word *trauma* has power. Even if your provider doesn't know anything about trauma, they'll often slow down because they feel like they should provide trauma-informed care. At the same time, this gives you an opportunity to be a compassionate witness to your own trauma and sensitivity, and to advocate for yourself as an authority.

Racism's Intersection with Body Shame

When I began working with Jasmine, she was forty-one years old, and she worked at a company where she was one of only three Black women out of 150 employees. She had been experiencing a pervasive desire to be smaller—ostensibly by losing weight.

At the beginning of our session, she told me about a recent dream in which she was trying to get away from the police who were chasing her. A friend said, "Here is a car for you." It was a beautiful, colorful Cadillac convertible. She wanted to take the car, but she thought that if she did, she would certainly get caught because it was so flashy. She thought, "I should drive a PT Cruiser instead," although that car didn't appeal to her.

This dream turned out to be quite prescient. It showed her being chased by something and that she had two alternative modes of responding: showing up bold and flashy or blending in and being less visible. This is a decision almost all members of marginalized groups face: *How much will I assimilate, accommodate, so I, as an innocent person, don't get caught?* "Get caught" includes everything from getting dirty looks from a stranger who thinks the person shouldn't exist—let alone be flamboyant—to getting pulled over by a police officer who shoots them without provocation.

Jasmine said to me, "You can put yourself in a less flashy car in life, but can you get away with that? I don't think it will feel very good. But, on the other hand, if you take the Caddy, you'll get caught."

I said, "I'm thinking that race and racism is part of talking about weight for you."

"Absolutely."

We then spent time talking about Black women and men who are powerful—resplendent, expressive people like Maya Angelou and Cornel West. Jasmine didn't feel comfortable behaving that way. We decided to focus on her struggle with her size and weight as a manifestation of this central dilemma of being a person in a minoritized group.

When Jasmine was twelve, her older sister died. For years afterward, Jasmine told people she was an only child, trying to act like her sister had never been there.

"She killed herself. She was very thin, a size six," Jasmine recalled. "I remember thinking, 'Wow, I can't even fit into her clothes,' when she was ten years older than me."

I heard this intelligent message through her story: "Listen, David, this is a life-and-death issue. People can die. Even being thin won't prevent that." Again, unshaming involved bearing witness to what she was bringing forth.

Jasmine's perspective about her body size was influenced by her sister's struggle—a chasing of thinness in response to the dominant white culture's values. At the same time, Jasmine was also influenced by her family culture. "My parents never worried about weight or talked about size," she said. "My mom believed in meals, not snacks. In the morning, we had eggs, toast, cream of wheat. I filled up on real food, not snacks and desserts. Outside the house, it was a different story. In second grade I remember boys bullying a girl on the playground for being fat. The boys called her Fatty, Porky. I felt bad for her because they were hurting her feelings. And then I thought, 'What about me? Maybe I'm fat.' I was a solid, healthy kid. I didn't think about it a lot or come to a conclusion about my weight. But the seed was planted."

"You say your sister was thin, a size six. What does it mean to be a size six?"

"Thin, white—it's the way it's supposed to be. It's control, not only over other people. It's control in that things come to you more easily. You don't have to work as hard. It's lighter, not as heavy."

Of course, Jasmine feels drawn to the privileges of being thin and white. She would not be racially targeted; she'd be allowed to be more visible, supported, flamboyant, and fierce.

I asked what felt heavy about her life. "I have to suffer indignities, big and small, all the time," she said. For example, I got an email at work that was addressed to one of my Black woman colleagues. There are only three of us out of 150 people. It's like, 'You motherfucker.' I always have to hold myself in check."

The person who emailed her couldn't keep three Black colleagues straight. This is a common microaggressive behavior in which Black people are seen as Black first and as people second. Mixing up Black people's names is one way this racialized perception shows up.

I said, "You didn't say anything, even something far less inflammatory, because that could be deadly to your status at that company. To keep your job safe, you didn't take the Cadillac."

"Exactly. I took the PT Cruiser."

When Jasmine chose the PT Cruiser instead of the Cadillac, even in her own mind, she was stifling and suffocating the part of herself that identified with the Caddy, out of fear of what would happen to her—discrimination, ridicule, harassment, death—if she went ahead and embodied her size and boldness. She and I witnessed what her unhappiness with her body was really about and why she wanted to be thin, not big and bold. If I didn't make the effort to understand her experience and the world she was forced to contend with, and focused instead on helping her lose weight, I'd be turning a blind eye to the complexity of her subject position. I would then become a shaming witness, complicit with oppressive systems. Any weight-loss program that didn't acknowledge its racial implications—and their shaming impact on Jasmine's sense of herself—would deny, dismiss, and gaslight Jasmine's experiences.

"As I got older," Jasmine said, "I noticed thin white women, their body types. I will never be a size six. However, some part of me absolutely wishes I could be. Does that mean I want to be like a white woman? Isn't that self-hating? That's really disloyal."

I asked Jasmine if she felt comfortable role-playing to investigate this double bind of either feeling discomfort for having a large Black body or feeling disloyal for wanting a thin white body. She agreed, so I began by saying, "'I wish I looked like the thinner white girls and women.' If I were a Black woman who said that to you, what would you say to me?"

"You can't think that way, that's so unhealthy," she replied. "You have to find a way to feel that you are beautiful."

"I can't do that," I said, continuing to role-play. "I absorbed this belief my whole life. I don't know how to do that."

"I don't either, but we have to find a way," Jasmine said. "I tell people that I weigh between one-eighty and one-ninety, but I actually weigh two-twenty-five. If I could get down to a size ten, that would be terrific. Size six would be even better. Size ten is okay, but it's not my ideal." Even in telling people her weight, she tried to shrink herself. By wishing she were thinner and smaller she was thinking of her body as if something was wrong with it, instead of listening to its story and experience. That's what shame does. And her internalized need to be smaller was influenced by racism that sought to diminish her presence, soul, and humanity.

"The story you told me about your sister shows the potency of that particular size," I said. "When you tell people you're thirty pounds lighter than you are, that's a little death of that unaccounted-for part of yourself. It's an accommodation to a norm and culture that are not truly your own."

Jasmine wouldn't identify as suicidal, nor would she see herself as following in her sister's footsteps. But there are other ways of killing oneself a little bit every day, such as covering up, blending in, and not showing up as we truly are. That's what shame does. Externally, racism kills people directly through bodily violence and a steady drip of hatred and the inducement of fear. Racism also kills from the inside when it's focused on the body's size and shape, and it's been internalized and unwitnessed.

"I get the appeal of being thin and white," I said. "Control, ease, power, freedom. That's a very compelling offer. Who wouldn't be seduced?"

"Right?" Jasmine said. "And you'll be safer too. There's a sense of being protected. You don't hurt things that are beautiful in your environment. Men protect you! You can even use your power for good, to do things. It's an all-around good thing—it's a panacea!"

Although the reality is not nearly so ideal—men beat up, rape, and murder beautiful, thin white women every day—the belief has power, both for women who are relatively more protected and for women who feel like they don't fit into a protected category.

"Wow, it's like being thin and white is the answer to life," I said.

"Absolutely," she said, comfortable and clear, "because when your life is easier, happier, you put beautiful things into the world. You get all the other things out of the way." As she said this, I saw the colorful Cadillac of her dreams and wondered what form the beautiful things in her would take.

"What could you do if you had this safety and ease?" I asked.

"I'd be kinder and easier on myself. I wouldn't struggle so much with feelings of worry about what's going to happen next. I would really be able to help people who need help."

"I see. First it would ease your anxiety, and then it would free you to help people. How would you help people?"

"Through my love, my kindness. There's a lot of love in me." Her eyes filled with tears. "Wow, that's emotional for me. I think it doesn't come out very often. I worry that it will be damaged. My love wants to come out, but it's not always safe."

This revelation blew my mind. Our unshaming process had made it clear that her desire to be thin was a desire for safety and support that provided the right conditions for her to express her love. That project had been distorted by shame. What she needed in her life was increased safety and support so she could embrace the fullness of herself: the resplendency, style, and flair expressed in her Cadillac dream, and the freedom to love. How will Jasmine get there? She needs the help of allies, internal and external, in pushing against the system that oppresses her so she can move, love, and create in the world as the resplendent person she really is.

Confusion: The Foe of Inner Authority

When shame infects our system, we leave our self-knowledge behind. In its place are questions and ambivalences: "Why am I so depressed, angry, sensitive?" "How come I'm still grieving/can't let go/feel upset with my family?" "I'm hurt, but it's really all my fault."

I've worked with person after person who came to me saying, "David, I have to get over being so triggered." And when I ask about the event that triggered them, it's a genuine, healthy reaction to being disrespected or mistreated. Shame teaches us not to trust our feelings. Instead, we ask why we have those feelings, as if they're symptoms of an illness. We ask why they still arise, as if we were doing something wrong. Rather than trust our body's feeling experience, we apply theories and opinions to our feelings, like, "I'm not really upset with my parents, because I understand why they were so abusive."

When I work with people on body shame, they mostly talk about what they don't like about themselves, the efforts they've made to change their size and shape, or the various reasons for their "failure" to change. However, when they make contact with their actual body experience instead of shame's bypassing opinions and judgments, they notice that they are filled with fire, power, grief, hurt, resentment, jealousy, or other feelings. Unshaming the body starts with making this kind of direct contact. When this contact is not made, it's impossible for the person to access their own knowledge. Their authority is all projected outward onto other people and organizations that supposedly know better. They're not rooted in their own earth: their body, their truth. Their inner authority, which comes from a deep trust in one's own experience, remains fallow.

My session with Daniela reminded me of what a powerful role confusion can play in shamed systems. She began, "There's this one gigantic, oppressive force that has been with me for as long as I can remember. I know I'm not going to be cured, but any insight you can give me, any little fleck of gold dust, I'll take it." She was already projecting her authority onto me, even though the insight she was looking for lived in her.

"In your wildest, freest imagination," I asked, "what would a cure be like? What would happen next?" It was important to get to know what this "cure" meant to her so we could assess whether her ideas about it were informed by the outer authority of a culture or family, rather than being based on her own truth.

"I would be exercising regularly," Daniela said.

"What's so good about exercising? Is it being more in shape, losing weight, feeling stronger?"

"All of it. I've often wondered if my resistance to exercise is a giant 'fuck you' to the system that tells me I'm overweight and not fit. I don't know if that's it. I eat well, I sleep well, I do all the other things for myself, but I just can't seem to exercise. I don't know. Maybe what I just said is a sound bite. Maybe I heard it somewhere and latched on to it."

I said, "The system sounds really sexist—something that evaluates you and your body and tells you how you're not good enough, that you have to change yourself. I can see how that would prompt a healthy self-protective response of 'fuck you.'"

"The culture tells me the way I am isn't okay."

"I hear you. I noticed you were saying 'I don't know' and 'maybe' it's a sound bite, and 'maybe" it's a 'fuck you.' That reminds me of a professor who told me about a study that found that among women, one of the most commonly used phrases is 'I don't know.' For instance, a woman might say, 'This is what I understand about life,' and then she'd say, 'I don't know.' Can you hear the internalized sexism? It's like women aren't allowed to say, 'I know this. This is smart. This is my idea.' Or even, 'This is what I know about myself.' One part of you is quite clear about what's going on—you have a giant 'fuck you' to an oppressive system. But then you say, 'I've wondered if it's true,' and 'I don't know,' and 'maybe I appropriated a sound bite.'" These words of doubt dismiss Daniela's truth and disconnect her from her own authority. They act like microaggressions that go unnoticed; they are the result of shame. Daniela was switching between someone with strength and authority and someone who didn't know, who thought she might be passing off someone else's insight as her own.

Daniela continued, "I know for sure there's a giant 'fuck you' in me. What is it toward? Is it toward society, myself, my parents?" Daniela was now standing more in her authority but was still questioning the direction of her "fuck you." One might think that she really didn't know, but that wasn't true. She had the self-knowledge within her; shame kept her from it.

"In an unshaming process," I responded, "my answer is that I don't have to know, because all I have to do is listen, believe that intelligence is pouring out of you, and see what you do with that intelligence. Where is this giant 'fuck you' living inside your body?"

This insight, which many of us need to learn again and again, is essential to unshaming: we needn't figure out what's right and wrong, how we should respond or feel. We simply need to pause and check in with our body's intelligence, listen, and trust.

Daniela put her closed hand on her chest and rubbed in a circular motion. "Right now, it's here."

"What's your hand like? Is it clenched? Is it just closed?"

"It's not tightly clenched. It's closed, and my knuckle is causing a tiny bit of pain."

"Is the feeling of your hand relieving? Is it soothing? Is it pushing?"

"It's pushing the 'fuck you' up into my throat so I can say it."

"Smart hand," I said. "Some people would put their hand on their chest as an act of soothing, to make something go away. Your body is saying that something needs to be brought up from the chest into the throat. What's the energy that lives in your chest like?"

"It feels electrified," Daniela said. "It's got a lot of energy to it. It's in this spot right now, but I sense that it travels and that it's ready to go again, and it wants to move."

Daniela was now staying with her body experience. There was no need to doubt it or question its validity. It just existed. Supporting her in doing this and witnessing what she did and felt would lead her to the answers she sought while also showing her how to get to those answers: by trusting herself and connecting with her inner authority.

"Let's imagine that your hands could move it up into the throat," I said. "If you could make a sound from your throat, what would the sound be?"

Daniela made a growling sound.

"Wow. Would it be okay to try just maybe two or three more times? Because I want to really get to know that sound that's inside of you."

She growled more. The sound was ferocious and bold.

I said, "That's a real sound from a real person who lives with this gigantic, oppressive force. This growling energy is part of the cure or medicine; it lives inside your heart." We no longer needed explanations; ambivalence was a thing of the past; doubt didn't even exist at that moment. The 'fuck you' that she once had doubted was her truth had become a growling energy rising up into her throat.

"It's dropping," Jasmine said. "It's moving into my belly now, which is where it usually lives."

"Fascinating. It lives there and sometimes it moves up into the chest, and sometimes it's in the chest and wants to come up into the throat."

"I think it moved up because you're giving me an opportunity for it to come out," Daniela said.

"Right! It moves up when it has more of a space and permission. It doesn't need soothing, like, 'Oh, sweetheart, you're okay.' It needs knuckle support. That makes you smile. Why?"

"'Knuckle support' is a great term. It made me think of literally punching someone and knocking them out. You'd use your knuckles to really do damage." She paused, worried. "Look where I'm going now. It's not kind."

"No, it's not kind," I said. "If this energy within you were free, it would do some damage. It would punch."

"Yes. What's living inside of me is an unkind knuckle punch."

Words can be interpreted, but punching knuckles are pure, unshamed experience.

"Well, I'm glad to meet her," I said. I wanted to support Daniela in identifying and accepting this disowned ferocity. I continued, "Could you be in touch with that energy again in your hand and in that sound? Feel the knuckle punch, and just for now, believe in it. I'm going to say some of the sexist things you hear from society. It's not going to feel good, but it will help the medicine to emerge. Is that okay?"

"Yes."

"Daniela, you're not okay as you are."

"Fuck you," Daniela said, and then looked pained.

"I know," I said. "Super painful. Don't forget the fists and the knuckle. This idea that you're not good enough as you are is a gigantic, oppressive force. You have to know what it is; otherwise you can get confused by thinking it can help get you to exercise or that you don't have a 'fuck you' toward it. So let's role-play. You be the oppressive force, and I'll be the 'fuck you' energy."

Daniela nodded and said, "You're not good enough the way you are."

"Fuck you," I said, responding as Daniela's fierceness.

"You need to get fit and sexy," Daniela continued, "and lose weight, and be toned."

"I will damage you," I said to the oppressive force. "I will destroy you. I will rip you to shreds."

"There's something wrong with your stomach, lady."

"Fuck you. You have no idea what's in me. No more will you live in my system. You are over. These fists are not going down. I'm owning them. These are mine. These knuckles are mine. You used them against me, but they're my hands now. You know what? This 'fuck you' is my exercise, and I'll decide how I'm going to do that. Not so I can be healthy. I'll get stronger and stronger, and I will beat you. I guarantee it."

Daniela's face lit up with a smile. "So much resonance. I want a punching bag right now."

Nobody had ever protected her before or had shown her that protective instinct belonged inside her.

"Yes," I said, "get something like that. If it's a dumbbell, then each rep can be an expression of 'fuck you.' If it's a push against the wall, if it's a punching bag, it's 'fuck you.' If it's a walk, it's not a lovely walk. It has to have that fierceness to it, because that part of you is the cure."

"Exercise as a giant fuck you to exercise!" Daniela said, exuberant.

"Yeah. That's the crazy wisdom of it."

"This feels really good, David. I'm imagining myself walking ferociously, putting on gloves and whaling on a punching bag. I feel an excitement and a peaceful energy now flowing through from my throat down to my belly. It's like an open channel."

Some people think a cure is like a pill that eliminates the situation, but many cures are things you have to live. The issue, like Daniela's oppressive force, comes up over and over. Daniela will need less "fuck you" some days, and more on other days. Whatever your biggest challenge is does not go away completely. Why? Because something else wants to happen in your life, and you need the cure again. The cure is you being more you. It's not a one-time thing. It's a living thing.

This cure belonged to Daniela, but because body shame is a social issue, a gender issue, and a sexism issue, it also belongs to the world. The world needs this as medicine, as the cure. Like Daniela, the problem needs lots of love and self-love and compassion, and it needs something that says, "Fuck you, I'm not going to take that." Bringing that out in the world is also good exercise.

When I said this to Daniela, she said, "Yes. It's activism."

Just like in chapter 4, where I talked about having an inner boundary regarding being an elder, and about how listening to people talk about their marginalization can effect social change, unshaming body issues can also shift a victimized person, like Daniela, into an activist role. It could never have happened if she had stayed confused.

If she stays confused and unaware, she remains powerless against oppressive systems. If she becomes clear about what's going on, as she did in this session, she's dangerous to these oppressive status quos. She's not going to help a gym's bottom line by paying for a membership. She's not going to keep buying clothes, because nothing she wears gets rid of the message that she's not okay as she is. She's not going to be pushed around at work or in romantic relationships because of low self-esteem.

Our bodies are ever present, expressing themselves via their size and shape, their curves and stances, their movements and hungers. Because we live in a shame-based culture, certain body expressions are seen as "not normal"—something to be fixed and corrected instead of listened to and understood. This came up in a relationship I had some thirty years ago now with a dear friend named Makwa, who has since passed on. Makwa was Native American, and his name means "bear" in Ojibway. He was large, round-bodied, and hirsute.

One day when I was at his house, I asked him, "Makwa, what's it like to have your body?"

He looked at me with stern eyes, seeing that I truly didn't get it. He got up, brought me a pair of his overalls, and said, "Step into these."

The legs were two or three times the girth of my legs, and the bib sagged down. He took out clothes, pillows, and sweaters and stuffed them into the open spaces inside the overalls until they were filled up.

Then he said, "Go to the kitchen drawer and get a fork for me."

"Why do you want me to do that?"

"Just do it."

I went to the drawer, but I couldn't reach it because the stuffed clothes got in my way.

Then he echoed my earlier question by asking, "How does it feel?"

"It feels like I'm a person inside a huge covering around me."

"That's how it feels to be me," he said. "I'm in here, but people don't see me. They see all their projections and notions. That's just the way it is."

Makwa's lesson was profound. He felt great pain living in world of bias, bigotry, and dehumanization of our bodies and cultures, but no shame. That was just the way it was.

If you get the urge to criticize or change your body, take time to reflect on this impulse and be curious about it. What are the ideas based on? Are they introjections of oppressive societal beliefs? What intelligence is living inside your body? Being curious paves the way to encounter your gifts, medicine, and power.

EXERCISE

Unshaming the Body

1. What part of your body do you feel critical of?

2. Listen to the judgment and say it out loud, clearly and critically, as we have done in earlier chapters. It's important for our ears to literally hear the inner voices in order for them to be witnessed.

3. Now put that aside and notice the qualities of what you don't like: the shape, the sharpness, the wrinkles, the sagginess, the softness or firmness, the smallness or bigness. Pay attention to those qualities, not the world's judgments, as if you're describing something that can be found in nature.

4. Now draw a picture of that quality. Don't take long, maybe twenty seconds at the most. Then amplify the picture: add detail, thicken some of the lines, and/or make it bigger. Let the child in you play; it's easy.

5. Stand up and use your hands and arms to make motions and gestures that are like the picture.

6. And now—guess what?—we're going to amplify that motion. Make a dance by continuing to amplify the motion you're making, letting it become freer, weirder, more exaggerated. If there is a pattern, focus on that pattern, and let your body dance that pattern over and over.

7. As you dance, hear a song in your mind. Begin humming or singing it. You can't get this wrong; even if the song seems like it doesn't fit, sing it anyway.

8. Shape-shifting: Ask yourself, "Dear Dancer: Who are you? Where did you come from? What message do you have for me about how to live my life differently?"

CHAPTER 8

Unshaming Disturbing Feelings

In a session, my client Avril said, "I don't feel like I belong here."

"What do you mean by here?" I replied. "Like on this planet? Do you not want to live?"

"No. It's in my community, in the area of the country I live. I've felt like this for years. I've moved to new places to escape it before. It's a heaviness, a weight. I don't feel happy or well."

What does this have to do with shame? She didn't say she felt shame; she said she felt a sense of not belonging. This shame that hides in our blind spot, that doesn't appear to *be* shame, can be most insidious when it comes to our feelings. Shame labels our feelings before we "feel" them, and it pathologizes them as if they are problems, which stops us from exploring them for their deeper intelligence. When we don't want to have a feeling, the feeling is often unknown, veiled by shame.

I suggested that Avril enter the somatic experience of "not belonging." She did, and then she said she felt a weight in her feet as her head began to tilt to one side.

"Let your head continue to tilt, let your body go with the feeling," I suggested, as she leaned over more and more, following the intelligence her body communicated to me.

Her eyes closed. "I feel sleepy. I feel peace. Relief. I'm like a bird in a nest."

When we didn't treat her feelings like a problem, she felt supported, as if she was in a nest. Once she had embodied that feeling all the way, I asked, as if I were her normal self, "What should I do with feelings of not belonging? Can you advise me from your nested place?"

"Yes, I can. You belong everywhere." That's the kind of answer unshamed feelings reveal.

Feelings are often policed, criticized, and told to get lost, first by our parents, and then by ourselves and the people close to us—or not close at all, as when men obnoxiously interrupt women on the street to tell them to smile.

With Avril, when we unshamed her initial feeling, she discovered that the feeling wasn't a problem, but a doorway to her deeper truth. After feelings are unshamed, we learn that the answer to a difficulty lies within us, not in an external fix. As the ecstatic Sufi poet Rumi wrote, "The cure for pain is in the pain." What seems to be something wrong with a person often blossoms into an understanding that something's *very right* with them.

I remember seeing this principle illustrated at a large-scale conflict resolution forum in Northern Ireland, as Arny Mindell worked with groups of Catholic and Protestant people who hated each other. Members of each group had killed people from the other group.

Mindell said to a member of one of the groups, "You want to kill that person," indicating someone from the other group. He said that not to support taking that action, but to witness the feeling behind their words.

The person Arny addressed said, "I do!"

Someone else responded, "This is too much. We need to make more peace out of this."

"You're not going to make a sustainable peace by suppressing these people," Arny replied. "They may have to use words and tones that are consistent with how it feels for them. They need their feelings seen and understood. If that doesn't happen, their words may turn into actual bullets or bombs."

We need people who aren't afraid of feelings. The belief that feelings are problems to be dealt with is biased and unhelpful—and it can be deadly. You can deny and suppress them, but they'll come back: *Remember me? I'm going to keep you up all night dreaming about this problem.*

You have to ask the feelings themselves to discover their intelligence, and not only with words. Feelings live in the body. We've talked about different channels for unshaming; now we'll review them through the lens of unshaming disturbing feelings.

Somatic: where the feeling lives in your body

Movement: dances that are sad, happy, or angry

Sound: sounds that are sad, happy, or angry

Drawing: depressed, fiery, ecstatic strokes of pen and color

Facial expression: scared or fierce jawbones, glaring eyes, pursed lips

It's amazing how able people are to do this. For instance, when I ask people to make the sound of their feelings—"Just make one up"—they always hit the spot. It's something very specific. The sound is instantly followed by a cry or a laugh, meaning something in them recognized its accuracy. Expression of feelings allows them to be witnessed, and just being witnessed is medicine for a person. Words alone are rarely sufficient.

Empirically speaking, what actually is a feeling? It is an organized set of sensory body experiences. Most people use names of feelings in ways that are not helpful because feelings are not the same as our labels. Neither are they solid states; they're in motion. When a feeling arises and gets expressed, it starts shifting into the next thing and the next thing and the next thing. For instance, someone might feel powerful, then at ease, then at rest, then safe.

Stuck feelings create problems. If you put a feeling in a box and lock it in (through denial, suppression, or pathologizing), you're not experiencing the true essence of the feeling. You're experiencing a feeling in a cage. A caged animal acts different from a free animal. They're experiencing a shamed feeling that's caged. The animal might snap at you, act depressed, or show up in distorted forms like moods, body symptoms, or even addictive tendencies.

The experience of the feeling is much more important than the feeling's label. Don't worry about the words people use. Move from the label to movement or another form of expression. Even ten minutes of experience through one of the channels listed above could help with an issue that's been plaguing you for twenty years. You can't find the intelligence of the emotion without letting it take you somewhere new. Once it flowers, it can tell you something.

Join me in this quest. Let's stop suppressing anger as people and a culture, especially in those most marginalized by that culture, as with the "angry Black woman" trope that seeks to mute women's righteous response to bigotry.

Anger, depression, and tearfulness can be signs of suppressed, shamed personal power. This is rarely conscious. As long as the person is trying to manage their feelings, they marginalize their power. People need that power—their birthright—to live more fully and authentically, to leave or enter a relationship, to set boundaries with people or boundaries inside themselves against inner criticism, to willingly take on a project, or to resist external or internalized oppression. In this chapter, I share how to unshame pathologized feelings—which can include anger, jealousy, grief, resentment, and even "good" feelings like pride or happiness—claim their power, and discover what our feelings flower into when they become unshamed. Every feeling has a natural intelligence and a message. You just need to be curious, go deeper, and let it tell you.

The term *emotional intelligence* has become commonplace, but seen through the lens of shame and unshaming, it becomes clear what we're actually talking about. Emotional intelligence is simply the intelligence of our emotions.

I taught a course in critical thinking for eight years at the University of Phoenix. The textbook represented feelings as something that can get in the way of good thinking. But have you noticed how strong thinking can also get in the way of clear feeling? People often try to think their way out of their feelings and then miss the intelligence their feelings are bringing forward. If we tapped into our true emotional intelligence, it might say things like:

"I'm scared because there's danger around."

"I'm hurt because something happened that was hurtful."

"I'm nervous to speak in front of a group because there are people in that group who are critical of me, or because I've been put down in the past."

"I'm proud because I'm in touch with my specialness, not because I have a moral defect."

Instead of pushing our feelings away, denying them, ignoring them, blunting them with substances, or distracting ourselves, why not be curious and attentive instead?

You may be wondering why I'm not one of those who suggest that some emotions are "better," preferable, higher order, higher frequency, spiritually or psychologically superior, or even more healed than others. It's because once this kind of belief system is in place, one begins to push away, marginalize, or go to war with the "lesser" emotions. This happens even when this marginalization is subtle or driven by compassion for the person having uncomfortable feelings, although it's ultimately not a compassion for the emotion in question.

When this bias exists, the person no longer follows the path of their emotions, relating to them so that they naturally deepen and unfold like the flowers (or thorns) they are and thus transform into the next state of feeling. Making matters worse, a bias in favor of "better" emotions leads to a suppression of both the feeling and the path that would have unfolded, resulting in symptomatic expression of feelings and disturbances in relationships and the soma, which are expressions of a split-off and disowned shadow. Does that mean it's never appropriate to go to war with certain experiences, whether they're feelings or something else? No, some experiences unfold when we take them on as enemies to battle with. But this must be done consciously and organically; otherwise, the alchemy doesn't take place, and the symptoms arise unbidden. What is the essence of almost all of these bias systems regarding feelings? You guessed it: shame.

Anger

Emily Dickinson wrote:

Anger as soon as fed is dead—
'Tis starving makes it fat—

With anger, as with an animal in the wild, the best way to stay safe around it is to be aware and respectful of the animal's nature, not to cage it or anesthetize it. However, most of us have been taught to respond to anger in ways that starve it by suppressing it, treating anger as an enemy with nothing of value to offer. I view anger shamanically, like an animal coming to us in our dreams with a message on its lips and power in its stride. That perspective unshames anger, revealing its true power, intelligence, and spirit.

Most people meet anger with a shaming attitude. What does a shaming attitude look like? It often looks like suppression: "Do something with your anger to make it go away!" People suppress anger by holding it in, or by trying to let it go before it's ready for that. They might do a spiritual bypass: "I'm going to meditate these feelings away." Meditating is great, but not as a substitute for communication or working out relationship issues. From a cultural standpoint, repressing anger can be less disruptive than causing problems by speaking up. This appeases the demands of a dominant workplace, family, or relationship culture, but it also supports harm and homeostasis instead of change.

When people talk about anger, they say things like, "Why am I getting angry? Why am I still angry? I keep getting triggered." This is also a shaming attitude. People in sessions almost always see it as a problem, a bad thing, instead of meeting it with curiosity. And some say, "Mad hides sad," implying that anger is not an important feeling in and of itself and that we have to get to the real issue: sadness. But this kind of truism is not helpful. Sometimes anger turns to sadness; sometimes people are more comfortable crying than expressing anger, in which case their sad is hiding mad. Nevertheless, anger is always just one element of the great diversity of our feelings, not because it leads to anything else; just for itself. Being angry does not mean something is wrong with us.

When speaking with clients about their anger, I refer to it as a "thing," and I ask them, "What is this thing like, and what would it do if you could consciously use it?" One client told me this anger "thing" would protest the norms of her marriage. Sometimes anger is actually a suppressed freedom song.

When in an unshaming process with anger, one thing I often do is engage body experience, perhaps through hand movements and voice. Anger moves if it's free. It has energy; it thumps. Movement is an important way to get to know it, to become intimate with this thing. Voice is also an especially important channel. I ask clients to make a sound, go into their bodies to feel the noise vibrating inside them. I want them to make sounds so they can use anger to support them in their lives, not only to let it go. Some people think the goal is release. But "Hit the pillow to release your anger" has the same biased and shaming function as treating anger like it's something we should get rid of, instead of heeding its intelligence and power and then integrating it like a friend we now have access to.

Express it, explore it, befriend it—and do something with it.

For some people, it's difficult to make sounds in relation to anger. The idea that anger should be expressed is so taboo that they can't even bring themselves to make an angry sound. That makes working with sound even more important if the person's life calls them to use their voice.

Perhaps they're suppressing their anger because they've been hurt by an angry person, or they saw someone get hurt by an angry person. Yet suppressed anger that breaks out hurts people. If a parent doesn't feel like they have any way to express discontent at work, the expression of that feeling might get displaced onto their children, who would be an inappropriate target for that emotion. Channeling anger about workplace conditions into finding a new job or negotiating better circumstances is good for the worker and their family, whereas taking it out on their children is harmful and causes regret, creating yet more shame.

When you start to get angry, ask yourself, "What is the essence of this feeling in my body?" Feel it with all the awareness you can muster, and then decide what you really want to say instead of the nasty thing at the tip of your tongue. Come out with it intentionally, consciously. Otherwise communication will get messy, and conflicts will likely escalate.

I once worked with a couple on their relationship issues, and during our work together we discussed how one partner threw things when she got angry. I gave that partner a crumpled piece of paper and said, "Now stand up and throw it against the wall. Make some noises as you throw this ball of paper." I wanted to help her come to know her anger and then what else she could do with it. We needed to give her some options for handling her anger, but in order to do that she needed to connect with it first, not just be ruled by her anger or try to get rid of it. Then she could try being more direct with her partner by saying something like, "This is not okay. I need you to hear me. Stop treating me like I don't get it."

Some people need to learn to suppress anger to keep themselves from hurting others, and I support that. In such cases, I'll say things like, "Walk away, count to ten, don't you dare abuse that person. . . . Okay, now let's unshame the anger." We still need to unshame the anger and discover its meaning, power, and message; otherwise it will simply find insidious and unconscious forms of expression.

A lot of men grew up with angry, abusive fathers, so they suppress their own anger in an effort to never be like that themselves. This can lead to them being disconnected from their own power. It can also interfere with them creating fulfilling relationships and life paths that are true to their calling, rather than obeying societal norms.

When I got involved with Robert Bly's men's movement in the 1980s, I saw that there was a genuine hunger and a need for men to be able to access appropriate anger. Because they didn't want to be like their fathers, their anger came out in weird ways. They couldn't stand up for themselves. In my case, I was in a doctoral program for four years, but I didn't finish it. I needed what I had disowned: my father's abusive anger, which contained the fire and grit I needed to push through hurdles and criticisms. If I had integrated the power of my anger, I could have used it to drive my studies to completion. Since then I have integrated it and have completed law school, and I use the power of my anger about injustice to fuel my social activism, write books, and express controversial viewpoints. In short, pathologizing anger, shaming it, doesn't work.

A Place for Anger

Everyone holds anger differently. You need a culture that helps to support that. For example, younger people often have to go through the anger doorway to find and get in touch with their power. Social change is often catalyzed by acts of anger, frustration, even desperation. The opening lines of the Declaration of Independence are fueled by anger: "When in the Course of human events, it becomes necessary for one people to dissolve the political bands which have connected them with another, and to assume among the powers of the earth, the separate and equal station to which the Laws of Nature and of Nature's God entitle them, a decent respect to the opinions of mankind requires that they should declare the causes which impel them to the separation."

Without the fire of anger, those lines don't get written. As the Declaration of Independence states, "All experience hath shown, that mankind are more disposed to suffer, while evils are sufferable, than to right themselves by abolishing the forms to which they are accustomed." In other words, experience has shown that we'll suffer evils for as long as we possibly can—way too long—until we come to a breaking point.

Martin Luther King Jr. wrote the book *Why We Can't Wait* from a Birmingham jail cell. In it he wrote, "Three hundred years of humiliation, abuse and deprivation cannot be expected to find voice in a whisper." We need the fuel of anger to empower our voices, stiffen our spines, elevate our courage. Women are told from earliest childhood to be nice and only say positive things: "If you can't say something nice, don't say anything at all." As we've already discussed, the "angry Black woman" stereotype is consistently weaponized to dismiss Black women's valid individual and collective reasons for anger. Palestinian people speak up and are viewed as potential terrorists; LGBTQIA+ folks speak up and are accused of trying to sexualize children.

"Do it nicely" means "Never do it." We need a lot of anger—and we need to know what to do with it—instead of being trapped in a shame cycle in which tone and apologies take center stage, while the issue at hand melts into the background, unresolved, unseen, its message unheard. Anger not expressed will almost always express itself somatically. People with unexpressed anger develop symptoms like stomachaches, acid reflux, or tight muscles.

We've been talking about anger as a valid form of resistance, but not all anger is related to resistance. People also express anger in abusive ways. Whether you are the one bearing the brunt of someone's abusive anger, or your anger is crossing over into abuse of others, unshaming can help.

If you're in a relationship with a person who is verbally or physically abusive while angry, consider the likelihood that they will not change. Consider that you may be drunk on hope for what you want reality to be and are thus not seeing them with sober eyes. For people in this position, I lead them through the following exercise:

> Get in touch with your anger for this person who is hurting you over and over. Let your eyes embody some of that anger. Now look at them through these angry eyes. What do you see now? What is more clear? What can they do? What can't they do? Will they ever change?

Once they've come up with some answers to these questions, I work with them to reshape their relationships accordingly. Knowing what they accept now, how can they be safer? How can this other person have less access to them in key protective ways?

Why is the exercise's focus on eyes so important? We can be a little bit blind about people so close to us, especially when it's a family member. Admitting they they're not giving you reason to believe their abusive behavior will stop is a kind of death, which brings with it the corresponding grief. It's not easy to digest.

If you're expressing your anger in abusive ways and you want to change, you can. It's healthy to feel remorse and regret, guilt and accountability; but to shift your relationship with anger, you need to be able to examine your anger without feeling ashamed or being shamed. You may have an internalized shaming witness, or people around you who are saying variations of "Shame on you." A shaming witness teaches people to suppress and be unconscious. Nobody ever gets smarter, wiser, or more adept at navigating emotions amid suppression and unconsciousness. Shame doesn't lead us to be less abusive; it actually causes us to be less in touch with ourselves—our compassion, our empathy, and the shadow we've denied. Experiencing anger while no longer being abusive requires a lot of awareness.

I've worked with many parents whose children behave in hurtful, even abusive ways. The parents get angry, but they say, "I must not get angry at my child."

I reply, "First, feel your anger with me. Express it in movement, express it with your voice. Get to know what it feels like in your body and tone."

Once they build that conscious relationship with their anger, they can decide how much of it they need to express to have an impact. Perhaps they offer stern words, such as "That's not okay." Perhaps they make a firm boundary, or they say, "Stop, that hurts." When parents can't do this, they often rely on moral lectures that don't build a genuine relationship with their child. These lectures are often shaming: "You are bad." Children are most moved by efforts pointed toward building a genuine, nurturing relationship.

You'll need to become more expressive of strong feelings *before* your emotional state reaches a point of no return. When I was a child, the conventional wisdom about people who restrained themselves and then blew up was that they "had a bad temper." You'll also need to embrace and express your own power in ways that do not violate others. Your anger needs to coexist with safety. The greatest safety comes from witnessing. A full awareness of who we are and what is inside of us is the greatest preventive medicine against injuring others.

Becoming more expressive about anger flies in the face of conventional thinking. The most common response to anger is to deny it:

"I'm not angry anymore." "I'm over it." "Water under the bridge." "I've released it to the universe." Or we say, "I'm not angry," although our clenched jaws and tightened stomachs betray our truth. People who say this may be telling what feels to them like the truth, because they're not in touch with their anger. Denied anger doesn't just show up in relationships; its energy also intensifies inner criticism or body symptoms. The person's anger isn't dealt with, and neither is the thing they were upset about; and their anger comes out sideways. I see it happen in my own relationships. It helps to be curious about yourself at these times: *There's an edge to my communication with my wife. I've been a little sharp. Am I angry with her? What about? What do I need to say?*

The next most common solution is to consciously suppress anger: "I know I'm angry, but I'm going to not take it out on you." This response is more useful than denial. Denied anger erupts and shows up outside one's awareness. Suppression has awareness. It also creates pressure, but it's more safe to the self and others than eruptions of anger. When you suppress your anger, you have the composure to ask, *What will I do with this? I'm not going to say something in rage that is damaging.*

If anger arises regularly in certain contexts, that's important information. It gives you a place to focus on as you begin the unshaming process. This is a safe alternative to suppression and denial, because self-awareness and the capacity to witness and hold one's actual experience provide the most safety to yourself and others. If you're not clear on what your anger wants from you, and if you're denying it and fighting its existence, that's unsafe. When you can truthfully say, "I know this anger and its energy. I'm not in a war with it. I know how it belongs to me and my story," you're a safe person. When someone else in your life is in this position, that's a safe person to be around. The compassionate, unshaming witness makes you safe. Then you can say, "I'm really upset and angry at you right now, and I care about you so much at the same time. I want to be able to work through this with you without hurting you or our relationship."

When anger is shamed, the choices are "I'm not going to say anything" or "I'm going to say whatever and blow things up." There's a sense of being drunk on anger, with drunkenness's lack of inhibitions and boundaries. That's when you're a weapon in anger's hand.

If a feeling is only something that causes you to be judged, or something that's wrong with you, it gets thrown in the "shadow bag," as Robert Bly puts it—outside of your awareness. You carry that bag around unconsciously until it leaks out in the form of eruptive rage, or you take it out on yourself, because you don't have an awareness that accepts and witnesses it. Without acceptance and witnessing, it overwhelms the system like drunkenness. There's no relationship with these feelings because they were once shamed, and they stayed shamed.

Vengeance

What do you do with the desire for revenge? As with any shamed feeling, look at it, go inside it, feel it, and express it, perhaps first in a space that's safe for both you and others. Like all feelings, it will start to show itself and transform, like a flower blooming. Unshamed, the desire for vengeance almost always unfolds into desire for justice and empathy. If our desire for vengeance could talk, it might say something like this:

> You have hurt me, and I want you to suffer. It's not fair. I want to wake you up. I want you to feel what it's like to be me. If I can hurt you, you'll know how I feel. I want to wake up your feelings and force you to empathize with me; then you'd get it. You'd notice and connect, and we'd be joined by the pain.

Like anger, when the desire for vengeance is shamed, it goes underground, and its fundamental motivation doesn't do the work of building deeper and more sustainable relationships and a world that's more just. It seems paradoxical that unconscious and shamed desire for vengeance maintains cycles of violence, while unshamed desire for vengeance builds bridges of understanding, helping cycles of vengeance come to an end. I have seen this countless times in working with people on their abusive childhoods. When they make full contact with their feelings, they may want to strike out, saying: "Do you have any idea how you hurt me? Don't ever do that again." Initially they were forbidden to feel this way; "Vengeance is wrong," they say. But when the desire for vengeance is unshamed, they get in touch with an essential healing need—the need for someone to stop, feel, and say, "Now I see; now I get it. Oh my god, I see how I hurt you." That's the medicine of the desire for vengeance.

Cecelia's Story

Sometimes our feelings are the doorway to change, even if that's not how we initially frame our difficulties. That was the case when I had the privilege to work with Cecelia, a woman of color who told me she was wrestling with how to communicate effectively and compassionately at work. She wanted help with her voice in the world.

Cecelia began by saying, "I've failed at communicating well with people."

Statements like that put me on alert. They're inner criticisms that may or may not be true and always have another side. When someone presents a criticism of themselves as the reason to make an effort to change, more exploration is needed so that we don't simply reinforce their shame.

"My voice wavers and I get self-conscious about it," she continued.

"You have feelings in your voice," I said, reflecting what she said without pathologizing the work she wants to do on her voice.

She went on to say that she wanted to communicate compassionately, but she was fearful of having her feelings come out. She gave an example of needing, as a leader, to tell people to show up on time. She said, "I want to both be kind and make a request." Cecelia thought she should be compassionate, but her idea of compassion didn't support making that reasonable request. This idea hampered her ability to be direct. Her idea shamed her feelings.

I said, "What happens if you are not kind in making your request?" This request opened the door to her free expression.

"I get hostility from people," she replied.

"What do you do with that hostility?" I asked this because I wanted to continue exploring what it was like to be her, rather than what I thought—or what she thought—would be a better way to be. "Are you free to be hostile back?" And I asked this question because hostility is an energy in her field, and shame may be veiling her access to that energy.

She pursed her lips tightly and shook her head no. "Mm-mm," she said.

I said, "You may need to feel a little hostile; you may need a bit of that energy. Something says, 'You need to be compassionate, you are failing to communicate, you shouldn't be hostile, you're too fearful.' That sounds like a suppressive response, shaming the intelligence of that feeling. It sounds like inner criticism that needs to be responded to."

"Thinking about it, I realize that I developed a survival strategy," she said. "I tell myself to stay calm, be compassionate, that others are going through things. This is what I do to justify whatever is happening so that I can get out of there alive." As she spoke, her voice shook and quivered with feeling. Her belief in compassion was actually a survival strategy, marginalizing other feelings that were medicine for her voice. What started as fear of her feelings, treating them as the problem, turned out to be a survival strategy that aimed to suppress her feelings. That's how shame takes over our feelings for many of us.

Can you see, reader, the possibility of internalized sexism? Racism? I felt the power of her vulnerability and insight, recognizing it as an opportunity for people like me—white men—to wake up to how people from marginalized groups must put away their feelings to navigate even the simplest of communications. For Cecelia and people like her, turning against one's feelings is actually a form of internalized oppression (which we discussed in more detail in chapter 6, "Social Issues and Shame"). It's common for people to shame their feelings of hostility, resentment, jealousy, vulnerability, and fear in a culture that lauds being logical, productive, open, and strong.

I said, "I can see why you'd be afraid; you're afraid for your life." This is not the kind of fear that needs soothing, like a child who needs to be held until the system regulates and eases. It's a fear of being her "unkind" assertive self, a fear of her authentic feelings, a fear of her voice—a kind of self-phobia. Given that, she needs support for her voice, not for her fear.

"It's scary to be unkind," I said. "I understand that can be dangerous. Someone can hurt you. It doesn't mean you shouldn't show your hostility, but in the world we live in, some people, often people of color, are killed when they do." I shared with Cecelia that even when it's dangerous to be direct and forceful, it's vital for her to be in touch with her feelings. "You must know that is *you*. If you're in a situation where the force behind your hostility is called for but it's dangerous, and you choose to perform gentleness while also knowing who you are, shame will not enter your system. However, if you think, 'Wanting to be firm and stern is wrong; I should be compassionate,' shame will enter, and you will search out remedies to cure yourself of your unkind feelings or simply decide that they, and you, don't really matter. That will harm you."

To go further with the unshaming, I led us into her body experience, where our feelings live. I asked her, "Where does this feeling—the less kind, less compassionate part of you—live in your body?"

"It's most alive in my legs and feet, and sometimes in my chest and belly," she said.

"Feel it. What do you notice?"

"I feel a tension or squeezing in my legs."

"Slowly allow your legs to be more like that: squeezing, tense. Now, intentionally and consciously, add to that."

As I've explained earlier, shame suppresses, denies, and minimizes. Amplification through the body counteracts that effect, and it allows us to witness and become more conscious of the somatic sensation of Cecelia's power. I want her to begin a kind of shape-shift, bringing more awareness to a quality and allowing an expression she fears. Then she and I can witness it.

I said, "Now allow it to move up to your belly, your chest. Let it change you." She nodded, and I said, "Now allow the squeezing and tension to move up to the back and neck."

I kept using the words *squeezing* and *tension* because they were her words. I witnessed her, trusting her intelligence, her authority, not my intelligence or authority, or some idea about her feelings. Unshaming a disturbing feeling in yourself requires developing a compassionate witness, an unshaming belief system through which you look at yourself.

At this point we had already done some important unshaming that involved shifting her view of herself. Instead of Cecelia continuing to think, "I fail at communicating," she now had access to a different perspective. If that viewpoint could speak, it might say, "I look at my fear, and my desire to be compassionate and understanding to others, and I don't think I'm screwed up. I am strong and wise. I developed this method of communicating to survive, but it has limits, marginalizing other feelings." There was a huge difference in how Cecelia now experienced herself and walked through the world. It would affect how people approached her, and it would resonate in her interactions in the world. She was a powerful woman who lived in a world in which she sometimes needed to put some things away to survive, and she would do so consciously, without shame. She could now make conscious strategic choices. Beforehand, her shamed inner belief system made choices for her; but now she could come out more and take risks, like Jasmine in chapter 7, "Body Shame."

Going further, staying with her feelings in the body, Cecelia's eyes begin to water. "My jaw and throat want to get more tense, begin to clench, but this is hard for me," she said. Cecelia was getting to the edge of her comfort zone, a comfort created by an old belief.

"Go ahead and use your hands," I told her. "Let the clench take place in your hands, so you can express the energy." Her two hands rose up in fists. Her face was now gleaming and smiling, indicating that her system was experiencing the wellness that unshaming brings.

I asked, "Do you grind your teeth at night?"

"I have been."

If Cecelia integrated this energy into her life and expression, she would be less likely to somatize it and express it during sleep. Why express it overnight? Because when our conscious mind and its biases and shame dissolve, the body is free to express the feelings that were shamed during the day.

She began to globalize the expression of these feelings: making a face, glaring with her eyes, crunching up her face, showing her fists. That's what this energy looks like; this is an expression of the feelings that she has been afraid of and later became shamed as uncompassionate and unkind. She was embodying her feeling.

"I'm a woman," she said, "a woman of color, and it's not comfortable to be in my power. This is what's coming up for me."

"Tell me about this part of you. This woman of color with this energy."

"I just want people to stop telling me who I am. What I should be doing. Just stop. Fucking stop. There's so much out there telling us who we are. Just fucking listen. At some point, I just stopped talking."

Cecelia was full of feeling, clarity, fierceness, tears, grief. This was the voice she was needing to connect with, that other people needed to listen to. That she needed to listen to. Unshaming her feelings showed us her path, her truth, and revealed the story of her voice.

After that session, Cecelia sent me an email:

I had a friend (another woman of color) watch the video of us working together. She gained so much from it and is experiencing so much freedom. And a few days after our session, I was invited to open up a festival, Viva Mexico, a celebration of Mexican Independence Day, so the timing of your support was impeccable. This experience and invitation were a huge homecoming. Initially I was to do a dance and blessing, but the plan changed last minute, and I had to use my voice in real time on a mic to start the festival. I did what felt right and it was super well received. Some said they cried. I can see now how liberating ourselves makes our voice transmit something that can be felt and tapped into by others. My next project is to put together a book, a body of work. It feels like I can just get on with what I'm here to do.

Notice how once Cecelia's power was unshamed, she could "get on with what I'm here to do." In other words, her shame had been interfering not just with her voice but also with her story, her gender, her race, her lineage, and her life mission. Once she unshamed the feelings in her voice, she gained clarity and momentum. This will hold true for all of us.

Depression

Depression is more than a feeling. For some, it's a mental illness, and as I explained earlier, I have no hesitation in affirming the use of anti-depressants if that is right for a person. Unshaming is not a substitute for other interventions, including medical ones. However, depression does have strong feeling aspects. People often experience depression as feeling down and heavy and having no energy. I've noticed that when I begin the unshaming process with a client, there are two main kinds of depressive directions or energies: feeling an urge to sink down, and being pressed down, oppressed, by an external force.

When I work with someone who feels like sinking or dropping down, I help them sink down with the heaviness, following their body: "Lie down, close your eyes, let go, drop down." In an unshaming process, it's crucial to support the person in sinking down, because in the everyday world, they're being urged to be more up and have more energy, which shames their depressed feelings. Most of us have internalized the belief that it is good to be "up," energized, bright, and light.

Once they go down far enough, the intelligence of that depth starts showing up. People often say things like, "The way I'm living is not working for me. I want to drop out of it. How did I get this life? I don't know if it's meaningful. I'm doing things I never meant to do." I once did a "drop down" with a client who remembered during that experience that when she was a child, she believed in angels. She started crying and said, "I forgot about the angels." Down there are connections with things we've lost: our natural gifts, sensitivities we've pushed past, even our true selves. Some people simply sink into the earth and report feeling at home. Their depression was a kind of homesickness; they needed more connection with "home" and the earth in their lives.

The other manifestation of depressed feelings is a feeling of being pressed down: "Something's on top of me and I can't get it off. It's pushing me down." Rasta culture aptly refers to *oppressors* or oppressive forces as *down-pressers*: such forces are (de)pressing us. Minoritized individuals who live in racist and postcolonial systems, like Rastas, can't bootstrap or will themselves out of institutional oppression/ down-pression. They need to unshame this feeling of being down-pressed, especially because it has nothing to do with them as individuals. In an unshaming process, people connect with the reality of intersectional oppression and stop blaming and shaming themselves. They *believe* how difficult major aspects of life have been for them because of their subject positions, instead of asking, "Why can't I do this? Other people can do this." They may have read books about it, but it doesn't necessarily land until they receive the intelligence of their down-pressing/depressing feelings.

Once when I asked a client about her feeling of being pressed down, she responded with frustration and resentment. She didn't want to be pressed down; in her frustration was some resistance, some fight. To help her tap into her emotions on a more intense level, I asked her to imagine I was pressing down on her shoulders.

She responded by crying out, "I'm pushing back!" She accessed the strength she needed to resist.

When a down-pressed person pushes back, they're accessing their resistance. Some people need the resistance inside their depression to fight against the forces that oppress or depress them. If I had merely tried to "antidepress" this woman with a pep talk, I would have missed the fact that in her depression was the very power she needed to make a better life. I might have made her momentarily feel better, but I would have failed to connect her with the power she needed to find support and change her life.

Approaching depression in a nonshaming way instills the confidence people need to begin to trust the direction and wisdom in those difficult feelings. Such confidence helps them be brave enough to dig into their feelings for a closer look and pull out the healing gems hidden within. This level of introspection gives a person the self-love and understanding needed to keep their mental scales properly balanced. They're able to see all their feelings and experiences—not just the good ones—as playing a vital part in their emotional well-being. This will encourage self-acceptance and open the way for expanded respect and compassion for others' emotional states, a vital necessity for becoming an unshaming witness to the world. This is the essence of emotional intelligence.

The brilliant Jungian analyst James Hillman said,

> Through depression we enter depths and in depths find soul. . . . It moistens the dry soul, and dries the wet. It brings refuge, limitation, focus, gravity, weight, and humble powerlessness. . . . The true revolution begins in the individual who can be true to his or her depression . . . discovering the consciousness and depth it wants.

Jealousy

Jealousy often arises when a person doesn't have enough passion around their strong needs, wants, and desires. If I'm jealous, there's something I want that's living in shame's prison. I see it in others, but shame stops me from intensely, passionately advocating for it myself.

In romantic relationships, a lover might say, "I want to be the only one you think about." As a demand, it's suppressive (and impossible, and impractical). But as a purely expressed feeling, it's a love poem or a song. "See only me," Tony sings to Maria in *West Side Story*, telling her that he wants to be her true love. When people are taught to actually feel their jealousy, sound it, even sing it, I hear their hungers—fervently, desperately alive.

When people are jealous and can't express it honestly because jealousy is shamed, how much does that cost? For example, if a parent is jealous of a child's freedom but can't unshame that feeling and become conscious of it, jealousy remains a feeling in the form of a caged animal. Instead of saying, "I'm so jealous. I wish I could have had the freedoms you do. I am going to become more free like you," they withhold praise, undermine choices, and criticize their desires. They do things that are hard to identify as jealousy because they can't feel it and say it. The child later reports being criticized or lacking esteem, almost never realizing a parent was jealous of them.

It's hard to see someone have a life you really wanted and didn't get to have. Sometimes one generation of a family, such as first-generation immigrants, is in survival mode. It can be hard for that generation not to teach their children to live in survival mode and to instead say, "Maybe you can write poems instead of becoming a doctor," or "Maybe you can just do what you want."

When I was in my twenties, I asked my father, "Did you ever want me to come into your business?"

"Yes, I asked you once and you said no."

"I don't remember that," I replied, surprised.

"You were thirteen years old. You said no, and I said I would never ask you again."

I didn't know then that his resentment of me had arisen because he was jealous of my freedom, a freedom to say no and follow my desires—a freedom he didn't have.

Anxiety

Anxiety often has shaking in it. It sometimes turns into shattering, in the form of fragility or sensitivity. I remember one person's teeth literally chattering as they allowed their feelings to become more embodied. Sometimes anxiety erupts into something more volcanic and furious. This is often the case when anger that has a lid on it literally shakes the person, but they interpret it as anxiety because anger is shamed and forbidden.

Once I work with a client and go into the anxiety with them to unshame it, it starts to share its intelligence. If a person is overriding and bypassing their sensitivity in a "stiff upper lip" way, they're out of touch with it. Because sensitivity is an intrinsic part of all of us, suppressed sensitivity can show up as anxiety. For instance, when I first began teaching at the University of Phoenix, students would regularly report in their teacher evaluations, "He seemed nervous at the beginning of the course." This was not a good thing in their eyes. After I read these evaluations, I acted out of shame by trying to present myself more confidently, but eventually I gave up. I simply couldn't consistently muster the confidence that I thought I should have at the beginning of a course.

I decided to unshame this experience: "This is me. I like me. I like my nervousness." In the first class of the course, I began to ask my students, "Does anyone get nervous when they first meet people or speak in public?" Everyone raised their hands and shared giggles of acknowledgment. "Me too," I said. On the next set of teacher evaluations, the students said, "David's great; he's so vulnerable and authentic." I didn't change anything. I simply unshamed my anxiety.

Emotional Truisms

There are some common notions about feelings that I find unhelpful. One is: "Behind all anger is grief." Sometimes grief *is* behind anger. And sometimes, grief and sadness have anger underneath, a common dynamic in a culture that so thoroughly shames anger, making it more acceptable to cry than to confront. At other times, anger is fueled by jealousy, not getting enough sleep, unmet needs, being mistreated, or other causes. Another common notion is that some feelings are negative and some are positive. Ideas like this and other truisms often carry a dismissive attitude that shames a person's or group's experience. The biggest problem is that truisms stop us from dealing with the feeling *as* the feeling. Truisms can throw up a wall between the person and unshaming, between an emotion and how it changes once it's given attention. Unshaming means making a safe place for a feeling to do its thing so we can get to know it, not so we can marginalize it, fix it, or make it go away.

I remember shyly telling my therapist, Salome, that I reread praising comments on my social media posts. I was ashamed for needing external praise.

"What's it like when you get those?" she asked.

"It's like a cookie."

"You need more cookies," she said, unshaming my enjoyment of the sweetness of praise. "What would those cookies be?" She wanted me to think about other areas in my life where I could be receiving rewards for my actions. I realized that inner criticisms often followed my creative expressions. I simply needed to focus on what I liked about my writing or ask Lisa, my wife, to tell me she loved me more often. I simply wanted to feel good about my work in the world; no shame necessary.

Hurt

Along with anger, one of the most important shamed feelings is hurt. You may think, "We all know when we're hurt, don't we?" No. People get hurt all the time and don't know it. We think we should develop thicker skins, not take things personally, brush things off, not complain, let go of being mistreated, get over it, forgive and forget. We push forward under oppressive conditions. We endure, try to be resilient. We smile for the world's camera. These notions are so powerful that people not only suppress their hurts; they lose touch with them completely, leaving them to express themselves in the body through aches and pains. Shame doesn't just hide parts of ourselves from others; it hides parts of ourselves from ourselves.

I once worked with a student who told me a painful story. "It sounds like that really hurt," I said.

"Not really," the student said. "It was a while ago."

But when we went into his body experience, he moaned and began to weep. The hurt was still inside him.

In another instance, I had the powerful privilege of working with a woman who had an infection so virulent that she died of it a few months later. When I worked with her, her body was inflamed, but she held it together.

I asked her, "What's the pain in your body like?"

"I can hear the sound in my ears," she said. "It's a howl." I then suggested we howl together. We did, but it was a rather muted howl until her dog walked into the room and showed us what a real howl sounded like. We howled away, laughing and smiling together. The hurt didn't disappear; it was not "healed." But it was being held with the wellness of being unshamed, allowing her to feel known and helping us deepen our connection. It was agony *and* it was beautiful.

We live in a culture sorely in need of emotional intelligence. Reading about emotional intelligence can make this sound like quite a complicated project. But in reality we can learn as children do, as the child we all are. Feelings are experiences, not problems. It's shaming to treat feelings like problems to solve. All we need to do is drop our ideas, opinions, criticisms, and evaluations of our feelings and actually *feel* them. How do we do that? It's simple: feelings live in the body as sensory-grounded experience. And when we go into that body experience, amplify it, move it, color it, sound it, we allow it to shape us into that feeling. And then, magic happens: the feeling says, "Here I am. Here's my message. Here's where you need me. This is what it's like being you. This is how you really feel. Sing me. Dance me. Assert me. Cry me. Love me."

EXERCISE

Unshaming Feelings to Discover Their Hidden Messages and Gifts

1. What are some emotions or impulses you've experienced that you've been taught are "bad"? (Hint: think of things you've tried to fix, change, transcend, or overcome.)

2. What are some ways other individuals, ideologies, or institutions have tried to educate/help/coach/heal you out of it?

3. Now bring to mind one feeling you've had trouble with—perhaps a feeling that you tried to make go away or that you think is bad or problematic.

4. Take your time and remember a moment when you felt that feeling. If you feel it in this moment, even better.

5. Where in your body is that feeling manifesting? If it manifests in multiple areas, choose the one where its manifestation is most clear or pronounced.

6. Bring your attention to that area of your body. Explore the feeling somatically in terms of its sensory-grounded experience.

7. Slowly allow it to grow and expand.

8. Let's use the sound channel now. Begin to make a sound that goes with that feeling, and then amplify the sound. Don't be shy; exaggerate it. If there's something unusual about that sound, focus on the unusual component and amplify it. And, importantly, enjoy the sound, like a child would enjoy playing with sound.

9. Integration: how is this sound different from how you usually show up or try to show up in life? Give your normal self a message: "Dear normal self, if you could sound more like me, you would . . ."

CHAPTER 9

Shame and Abuse

Victims, Perpetrators, and the Witness

Larry Nassar spent eighteen years as the team physician of the United States women's national gymnastics team. During that time he sexually molested an uncounted number of young gymnasts under his care. In overlapping court cases in 2017 and 2018, Nassar was convicted of possessing child pornography and multiple counts of sexual assault. During his various trials, over one hundred and fifty women and girls whom Nassar abused filed victim impact statements with the court. Consider their words:

Tiffany Thomas Lopez said, "The army you chose in the late '90s to silence me, to dismiss me and my attempt at speaking the truth, will not prevail over the army you created when violating us."

This army comprised witnesses who shamed by silencing and dismissing.

Marie Anderson said, "My parents, who had my best interest at heart, will forever have to live with the fact that they continually brought their daughter to a sexual predator, and were in the room as he assaulted me."

Marie's parents were silent witnesses. Even when a witness means well and is simply unaware of the abuse, the abused person still internalizes a witness who does or says nothing. That's shame.

Jamie Dantzscher said, "I was attacked on social media. . . . People didn't believe me, even people I thought were my friends. They called me a liar, a whore, and even accused me of making all of this up just to get attention."

People who attacked Jamie tried to silence, blame, and further abuse her for speaking up—all forms of shaming.

And Amanda Thomashow said, "I reported it. Michigan State University, the school I loved and trusted, had the audacity to tell me that I did not understand the difference between sexual assault and a medical procedure."

The university's staff gaslit Amanda. Internalizing that kind of treatment forms the core of shame.

The abuses these women suffered at Larry Nassar's hands are egregious forms of assault and violence. The people who witnessed the violence and then denied, dismissed, silenced, gaslit, and otherwise supported the abuser actively cooperated and were complicit with Nassar's horrendous, ongoing, institutionally protected abuse. They function as shaming witnesses.

When victims of abuse internalize the viewpoints of shaming witnesses, they live with shame, meaning that they treat themselves as if something is wrong with them and they don't matter. Further, when their bodies express emotional or physical symptoms of having been abused, they often punish themselves: "Why am I feeling this way? How did I let this happen? Maybe I'm making it up. Why am I so sensitive? I should stop being such a victim. People won't like me if I complain too much." All the while, the Larry Nassars of the world go unconfronted, and they continue to abuse. The dominant culture's bias toward shaming witnesses is evident in the fact that reports about Nassar were first raised (and ignored) in 1997, twenty years before he was convicted.

When there is abuse, we need a loving witness. When we are denied, dismissed, or gaslit, or when there is simply no witness, we internalize a shaming witness. That is how shame is created. One of the greatest injuries of all abuse is the shame we are left with in its aftermath.

What Is Abuse?

To really understand the impact of abuse, we must look beyond victim and perpetrator. One more component must be identified and highlighted: the witness. The term refers to the people, institutions, and other parties (such as colleagues, police, or family members) who saw, were informed, didn't see, or heard the story later and denied, dismissed, and gaslit, or who received a report of the abuse without taking appropriate action. The way abuse is witnessed invariably becomes the way victims witness themselves. In cases like Nassar's, victims treat themselves as if something is wrong with them, as if they and their suffering don't matter, instead of understanding that something happened to them.

The term *abuse* is used in all sorts of ways, so it's important to define it in this context so we can clearly see how shame is created and internalized and how the unshaming process needs to proceed. Abuse is when one person or system with greater social or personal power assaults another person, such as parent vs. child, teacher vs. student, or straight person vs. queer person in a conservative organization, for example. This leads to the next identifying aspect of abuse: a lack of consent. This is often because the person being abused doesn't feel free to withhold their consent. Finally, the abused person can't adequately defend themselves.

In the case above, Nassar assaulted these women, many repeatedly. As the team doctor for US women's gymnastics and a Michigan State University professor, he was in a position of power over the gymnasts he assaulted. The hundreds of women he assaulted could not adequately defend themselves, in part because of the power difference; in part because the assault was disguised as a medical procedure; and in part because when they spoke up, they were ignored, attacked, gaslit, dismissed, and threatened, among other assaults.

Discerning the presence of abuse requires attentiveness to cultural and diversity issues. In my Jewish home, our conversations had rough edges, and conflict was common and often unremarkable. Someone who grew up in a traditional WASP family might have found that environment to be too harsh, but it was my norm. The level of heat people can handle and are used to varies. For instance, when I told my father-in-law "You're really pissing me off," he was shocked and offended. In my family of origin, that comment would be on the mild side, but in my wife's family it was deeply disturbing.

I used to be involved in a process called World Work, conflict resolution gatherings offered in different countries, that was developed and offered by Dr. Arny Mindell and Dr. Amy Mindell. These gatherings were ten days long, involving many hundreds of people and many conflict facilitators. People gathered from thirty-five different countries, which allowed me to notice how differently people interact depending on their native culture.

For example, people from Eastern European countries interact very differently from those native to western Europe. Witnessing those differences helped me to notice how a person's unconscious supremacy interferes with their ability to recognize and name abuse. Some folks may criticize a verbal exchange as being abusive, but they are basically saying, "That way of communication is distasteful according to my comfort level and my worldview." I have seen the same issue arise in working with couples, where one couple can speak to each other fiercely, even angrily, and no one is getting hurt and there is mutual consent; whereas another couple may find the same language, tone, and volume to be abusive. In these examples, what may meet the definition of abuse for one person may not constitute abuse for another. In other words, we can't simply label something abuse based on the behavior alone.

Abuse is relational. The existence of an assault, a power difference, consent, and capacity to defend oneself make all the difference in how the person experiences the event and whether it lodges in their psyche in a way that requires psychological healing. What does psychological healing look like? It's a witness who believes, respects, and cares for the person's experience in a way that allows their organic reactions to the abusive event to unfold and express themselves. This allows what Peter Levine calls "incomplete actions" to be reintegrated.

The Minimizing of Abuse

Situations that "don't look bad" can seem too trifling to be abuse. For example, sometimes people frame forms of neglect as not being assaultive: "My father wasn't there for me, but he didn't beat me or sexually violate me." This is a minimizing statement. Whenever someone offers a dismissal of their experience, shame is present. Things that people call "little" or "small" are often much bigger or attached to a whole string of experiences. For some, their whole childhood may have been characterized by neglect, teasing, put-downs, and a thousand other cuts that many would say aren't abusive. One minimizing statement is often evidence of something a person has experienced a lot of in their life: that particular assault as well as a dismissive witness.

When someone says, "My father wasn't there for me, but he didn't beat me or sexually violate me," not being seen or feeling seen can be a very potent injury. People feel the absence of that experience. The reason why the parent is absent also permeates the atmosphere. Let's say a parent thinks, *I can't be with my child because I have to work. I hate my job, but that's the way it is.* The child doesn't just experience neglect; they also experience the aggressive energies of the parent resenting their own life.

Our American culture is a shaming witness to abuse. In the legal system, if there's no physical evidence of abuse, a claim is going to be less effective. However, words hurt, too. Ideas that minimize verbal abuse are shaming notions that we live with. Corporal punishment in schools continues to be legal in seventeen states and is often referred to as physical discipline. A culture that sanctions corporal punishment witnesses abuse by gaslighting the children by conveying the message "You deserve to be assaulted."

Another minimizing statement is related to the denial, dismissal, and gaslighting effects of comparison. This is something we hear from our internalized shaming witness: "Nothing really happened. I don't see why I feel upset; it's not as bad as what this other person experienced. What's wrong with me?" One person's more extreme experience of abuse does not magically cancel out everyone else's. If you compare your abuse to another's, shame is present.

People also commonly dismiss abuse by saying, "How can I work on it when I don't remember anything that happened?" Many people come to me and say, "What if I can't remember?" What people are saying to me is "I don't fully believe that something's happened because I can't prove it. I don't remember the details that could be evidence."

Why do they need proof? Because the witnesses in their life have required proof. The message is, "I don't trust you and your experience. We can't believe you, and you shouldn't believe yourself." That's where the shame enters, confusing the individual about what they know, just as in chapter 7, "Body Shame," Daniela was confused about what she knew and kept repeating, "I don't know."

For example, if a man was molested by his grandfather as a child, some immediate family members might have insisted it didn't happen. "Your grandfather could have never done that," his mother might have said when he was a child. Later, when he tells the story at age thirty-five, someone again implies that he is making things up by saying, "Do you have specific memories of the event? If not, maybe it didn't really happen." This shaming interaction directly harks back to the earlier event and earlier shaming, activating the early shaming and betrayal. Someone in this situation typically experiences great pain, debilitating self-doubt, rage, or furious inner criticism.

People don't need any visual memories to work on abuse. They just need to believe their experience and work on it in the body. Screams, terrors, freeze responses, and fight responses that live inside can be expressed. People can connect with and share nonvisual experiences. We need to come to believe our experience, especially as we feel it in the body. That's how we unshame and restore self-trust and wholeness.

As we know, focusing on a person's experience has unshaming power. Reconnecting to your experience allows you to work through it. Disconnection is ongoing because we live in a world invested in so many people not speaking up about what happened to them.

Early in Sigmund Freud's career, he gave a lecture, based on his research, in which he spoke frankly about the impact of childhood sexual abuse. However, he succumbed to the pressure of his male medical colleagues in Vienna by reconceiving these first-person accounts as erotic fantasies created by children. What was once witnessed as real stories of abuse were now officially declared to be fantasies, with the associated symptoms designated as pathologies. This endorsed the denial, dismissal, and gaslighting of childhood sexual abuse. This handed parents an institutionally vetted claim of innocence, and it blamed victims by defining any statements made by children or adult children as untruths that spiraled out of fantasies. This shaming became formalized as theory within psychology: we don't have a story to tell, we have psychological problems to fix. That's shame.

Power and Abuse

Powerful people often have very little awareness around power differences. In his book *Sitting in the Fire*, Arny Mindell wrote, "Rank is a drug: the more you have, the less aware you are of how it affects others." Rank feels really good. Anyone who has more power in a given situation is partially blind to that fact. A person at a lower rank will often be able to see power differentials, but those at a higher rank often will not.

I once worked with a manager who complained, "I asked my employees for feedback, but they never took me up on it. What's the problem? They should just talk to me." He was unconscious about his rank and how power dynamics were playing out. But when I asked him if he would give negative feedback to his boss, his eyes opened. "That's not easy to do," he said.

When I was teaching at the University of Phoenix, a student was scheduled to do a five-minute presentation at the beginning of class. That day, I forgot about the student's presentation and just started teaching. The class continued that way, and afterward the student approached me, upset that they hadn't gotten to give their presentation.

I said, "Why didn't you say anything at the beginning of class?"

I later realized I had higher rank, and for that reason, the student was more aware of our power differential than I was. Interrupting me would mean overcoming the effects of the power difference.

During my consulting work with organizations, whenever I worked with a boss and his employees in the same room, I would always start by saying to the employees, "It may be difficult to say what you really feel. I'll be aware of that." When I said this, people did one of two things: they either voiced appreciation, or they said, "I don't need your help. I can speak for myself." When I made that statement, it resolved the issue of rank for the moment, regardless of the response they gave, because the issue was out on the table. It's good to acknowledge power differences; too often they suppress authentic, deeply helpful conversations.

Because abuse and shame occur when there are power differences, those power differences need to be witnessed. When a child says to a parent "I hate you" after the parent forbids them to watch television, it's not the same as a parent saying to their child "I hate you." The parent is not likely to be as hurt; but more importantly, the parent is more powerful and can defend themselves. The child, however, may experience abuse.

Consider the example of a queer person in a meeting who may experience a group of people making jokes that injure. They may not be free to defend themselves or out themselves. They may laugh to hide their pain and get along with others. The same joke made to their straight peers may sting, but the laughter will likely be genuine. Or consider that a private citizen challenging a police officer is not the same as a police officer challenging a private citizen. In fact, that is the reason for the required Miranda oration: "You have the right to remain silent." The citizen doesn't have the same power to defend themselves or consent. The Miranda right witnesses the power differential.

When Clarence Thomas was nominated for the US Supreme Court in 1991, law professor Anita Hill came forward to testify that Thomas had sexually harassed her when he was her boss in the 1980s. Most people doubted Hill's testimony. Adding to that shaming was the question many asked her: "Why didn't you come forward earlier?" Not understanding power differences and the impact of shame still leads many to be suspicious of the fact that victims of abuse often stay silent for years or decades.

On the other hand, if someone cuts you off in traffic and you cuss them out from the driver's sea of your car, it's not an abuse problem. Someone cutting you off could be seen as an assault or a hurt, because it's rude and dangerous. Cussing someone out is an understandable response to them doing that to you. But as drivers, you're peers; you're not in a situation of unequal power. You can turn down a side street to avoid driving near this person; they aren't depriving you of consent or freedom of movement. You can adequately defend yourself (assuming it's a run-of-the-mill traffic experience).

When a person has the power to defend themselves and is free to consent, they can still be hurt. But their responses are not frozen inside, locked away until someone witnesses them and helps them complete their responses. When they don't have that power and there are no loving witnesses, shame manifests.

To unshame abuse, to witness it in a loving way, requires that we take full account of the power differences. Not seeing them allows shame's eyes to doubt, dismiss, and throw shade on those who tell their stories.

Unshaming Abuse

Unshaming abuse requires a compassionate witness who explicitly or implicitly recognizes the power difference, honors that you weren't able to defend yourself, witnesses the injury, believes the story, and asks, "What was it like to be you? What did you experience?"

This is often done somatically. Wanting to know the details of a person's experience, expressing empathy and compassion, and demonstrating a profound trust in the heart and story of the person combine to wrap their way around the heart and soul like a loving bandage. Witnessing a story makes the person a subject to be understood and cared for instead of an object of psychological analysis that focuses on whether the person should be believed and what might be wrong with them.

Identify the Internalized Witness

As you consider an instance of abuse in your life, the first step of unshaming is to identify your internalized witness: How have you learned to view your story with denial, dismissal, or gaslighting?

Ask yourself these powerful questions: Who was there, or wasn't there? Who did you tell? Or, often most powerfully: from whom would you want to conceal the details, and why?

"I would never tell my father. He would vehemently deny it."

"I would never tell my best friend. He would think I was being too dramatic and emotional." This person's response gives a clue that they also likely think they're too dramatic and emotional. When their best friend told them they were being too emotional, they accepted it as truth. This is how shame silences.

When I'm working with someone to help them unshame their abuse, next I ask how that witness's attitude lives in their life: "Tell me more about how you doubt your experience or dismiss hurts because you think you're too emotional. Do you not speak up because you don't want to complain?"

When they answer, a whole unshaming world opens up to them: "Damn! I'm always thinking I shouldn't feel hurt, that I'm too sensitive."

One person I worked with on unshaming told me, "I wouldn't tell anyone because I believe they would feel burdened."

I asked, "Where else do you not share your experiences and feelings because you don't want to burden people?"

"I'm like that all the time," she said. "I never want to burden people." She had internalized a shaming witness that governed much of the way she related, and it had influenced her to hide herself from others. The shaming witness we get to know as children takes a seat of great power in our psyche, our relationships, and our lives.

That witness governs our abuse stories. That witness says, "This is what's wrong with me; this is what needs fixing. This is why my experience really doesn't matter." Identifying that witness is key, because once you do, you can shine a light on the internalized witness and its messages, which changes the relationship. You become more self-aware, self-trusting, self-loving.

Discover Your Ally

The second step in considering your abuse story is to find your inner ally. I define the ally as a defender who could not defend you at the time of the abusive event. If you were unable to scream and kick when you were abused, your ally is able to scream and kick. If someone was watching and didn't intercede, your ally sees what happened and has the power to intercede on your behalf.

A loving witness is an ally who sees what's happening or believes your story, and responds compassionately by caring for your feelings (e.g., fear, hurt, anger) and acting protectively. The fact that this kind of witness is so often missing, or that there may have been no witness at all, doesn't mean we don't need that kind of witness now. We need to find it from the outside, even when we tell our story years later, and we need to develop that kind of compassion for ourselves. We need to internalize an unshaming witness. Otherwise, when abuses occur today, even if they're not as harmful as the earlier abuse, we don't respond to ourselves with compassion and protection.

How do we internalize an unshaming witness if that kind of witnessing wasn't modeled for us earlier? The response we need lives inside of us. We simply need to look at the scene again—from the outside this time—and trust our impulses. Why look from the outside? Because these events are so powerful that we get lost in them, we become them, we get filled up with the feelings and experiences of being victimized. In other words, when we enter the scene too quickly, we lose touch with our capacity to witness. In a real way, we dissociate. (We'll talk more about dissociation in chapter 10, "Witnessing Trauma: Unshaming Our Deepest Wounds.")

Here's how to proceed. First, lay out the fundamental details of the abusive event in a way that helps you stay distant from it. For example, I invite my client to spend thirty seconds drawing a picture of the abuse. We only need a basic image; they could draw stick figures.

For instance, when I was a child, my older brother used to tie me up and perform sadistic "experiments" on me. As an adult, after I had started my career as a therapist, I told my friend Marcus about this. He was a therapist too, and at the time we were both attending a therapeutic training.

Marcus asked, "Do you want me to gather people for community support?" I assented. Marcus gathered twenty-five other therapists to work with me on this, and we all convened in a room.

"Let's play out one of the scenes David went through," Marcus said. "Who's going to play David's brother?" Someone came forward, and Marcus said, "Okay, who's going to play David?"

"I should play myself," I said.

"I'm not allowing you to go back into that scene," Marcus replied. "You can design and choreograph it, but you're not going in."

Before we even started, he had already protected me from the events that nobody else had protected me from when I was young and vulnerable. In that moment, I knew that I mattered.

A group of process-work practitioners is usually not available, but drawing is an easily accessible method. Drawing a basic picture and looking at it invites the compassionate witness, which is a powerfully unshaming presence.

When I witness a client's drawing, I ask questions like: "What do you see?" "What happens to you when you're looking at that story, thinking about it with me?" "If you could enter the story, what would you do?"

My clients have said, "I'd hit that person." "I would take the person out of the room." "I'd hold them in my arms." "I would send that person to prison."

That powerful consciousness is the person's ally. This ally lived inside the person during the event, but it wasn't free to be activated; it got frozen. That ally lived in me. I wanted to hit the abuser, kick them out of the room, put them in prison, but I wasn't free to. In that moment of abuse, inner allyship and self-love were not allowed. My inner allyship and self-love got stuck under shame's veil for decades afterward. Now that I've identified my inner ally, I need to affirm and nurture our bond.

Once you discover that ally—that part of you that is free to respond fully and compassionately—ask yourself, "Where do I need this ally in my current life?" Where else do you need an advocate or friends to help you? I guarantee you will find places where you need more tenderness and protection, places where you're getting hurt and you need to take care of yourself better. In short, you need to integrate that ally, the one who wasn't there for you *then*, so they can be there for you *now*.

Feedback

Each of us has an inner guidance system, a knowing of what is right for us. As we discussed in chapter 4, "The Role of Boundaries in Healing Shame," my teacher, Arny Mindell, calls the communication of this knowing *feedback*: the client's communication of yes, no, or maybe. The client is always showing me whether the direction I'm going is the right direction for them. Mostly they show me not by telling me; rather, they either flow smoothly along with my suggestions, or their body language, pauses, confusion, or other responses indicate a better direction. When I train practitioners, I show videos and have them study moments of client hesitation, agreement, or other subtle cues expressing maybe or no.

However, when you work on unshaming yourself alone, without a facilitator or a witness, you need to become more consciously attuned to your own feedback. Otherwise, you'll bypass your own consent, and guess what that leads to: shame.

For instance, maybe you think you should meditate, but your body doesn't want to do that. Or maybe you decide to explore a deep issue, but then your mind jumps to thinking about an errand you should run. Please take yourself and your responses seriously. Be attentive to whether you're feeling yes, no, or maybe. Should you slow down, speed up, or walk away and get some support?

It's quite common for people who are working on themselves to ignore this fundamental kind of feedback. You may think "I gotta change this pattern. I'm going to figure out why I do this," but inside, a part of you resists; perhaps it feels interrogated or as if it got caught doing something bad. Or you decide, "I'm going to sit with these feelings and not run away from them," while some part of you feels punished and "made to look" at something. When we bypass this feedback, we abuse

ourselves without realizing it. Not only will this not help; it will perpet-
uate the abuse and create more shame. And remember, more shame
means you matter less to yourself and you treat yourself even more like
something is wrong with you.

Some practitioners are misusing somatic methods because they're
not sufficiently trained in issues related to abuse and trauma. This
sometimes happens when clients provide feedback that requires close
attention and adjustments. For instance, when the practitioner invites a
client to work in a certain way, the client may say, "Um . . . I guess so," in
a tone that says "No" or "I don't feel safe in my body; can we find another
way?" They may not be able to use their voice or even movement. They
may not be able to say "That's not right for me yet" because of the
practitioner/client power imbalance.

When practitioners are insufficiently observant, an attempt at heal-
ing can become an abuse scene, as the "no" that is getting overridden by
the practitioner's agenda echoes previous violations.

"That's not right for me" is an unshamed way of saying no.

"I'm not able to" is a statement that often arises from shame.

Accessing the Body's Experience: The Somatics of Abuse

The "energies, potentials, and resources necessary for [our] construc-
tive transformation" are held in the body, writes Peter Levine.

You are now prepared to go deeper into your abusive experience.
We didn't go directly into the experience earlier because going into
an abusive story when you're not ready will put you right back where
you were. If you don't have a witness or an ally, you will simply be
reabused, and no healing will take place. If someone punched you,
it would only be injurious to allow it to happen again unless you
reentered the scene able to protect yourself and to connect with your
deeper healing energies and experience. In essence, your efforts at
healing would not succeed or be sustainable, and you would be left
with more shame.

The somatic channels we've gotten to know in the previous chapters are powerful doorways for unshaming the "energies and potentials" needed to bring healing to abuse. Our goal is to connect directly with these experiences and amplify and unfold them. Shame minimizes and shrinks; it suppresses and hides experience from our awareness.

I worked with a man on this just the other day. He said it was hard to connect with his abusive experience because he was frightened. As he spoke, his body made movements as if pulling back and turning away.

"Your body is beginning to turn," I said. "Can you continue that movement?"

He turned away from me and drew back further.

I said, "Keep going. Allow your body to go as far as it wants."

"I would get up and walk away," he said, "but isn't that just escapism?" Can you hear the pathologization of wanting to get away?

I said, "What's wrong with escaping when you're in danger?"

His tears begin to flow. "I wasn't able to get away."

"Your body knows what was right for you then. And now, allow yourself to walk away from anything or anyone when you have that impulse."

"There are many moments in my life when I don't allow myself to walk away," he said. "I thought that was wrong." Can you hear shame's interpretation?

When we follow the body, we learn about impulses that we had earlier but that were denied, overpowered, or gaslit. Unshaming those impulses brings healing to the earlier abuse and allows those impulses to be integrated.

As we've already discussed, sometimes when I ask a person about their experience, they say they don't know what happened to them. Shame has robbed them of their bodily connection with the abuse, leading to dissociation. In such cases, what can we do? First, we can try to elicit more details: "Where were you? What do you remember? In your memory, do you see anything? Notice anything? What did your house look like? What was the day like?" As we recall details, the body will start going into the experience. It doesn't matter what details we recall. This is also the case when you're working on your own to unshame yourself. Follow the trail of details. They will unfold the experience in your body.

Once a client's body is activated, we slow down what's happening in the body. Feel it, amplify it, express it, unshame it. Stay with the experience. Shame will constantly attempt to doubt, deny, and minimize, so we keep on going back into the body experience. If you find yourself dissociating, don't shame that response. It's the body's intelligence protecting you from harm. (We'll talk more about unshaming dissociation in chapter 10.)

Taking Back Your Lost Qualities

In an abuse scene, power gets attached to the perpetrator. The assault consists of more than just the violating act; the redistribution of power away from the victim and to the abuser is also part of the assault. Afterward, the injured person often identifies with a disempowerment that did not exist before. We look at the world through the eyes of the victim we were, disidentifying with our power. Do you relate to this? If so, I bet you want your power back. You deserve it.

Unshaming includes wresting back those powers. We often think these stolen powers are bad because we identify them with injury and abuse: anger, ferocity, determination. I'm not suggesting that I become like my father and beat up children. But even if I never punch someone, I need to have the power to firmly maintain my self-respect. Even if I never snarl at someone, cuss them out, or tell them to get lost, I need the power to protect my boundaries. I needed that power to complete my law degree and write my first book; otherwise, outer and inner criticism would have stopped me dead in my tracks.

What are the powers the perpetrator took from you? How can you, with the help of your ally, recover those qualities and integrate them into yourself?

Working to unshame experiences of abuse does more than restore stolen qualities. It also builds empathy. Sharing our stories heals the world as it heals us.

One example of reclaiming our lost qualities came up in a session I had with a client named Kinsley.

"I have something I've wanted to deal with for a long time," Kinsley said. "You may have noticed already, but I deal with severe anxiety. It's so severe that I can't drive anymore. So I go for walks instead, but whenever I try to walk the dog, our neighbors make rude, mocking comments."

"You can't drive or leave your home," I said. "That's big."

"I had a panic attack when I was driving. Then when COVID was happening, our neighbors started attacking us; that's why I'm scared to leave my house." She started to cry. "And my son deals with PTSD [posttraumatic stress disorder], and he'd have attacks that look like seizures."

"I'm thinking of two things, Kinsley. I'm thinking about the anxiety experience itself, of course; I want to go further with that. And then the word *attack* keeps on coming up: panic attack, neighbor attacks, scared of being attacked. So that makes me think that something is attacking you."

"I do have a history of severe abuse and trauma," she said.

"Let's explore that. How have you been attacked? I don't need to access the most painful experiences, but I need to know something about being attacked. You talked about your neighbor, for instance. Let's think about Kinsley as a separate being we can talk about. 'Kinsley gets attacked.' Don't tell me how *you've* been attacked; tell me how *Kinsley* has been attacked." I first asked Kinsley to step outside of the experience, to witness the experience. She had already entered a difficult and anxious state that would prevent her from caring for herself if I asked her to go right into being in the experience.

"Kinsley has been . . . both parents and brother have attacked," she said. "And I didn't have any help anywhere. We moved when I was in the middle of first grade, second grade, third grade, fifth grade, sixth grade, seventh grade, eighth grade, and ninth grade. At home I was being attacked. I was bullied in school, as well. There was nowhere safe."

"I'm listening," I said.

"As an adult, I went looking for family. I got involved in church, and I became an ordained minister. But I was also a woman trying to function in the church, so I encountered a lot of sexism and marginalization."

"Say more about how Kinsley was attacked," I said. "Was she physically hurt?" I asked for some details so we could get to know more about her story and eventually her somatic experience.

"Her brother physically and sexually attacked her," she said. "Then probably the worst was that he blackmailed Kinsley. He told her that if she didn't do everything he wanted, he was going to tell Mom that she had been the one to approach him sexually. For about a year, I was doing anything he wanted, until I didn't." Not only was she abused, she was forbidden from getting a witness. That means none of her natural responses to the abuse—her hurt, fear, anger, freezing—can be supported.

"Let's slow down there," I said. "That's very powerful, what you're saying. If you can see Kinsley in your mind's eye and the brother who commits this betraying sexual violence, what is her body doing? Is she standing? Is she frozen? Is she curling up?" I still supported Kinsley in witnessing the abuse. We needed her witnessing capacity to come online in order to unshame, in order for her to be able to see and believe herself in her current life and have the freedom to respond.

"I'm kind of . . ." she began, with clenched, shaking hands. "I'm thinking of one particular moment. I'm wanting to fight, knowing if I do, it's going to get worse."

"There's fight in her, but it's not very wise to do that fighting," I affirmed. "I see your fingers clenching up, and your hands are shaking. Can you amplify what your hands are feeling right now?" Now Kinsley was doing more than just witnessing herself from the outside. I was there as a witness, which gave her access to her fight and her tears—things she didn't have access to then.

Her hands started making wild and furious punching movements as she sobbed. "I'm literally like this and with my knee sort of up because he has a knife in his hand," Kinsley said. "I'm trying to protect myself." Her hands continued to punch wildly at the air.

"Trying to protect yourself," I said. "I see it in your hands. I know it's not wise to fight with him, and I'm not thinking that you should have.

When I was a child, I got hurt and couldn't fight back, and I understand that I would've gotten hurt more if I fought back. I'm interested in the fight that's in you still." Kinsley's body system contained an energetic fight, and she needed to get to know that. It needed to be witnessed. Then she could decide whether to use it or not in different situations, at her discretion.

I said, "Can you feel your hands clenched and shaking? Allow that shaking to grow a little bit. It can be painful and emotional, but imagine your hands could be wildly free."

Her punching motions became even freer, as did the sobbing sounds. Then she stopped, indicating that she had gone far enough for the moment.

I said, "When you curl up in an anxiety attack, there's a lot of energy in the shaking. It's panic *and* an attack. There's attack energy in you. It was given to you in a violent, abusive way. And now it's yours. You've got to figure out what to do with it. You have to embody it and say, 'I also have attack energy in me that I need to get to know.'"

"Before COVID I had a personal trainer, and so I went to the gym every day," Kinsley said. "I think all that exercise in the mornings actually helped."

"Yes, activities that allow you to express the shaking, the punching, may be helpful. I would think about movement—making a dance of some of that energy. And if not, do something that has resistance in it. Push against the wall, do push-ups, get some barbells, because you want to start feeling strength in your body and in your psyche. It's not wrong to be scared; you mustn't shame that. Making movements like that could be useful for you. Singing could also be a useful tool. Get some songs that have good energy to them. Channel your attack energy through the songs."

Some time later she wrote to say, "Thanks so much, David. I don't have words to explain just how life-changing the work you do has been for me."

This was a big step. Kinsley got to witness herself, allowing her to be a better witness for herself in the future. She was able to have her sobbing and her terrified feelings without shame. She encountered some of her story in a new way, with the presence of an unshaming witness. And she also now has access to the fight in her anxiety. What she once witnessed as an anxiety to get rid of had a lot of energy in it: the energy of her wild, fighting, punching self, an energy she needed then and needs today in managing her relationship with her neighbors.

Remember that with such powerful experiences of abuse, we may have to go slowly, a little bit at a time, because it's a long-term process, not a one-time procedure. Often people feel that they've made a big breakthrough; but later, when old symptoms arise, they feel like they failed, and shame can take over again.

Unshaming an Abuser

You might be asking, "Why would you want to unshame an abuser?" Or maybe, like so many people, you're ashamed of having been abusive; or your abusive behavior is ongoing, and your ability to change and heal are mired in a shame spiral or suppressed. Yes, this book is for you, too.

The question of why we would want to unshame an abuser represents a common misunderstanding about what unshaming is. I never tell an abuser that it's okay to hurt someone or that they should forgive themselves. (That's a different process altogether.) In fact, I've worked with people who have injured children, who have social views that I find violent, and even those who have taken another's person's life. In this kind of work, I do not recommend that a person or group that has been victimized facilitate the unshaming of their abuser(s). That is a job for a facilitator who is not in an abuser/victim dynamic with the abuser.

And remember, I am not talking about shame in the conventional way: a sense of guilt, feeling bad, or responsibility for hurting someone. Unshaming is not the same as saying, "Don't feel bad about what you've done. It's okay; you're a good person." It doesn't mean bypassing the harm or the abuser's deeper experiences. When we abuse another, we have to become more conscious of our impulses, our inner critics, and our stories. That's what unshaming does. That's what true witnessing does.

How do I help people become conscious of the violence that lives within them, and then deepen their relationship with that violence? Let's say I'm working with a parent who physically abuses a child. I first tell them that I will do everything I can to stop them from committing that abuse. Once that's understood, I then help the person get close to that violence. What does the violent energy feel like? How does it move? What are the voices and sounds that live inside of the abuser?

Many people say about abusers, "They know exactly what they are doing." In a way, that's true. They must be held responsible. However, a person is almost never aware of the depths of the experience of the violence that lives in them.

We then keep going deeper until the person knows the underlying energy, need, power, rage, or hurt they have experienced that is connected to their violence. I am not saying that all violence emanates from being hurt; that is simply not true. We do this step because it has a healing impact. It also decreases the likelihood of future violence because the person now owns and intimately relates with the source of their violence.

Next, we look at where the essence or root of that energy properly belongs in the person's life.

"Did you need it earlier in life? How?"

"Do you need it to make an outer change?"

"Do you need it to take on an inner critic?"

"Do you need it to speak about your own hurts?"

"Do you need it because you're out of touch with your own power?"

"Do you need it to stand up for yourself in another area of your life?"

Often an abuser is unaware of their intense vulnerability, which, if owned and integrated, would create empathy that would prevent them from injuring others.

I follow these unshaming steps with the fundamental belief that at the root of an abuser's violence is an intelligence, a power, and/or a story. Unshaming in this way is not the opposite of punishment. It is the opposite of shaming, which is a repressive, suppressive act that does not create long-term, sustainable change.

It is also important to work with the abuser's inner critic. The inner critic can create guilty feelings. If the critic has something important to say, the person needs to listen to it and feel their reactions to it. When they do, this may be the first time an abuser actually feels empathy for those they've injured. If you hurt someone else, guilt is a worthy feeling, but ongoing self-excoriation and shaming does not benefit the perpetrator or those around them. In addition, a person made to feel guilty or bad about themselves can make a show of remorse without actually changing the underlying dynamic. Saying "I'm really sorry" out of a sense of guilt can actually keep a person from getting to know the violence that lives in them and what to do with it.

In addition, when the perpetrator brings their guilt (meaning their relationship with an inner critic) to the injured person, it never brings healing to the injured person or the perpetrator. In fact, it blinds the perpetrator to the one who has been injured because the perpetrator is in a closer relationship with their critic than with the person they've hurt.

Thus, if you have the opportunity to apologize, feel into the hurt of the other (not the guilt; that's a critic). Notice if empathy, compassion, or remorse arises. Express those out loud, to the ones you have hurt if possible, or to at least one or two others.

Ask your heart and soul what you must do in your life to live out this compassion and empathy in the world. This may be very little or very much, depending on the level of the injury you've caused.

If the injury is great, it can affect a perpetrator's life path. For instance, if a person has taken a life, no amount of therapy may be sufficient. The person may need to devote their life to certain causes related to the injury. This must not be seen as penance or punishment, but a beautiful, meaningful unfolding. For example, I knew a man who had taken a life when he was part of a gang. He later devoted a great deal of time to mentoring youth who were at risk of gang involvement. This is not about punishment; this is about unshaming the life path of the person who took a life, allowing their life to become meaningful by nurturing other lives.

Unshaming recovers the story, not of what's *wrong* with you, but of what *happened* to you, as clearly explicated by Bruce D. Perry and Oprah Winfrey in their book *What Happened to You? Conversations on Trauma, Resilience, and Healing.* Unshaming shows us the way to healing by focusing on how our abuse was witnessed, giving us access to the powers we needed at the time so we can return to the abusive events, and allowing the body to complete its responses. Finally, unshaming teaches how to experience the feelings and memories and to integrate the split-off powers and awareness—aspects of our wellness that we need to live the life that was meant for us.

EXERCISE

Identifying the Internalized Shaming Witness and the Ally

1. Remember a specific abusive moment—just one moment, even if there were repeated events. This will help you access your sensory-grounded experience.

2. Identifying internalized shame: Were there any witnesses present? Did you tell anyone at any time afterward? How did they respond? Did they do anything to deny, dismiss, or gaslight your experience? What message did they send to you about your experience? Do you deny, dismiss, or gaslight your experiences in your current life in the same way that you experienced earlier?

3. Identifying internalized shame: Who would you *not* choose to tell about this event today? Why not? What else do you not share with people for the same reasons? This could be *not* sharing your needs, feelings, thoughts, behaviors, or behavioral patterns. (This is how an internalized shaming witness affects you years later.)

4. Connecting with the inner ally: Imagine going back to that event as you are today. Look the scene; see yourself as you were then. Look at the perpetrator(s). Look at yourself.

5. Notice what impulses arise in your body. What would your hands do, your arms, your legs, your whole body, now that you are an outsider? Stay with your body experience first before moving on to question 6.

6. Would you protect yourself? Fight your abuser? Comfort yourself?

7. Where do you need that kind of support in your current life? Say out loud, "I intend to be there for myself in this way from now on."

CHAPTER 10

Witnessing Trauma

Unshaming our Deepest Wounds

The past is never dead. It's not even past.

—WILLIAM FAULKNER

Our greatest gifts and our deepest wounds reside in the same place.

—MICHAEL MEADE

My client Samara lived through some of the most painful childhood sexual abuse I've ever encountered, as well as severe violence perpetrated by the medical system. In a session, she said to me, "I'm working on reclaiming my agency in my healing from complex trauma."

"What would it feel like to have agency?" I asked, wanting to access her experience.

"Really good in my body. I would stand up straighter, breathe more deeply, feel free and safe."

I suggested that we stay in that body experience, as Samara was leading us that way.

"I enjoy feeling it," she said, "but then the shame enters. I'm not allowed to feel this kind of joy and wellness."

Shame wasn't allowing her to fully experience her life force. The unshaming process follows the river of experience, so I focused on wellness next.

"Let's drop the issue of agency for the moment," I said. "Let's follow the next step, into . . . what's wellness like?"

"It's like sailing; like we're all doing our jobs individually, and as a group. We're all connected. We get along, even if we come from different belief systems. And when the captain turns off the engines, we all start to whisper because we don't want to break the spell."

In following Samara's desire for the agency she lost in her trauma, we had arrived at a vision of a new world. She had moved on from thinking she wanted to recover the agency that was stolen from her by the horrendous abuse she suffered. Now she had arrived at a new destination: a vision of a better world, one of fellowship amid diversity, a world of spirit. Samara had been working on her trauma and teaching people about trauma for years now, and this was the process through which she had developed her inspiring vision. However, she didn't see herself as a visionary leader. Instead, she saw herself as someone who needed healing to recover what she had lost.

Like Samara, many of us are "wounded healers." In her case, a visionary leader was being formed alchemically in the midst of her traumatic wounding. Unshaming that trauma wound led her to integrate that aspect into herself and her daily life. We'll discuss this teleological function and process in more depth as this chapter progresses.

Clarifying the Differences and Relationship between Abuse and Trauma

One could write an entire book on trauma, given its significance and the wealth of evidence-based research findings on the topic. Much of this research examines the link between neurobiology and trauma and its impact on depression, suicide, addictions, psychosis, aggression, and various physical symptoms. One thing is clear: trauma impacts us at a somatic level, so healing trauma must involve our bodies. As unshaming trauma happens in the body, this method is especially useful for not only unshaming abuse but also addressing its related issues and manifestations.

Much has been written about trauma in recent years by authors including Peter Levine, Gabor Maté, and Judith Herman. In her book *Truth and Repair*, Herman speaks of how trauma shames those who experience it, and she acknowledges the important role of the witness: "The wounds of trauma not merely by perpetrators but the actions and inactions of bystanders—all those who are complicit in or who prefer not to know about the abuse or who blame the victims—often cause even deeper wounds."

Like the word *abuse*, people use *trauma* to mean many different things, so it's important to review what abuse is and define what trauma means in the context of shame and the power of unshaming. Abuse, as I define it, can include being overpowered by, injured by, and not being able to defend oneself against impersonal forces, including natural disasters. Social abuse—being discriminated against over one's lifetime—always begets social trauma because it is a long-term, unwitnessed experience.

Even one instance of abuse can have longer-term implications. Trauma is a long-term wound and process, often intergenerational. Thus, the distinction between the two is not a perfectly sharp line of demarcation. As we saw in the last chapter, people suffering from abuse experience healing when the abusive events are compassionately witnessed, which means that someone believes them, supports all their feeling responses—many of which have been locked up—and holds the person's story with compassion and a protective instinct. When this does not happen at the time of the abusive event, the system can't process the experience, which overwhelms the system and causes abuse experiences to become trapped in the body as trauma. Trauma is an abuse experience that doesn't have a sufficient witness.

In this chapter, we'll identify and acknowledge the effects of intergenerational trauma; how trauma and shame can interfere with becoming oneself; how issues related to trauma manifest for wounded healers;

the physical symptoms that can be connected to trauma; and trauma's relationship to the shaming inner critic and internalized oppression. We'll also honor the gifts and medicine of unshamed trauma; we'll unshame the trauma responses of dissociation and freezing; and we'll discuss shame in the context of detaching from family introjects.

Long-Term/Intergenerational Trauma

Recently a person reached out to me in need of unshaming, but she didn't call it that. She said it better than I could have: "I need someone to trust me so I can learn to trust myself."

A person's trauma almost always leads to long-term issues, which can cause their life trajectory to become seriously truncated, derailed, twisted, or even tortured.

Intergenerational trauma prompted my first foray into the study of trauma, although I realized that later. At the time, I was trying to understand my body's reaction to a friend's statement that Jews were always smart and successful.

I replied, "Even when projections onto a group seem to be positive, they are still dehumanizing and hurtful stereotypes, rendering the diversity of people within the group invisible. These kind of stereotypes are always dangerous."

It was the first time I had ever spoken up about the hurtfulness of Jewish stereotypes. Much to my surprise, my whole body went into a sustained shiver, and I felt as if I were hearing and seeing at a distance from my own body. I didn't understand it. Where did this fear come from? My friend wasn't accosting me, and I had never been subjected to direct anti-Jewish violence. Yet I was scared to death. It seemed that my emotional body held experiences with no clear associations or connections to my own lived experience.

Soon after that event, I began combing evidence-based journal articles to find explanations for my reactions. A plethora of studies attested to the impact of Holocaust survivors' trauma on their children and grandchildren. Since then, the scope of research findings on intergenerational and epigenetic trauma has expanded to encompass survivors of the atomic bombing of Hiroshima, the Vietnam War, domestic violence, and the children of perpetrators of violence, even when the children were not directly subjected to violence themselves.

My understanding of epigenetic trauma grew when I read the research findings of Kerry Ressler and Brian Dias, neurobiologists in the Department of Psychiatry at Emory University School of Medicine. In their studies, they gave mice electric shocks in conjunction with the release of a specific smell. The animals eventually began to shudder at the smell alone. The offspring of those mice, born after that phase of the experiment, also shuddered when exposed to the same smell, even though they had never been shocked or encountered the scent before. The third generation of mice inherited the same reaction. This suggests that humans can also experience inherited trauma responses.

At that point in my career, having already studied the issue of abuse and worked with many abuse victims, I began to make a new distinction between longer-term postabuse effects such as PTSD and the workings and healing of abuse as I discussed in the previous chapter. Healing abuse does not resolve all the symptoms of trauma or return a person to their wholeness, so trauma needs to be identified separately. This is why I make a distinction by devoting separate chapters to abuse and trauma.

When I'm working with clients on these topics, it can go one of two main ways, based on what they need. Some people need to work through their experiences of abuse, as discussed in the previous chapter. The other direction is when a client needs to work on the unfolding of their life paths after traumatic experiences; that is, they need to address how the unprocessed abuse has been preventing or thwarting their innate purpose and self-actualization.

Components of Healing Trauma

What else can happen if we work through our trauma in a way that relieves us of our symptoms, beyond making meaning and facilitating the flowering of our gifts? As people learn to unshame their traumatic stories and symptoms, their awareness—their ability to witness their suffering and story from the outside—grows. They can talk about it, sometimes laugh about it, and metacommunicate: talk about the ways they're communicating about traumatic stories and symptoms.

The healing of trauma involves several components:

- **Working with the body/soma.** Because abuse and trauma are interrelated, the healing of trauma also involves working with experiences stored or remembered in the body that need witnessing. We also need to complete our responses to the trauma that we were not free to express when the abuse happened, especially responses of pain, terror, and resistance (such as anger, rage, and pushback).

- **Witnessing our internalized criticism and oppression.** We internalized viewpoints about ourselves that were either explicitly stated or embedded in the traumatic experience (often abusive experiences.) Those "inner voices" almost always continue to live on in the person, mostly unconsciously, continuing the perpetration. When we make these viewpoints and voices explicit, they can be witnessed and responded to.

- **Alchemy.** The parts of us that are locked in trauma are often being cooked alchemically, even before we begin processing them. That means that our system—our psyche, dreams, and body—is actively working to heal the wound. This natural and organic alchemy yields a medicine that can be applied not only to our own wounds but also to the wounds of others who have had the same experience. Our greatest traumas are precisely the location where we can discover and uncover the wounded healer in us.

- **Loads of self-love.** This is particularly true when it comes to embracing the long-term healing process involved in profound trauma—a healing process that may take years or even generations.

An Unshaming Note on the Time Frame of Trauma Healing

Because healing trauma is a longer-term project, we need to have a realistic understanding of the time frame involved. Clients will often say to me, "I've been working on my trauma for so many years, and I *still* get triggered." In addition, they'll also report that they still can't focus, have physical symptoms, get depressed, have unsatisfying relationship patterns, have addictive and codependent behaviors, and so on. (Remember, *still* is often a shaming word; it carries the message that if the person were better at self-improvement, these troublesome, disruptive symptoms would disappear.)

In these cases, I point the client not toward their past or the causes of their suffering, but toward the future: who they are becoming and what they can make out of their story.

Trauma and Shame as Obstacles to Becoming Yourself

One tragic yet often overlooked consequence of early abuse and trauma is that certain aspects of our development get bypassed while the psyche's resources are invested in ensuring our survival and security. One of these bypassed aspects is the development of our natural gifts and genius, in this case defined as the unique spirit that guides the essence of our life path. Each life, through its genius, carries a medicine meant to heal the individual *and* to bring healing to the world around us. If the trauma doesn't get addressed, this healing doesn't happen. The culmination and fulfillment of healing our trauma is the connection with our genius and the orienting of our life in the direction of our true path of heart.

When I'm teaching students to work with abuse and trauma, the way I define abuse to them links directly to how to unshame the abuse and speak to the longer-term healing of abuse. To unshame trauma, we must anticipate and address its aftereffects and be curious about them to reveal a pathway to the person's birthright of unfolding, to their ultimate individuation—the project of becoming themselves. The medicine for that restoration exists in the individual; unshaming can unlock it. Taking this matter further, we'll focus on one specific aspect of this project: becoming a wounded healer.

Trauma and the Wounded Healer

Many people justify trauma and abuse by saying things like "What doesn't kill you makes you stronger." That is not my message. It was *never* good for Samara or you or me to suffer so egregiously; that idea brings shame to our wounds. We never needed the thing that caused our trauma. However, although we can't change the past, there is some alchemy to the life that follows an abusive event. It consists of us becoming who we were meant to be. Wounds are where we cook. Shame guards our wounds behind denial and dismissal, which leads to pathologizing and not mattering. Thus, unshaming must not only relieve and release, uncover and recover what has been stolen; it must also bring witness to the years of trauma in its wake.

It's easy to believe that such time has been wasted because nothing was happening in that terrible rupture. This is a shaming lie. Aspects of the person's gifts, their deep nature, often cook right there. I see that gift as a kind of medicine, which is the essence of the wounded healer archetype. Without this notion, trauma is viewed only as a pathology, something to get over so we can get back to normal life. That viewpoint shames everyone who has experienced or is experiencing trauma. It also neglects to see how some of the most gifted people rose out of the depths of trauma, and how our greatest and most needed leaders often rose out of great social marginalization—a form of abuse with inevitable generations of trauma in its wake. Working on trauma is more than a psychological and often physical healing; it is a sacred soul project.

The truth—frustrating in the short term but liberating in the long term—is that healing trauma is different from making your symptoms vanish in a short period of time. For many, it involves a lifetime of coming to know oneself, of gradual relief, of greater self-acceptance. In fact, because much trauma is intergenerational, it may take generations for symptoms to be released. When I say this, clients often sigh with relief: "I'm not broken, doing it wrong, defective. I'm not unworthy." I also share with them that I still suffer from certain trauma-connected symptoms, including waking up with fear in my body. These symptoms have *eased* over the course of thirty years of working on my trauma, but they still *arise*. Although modern medicine has immensely deepened our understanding of trauma, the medical model—"Take this drug, and your symptoms will go away"—isn't all that effective, and too often it's shaming.

If we can't relieve all or even most of our symptoms, what *can* happen in the longer term? People become fantastically creative, whether literally creative via an art form, or figuratively by creating a life of meaning. Consider this story about the early life of the legendary, brilliant Maya Angelou. When she was raped at the age of seven, she named her abuser. Soon afterward, her abuser was found dead, apparently having been kicked to death. Maya, in her child mind, concluded that using her voice had killed this man, so she stopped speaking and remained silent for the next five years. During this time, her grandmother, called Momma, said, "Sister, Momma don't care what these people say, that you must be an idiot, a moron, 'cause you can't talk. Momma don't care. Momma know that when you and the good Lord get ready, you gon' be a teacher." During those years she communicated by writing, and she spent countless hours under the porch of Momma's house and in the Black library reading everything she could get her hands on. She memorized much of what she read, including full Shakespeare plays and fifty sonnets. Thus, she later said, "When I decided to speak, I had a lot to say and many ways to say it." Her psyche did some powerful cooking in that silence, and afterward she did indeed go on to be a teacher, as well as a brilliant and successful writer, role model, cultural icon, and visionary leader.

Our wounds also hold our most sacred medicine and intelligence. Shame makes us forget or forsake our loveliness, in this case, the visionary healer aspect or other strength mired in a traumatic wound. This is why, instead of only looking backward to the cause of our symptoms, as we must while working on abuse, working on trauma requires us to look forward teleologically. The dictionary definition of *teleology* that's most relevant to an unshaming context is "the fact or character attributed to nature or natural processes of being directed toward an end or shaped by a purpose." These natural processes are growing in us—cooking in us as abuse survivors—as we get triggered, can't focus, have physical symptoms, get depressed, have relationship patterns, have addictive and codependent behaviors, or as in my case, wake up with fear suffusing my body. In fact, manifesting those creative gifts and lives of meaning almost always relieves our symptoms.

The archetype of the wounded healer is instructive here. Mythologist and storyteller Michael Meade asserts that ancient stories teach us that each person is born carrying a unique medicine, and facing our deepest wounds activates that medicine: "In that sense, the inner wound can be seen as a womb. In going through the wound we become reborn as an initiate on the path of healing." He also says, "Our greatest gifts and our deepest wounds reside in the same place."

From this vision of trauma healing, we look not toward the end of our symptoms, but an end result that encompasses the birth and fruition of the medicine we carry: living the life that is meant for us and bringing forth the gifts we were given. Often this means that we, like Samara, become healers.

Sensitivity as a Healing Superpower

I once worked with a woman who, as a child, had felt unseen. She came to me suffering from being regularly hurt by friends and peers in much the same way she had experienced hurt in her family of origin. That hurt arose out of abusive events that were left unprocessed, resulting in traumatic symptoms. Naturally, she wanted to overcome this pattern.

"How can I learn to be less sensitive?" she asked me, thinking that healing would arise from trying to overcome her sensitivity. This belief had been planted early in her life when her parents told her as a child,

"You're too sensitive. You need to develop a thicker skin." She, like many clients I have worked with, learned to blame and even hate her sensitivity, seeing it as the root cause of her suffering. She thought something was wrong with her (her sensitivity), that she didn't matter (because only the people hurting her seemed to matter and to have authority and credibility), and that her sensitive responses shouldn't matter.

Instead of agreeing to her agenda, I expressed curiosity. "Where does your sensitivity live inside you?"

"In my heart."

"What aspect of nature could represent your sensitivity?"

"The grass. It's so easily moved by the wind."

I guided her to move closer to her heart, to sense the flowing grass that symbolized her sensitivity. When she did, she reported feeling a sweet, easy joy. She also said her heart could feel the cool breeze or stormy tumult of another person's mood or manner, sometimes almost before she even encountered them in person. Her healing would not take the course of getting rid of her sensitivity; this path would only amplify her self-hatred. Instead, healing came about through her owning and honoring her sensitivity, and even further cultivating its delicate acuity.

When she was abused as a child, she was criticized for her sensitivity, leading her to turn away from it, when her sensitivity was in fact her gift. Perhaps her family and others were secretly envious of her capacity to feel so deeply and easily. Perhaps they preferred to blame her for her responses to their inconsiderate comments, instead of reflecting on their behavior and making changes. People who had disowned their own sensitivity may have even been jealous of her, which led them to disparage her gift. Regardless of what was driving their responses, the site of her wounding was the very seed of her gift. Her shamed feelings about her sensitivity had been leading her afield from her life path. Her sensitivity *was* her life path. Shame had disguised it.

Everyone who is suffering from trauma has a slightly different estrangement from their life path. The shamed trait should invite curiosity and admiration that lead to flowering and integration, not an agenda of removal.

Whether dealing with our own wounds or the wounds of clients and friends, we must be careful not to focus solely on their pain and suffering. When we do, we inadvertently patronize, condescend, and fail to bear witness to the power and capacity of the person's gift. We diminish them, reduce them, encourage them to be less whole, and bring a form of pity to the healing equation.

If we want to help ourselves and others, we must attend to the story, the hurt, and the wound with care, compassion, and love. And then we must ask, "Where is that wound in you? Is it in your sensitivity, your intelligence, your body, your connection with people? Were you attacked for your intelligence, your feeling, your sensitivities?"

Trauma and Physical Symptoms

The discussion in this section expands on the material in chapter 3, "Shame, Physical Health, and Symptoms." Unshaming trauma can also occur through unshaming of physical symptoms that arise from trauma. This was the case when I worked with Liana, a psychotherapist who had an extreme case of tinnitus for over three years. Tinnitus is a condition in which a person experiences a ringing or other sounds in the ear, even though nobody else can hear it. Liana's tinnitus was so extreme that she considered suicide just to stop this sound.

"I wish I had chronic pain so that I could numb it out with medication," she told me. "But I can't stop the freaking noise in my head. I am completely dysfunctional." She said that the only time she remembered it getting better was when she screamed into a pillow, yelling, "Just stop! Leave me alone!"

A conventional approach would compassionately seek to make the noise go away, but unshaming proceeds by witnessing one's experience with the underlying belief that it might reveal a story or a message. In an online session with Liana, I asked her to make the noise herself, for two reasons: so I could experience it, and so she could externalize it and get to know it.

"It's like a constant electric drill," she said. "I hear it everywhere. It's like someone getting their claws into my nervous system." Her hands formed into claws, and she began to make the sound. It got so high-pitched that our Zoom interface couldn't pick it up. I couldn't hear it, even though her teeth were gritted, her hands were clenched by the sides of her face, and she was obviously making an unbearably intense sound.

"I can't hear the sound but we can see your body expression," I said. "Can you continue to do that with your face and hands?"

"I'm so ugly," she said as she sobbed and started to gag, as if she was going to vomit. "I can't control myself. It's the only sound I know to make." Her hands were now beginning to flail, and her face became more contorted. "It's all the unwanted attention. All the broken boundaries. All the intrusion. I had no control. I was helpless."

"Why are you so loud?" I asked.

"The world needs her to set boundaries, to be loud," she said, talking about herself.

"Maybe you need to be loud because some people don't listen."

"It's very hard to get to know the sound," Liana continued. "To welcome her. It's one of the biggest challenges in my life, to show my ugly side. And I've had many challenges."

A lot of memories come up for Liana—abusive moments and stories. We could have worked with the abuse stories themselves, but her body said, "Get to know what's happening in my ears." And in those ears was a sound that only she could hear, a sound that she would have to make others hear. The ringing would become an alarm for the world; not just the resolution of an old wound, but a life path forward.

Even if we work to heal ourselves through allopathic or alternative forms of healing, or if we work on our childhood wounds and traumas in therapy for years, or we sit on our cushions or shape our bodies into postures on mats, or we go to a mosque, a church, a synagogue, or a tree, some of our deepest and most chronic difficulties may not disappear. What then is healing? Something quite profound, even marvelous. We can find the path of our own lives, our path of heart. We can use all that we struggle with as wood for the fire we need to heat our alchemical cauldrons. We can discover our deepest gifts and learn to bring them forward right in the midst of our suffering. We can titrate a medicine that others need for their own process of becoming. We can cultivate paths of power and vulnerability that allow for deeper levels of intimacy.

Trauma's Relationship to Shame and Collective Healing

Social trauma, including long-term racialized trauma, must include the issue of abuse while going beyond that understanding. Making matters more urgent, these forms of trauma-creating abuse are often still occurring. Resmaa Menakem, in his profound book *My Grandmother's Hands: Racialized Trauma and the Pathway to Mending Our Hearts and Bodies*, offers this medicine to Black people: "You are not defective." Menakem has hit upon the most important impact of trauma: our belief that something is wrong with us and that we don't matter. Menakem's method resonates with the unshaming approach by focusing on shame and the body. In an interview with Dominic Lawson on the podcast *Beyond Theory*, he says to Lawson, "Brother, you are not defective. You never have been. You never will be. You are not defective. Something has happened, and continues to happen, to your people, but you are not defective." He then asks Lawson to feel, in his body, how this awareness affects him. He calls this body-oriented unshaming practice "somatic abolitionism."

To review: when abuse is unseen, or denied and gaslit as social abuse is, then people suffer symptoms and don't know why. We don't often connect our depressions, anxieties, aggression, and illness to a story or a people. We are simply left to the dominant culture's analysis: "Something is wrong with you. You are sick." And if those symptoms are not taken seriously, or even seen as psychosomatic, then we are told, "Your suffering doesn't matter. You don't matter." This bears out Herman's observation that trauma shames.

The clear implication, which builds on the material in chapters 6 ("Social Issues and Shame") and 9 ("Shame and Abuse: Victims, Perpetrators, and the Witness"), is that people need to connect with the social story behind their traumatic symptoms, connect with people in solidarity and community, in addition to working with abuse and internalized oppression. Much of the trauma healing must be accomplished by the privileged witnesses outside those communities, who can change policies, hearts, and minds, and bear witness. Social trauma highlights the fact that much healing is not about the individual, but the collective. That notion alone is powerfully unshaming.

Unshaming Some Trauma Responses

Dissociation

Dissociation, a natural response to trauma, is regularly shamed when it is only seen as a pathology to overcome. When I was a child and my brother would hold me down, he used his knees and sometimes rope to prevent my physical escape, so I left the normal world. I went into the ceiling, perhaps looking for the stars, or even into the expression on his face or his deep brown eyes. This psychological response is commonly known as dissociation. It's often pathologized, although, like all natural impulses, it carries natural intelligence. When I work with people, I notice that the freedom to dissociate—to back away or remove oneself—is often linked to the freedom to walk away from unhealthy partners, jobs, and friendships. When you notice your consciousness has created distance between you and a harmful experience, flow with its current. Believe in it, unfold it, get to know it; and then you may find that your consciousness clears up and you become safer, or you discover a faraway place where you really want to be.

Reframing this state as creating distance unshames the dissociative response. It's not an illness. It's natural. It's like pulling your hand away from a flame. It's not dissociating to pull your hand away.

When a client comes to me asking for help with their dissociation, I say, "Let's dissociate."

When they do, they say, "I get blurry. I feel myself backing up and going away."

"Where are you going? Where would you go if you could go anywhere?"

"Let's go to the ocean together."

Isn't it amazing that we can travel through time and space to go to the ocean, or any other resource, when the present moment is unsafe? Your entire system is intelligent. There is nothing wrong with you. It has to be okay to forget about the trauma and do something else.

Learning to trust and believe oneself is a longer-term outcome of working on the abuse and associated longer-term trauma. In addition to the relief of symptoms, perhaps the most significant medicine that is titrated through the longer-term work on abuse and trauma is the ability to be intimate with oneself and others—the ability to love.

I once worked with a woman who sent me a book about child abuse before our first session, saying that it would be helpful if I read it. It was a horrific story. At our first meeting, I put out my hand to shake hers, and she responded by saying it was not okay for her to touch me and that she hasn't wanted any physical touch since she was a young child. I began by asking her about abuse; she refused to discuss it. I tried to get her to discuss abuse a few more times that day and even in the next session, but she never followed my lead, so to speak.

I told my supervisor, Max, about this situation, and he said, "Why are you trying to get her to talk about abuse?"

"How else will she heal?"

"If you continue to press her when she's saying no, that will be abusive. It's good that she is able to resist your suggestions. That is her work." She was resolving the longer-term trauma by reclaiming her freedom to resist, to withhold consent, and to trust herself. That was a fundamental wake-up for me. She wanted to go away from the abuse, not toward it. That was her natural intelligence, her unshaming way.

She later told me that the person who had abused her was subjected to an investigation, and caseworkers talked to the children who were suspected to have been abused, including her. She was a young adolescent when they interviewed her.

"How did that go?" I asked, wondering if she opened up to them.

"It was the worst experience of my life," she said. It resulted in her being committed to a psychiatric hospital.

When I'm teaching students and I have them explore their dissociative experiences by feeling into their body impulses, they report turning away, pushing away, or fleeing. I then ask, "If you could turn away, push away, or flee somewhere in your current life, where would that be?" Students often have tears in their eyes or joy in their voice as they list a myriad of spaces and moments.

About ten years ago, I read Arny Mindell's *Earth-Based Psychology*, in which he spoke about people feeling a special magic or medicine at certain spots on the planet. Afterward, when I had clients who showed signs of dissociation, I would ask them, "If you could go somewhere else, somewhere on this earth that you would most like to be, where would you go?" They answered with the names of faraway oceans or mountains. Some wanted to go into the stars. Other people named places like their grandma's house. When we imagine our way to those places, we end up feeling more than safe. We find a new kind of power, one that helps us walk toward or away from the violence that overwhelmed us.

Freezing

I later worked with Liana again because she had been encountering difficulty in moving forward with her dream of singing as a performer. Whenever she tried to advance on this path, she'd freeze up. Freezing is one of the responses to trauma.

"Shame has been a big theme in my life ever since I can remember," Liana said. "I find it challenging to express and show myself to the world, especially artistically, even though a big part of my real self and soul is related to art, music in particular. I've been taking singing and songwriting lessons and guitar and piano lessons. Professionals are encouraging me to get gigs and post my songs on social media, and I would love that from the bottom of my heart; but at that moment I become so activated. It's like, 'No,' because I'd be showing my soul to the world, and that's very vulnerable."

As I told Liana, a conventional approach would try to help her get rid of her resistance and might even pathologize it by calling it "stage fright." Unshaming says that resistance to performing is not a problem; unshaming is more interested in how that's the place where her soul is showing up, right in the middle of that difficulty. To unshame, we need to go right into the most difficult spot to find the intelligence living in that difficulty. Liana's cooking. Her alchemy, her medicine, is right there, not with the removal of the difficulty but right in the middle of the difficulty. That's where we want to look: in her activated self.

With her permission, I encouraged her to sing in public. "Liana, it's time to come out, do some singing, maybe post some reels, sing on social media. We'll go to a club or something like that, where you can sing and show your voice."

"Yeah," she said, "I can already feel it. Great. I tend to freeze, so there's a lack of movement, especially in my upper body, in my shoulders. I stop moving. But when I try to move again, I feel very afraid. I feel scared."

"One part of you wants to perform, and the other part freezes. Instead of getting rid of the freeze, I want to get to know the freeze. Where do you feel it the most?"

"It's more in my chest and my shoulders. Wait, something else just appeared. Right now, there's a wave of heat coming from the bottom up."

"Great. Two experiences. Let's stay with the freezing for a little bit longer. Breathe into that area of your chest, as if the freezing would become more freezing. I don't want to reduce it. I want it to get bigger so we can get to know it. Allow it to spread up your neck and into your jaw: frozen jaw, frozen cheeks, frozen eyes. What starts to happen as you do that?" Here, I worked with Liana to *amplify* the somatic experience.

"My fear is amplified," she said. "I am right at the brink of crying. I feel terror."

"Let's go slow. Stay with the body. Freezing tears, emotion starts to come up, and terror. If you could show me what the terror looks like with your hands, how would you do it?"

"Like this? It's like, it's even hard to breathe. My breathing stops like a deer who stops still in the road." Both of her hands rise up beside her face, slightly quivering, and her mouth is now agape.

"Amplify the hands and your open mouth," I said. "I hear a sound coming out. Let's do that a little together. Teach me that way."

Liana's sound was a barely audible halting sound: "Uh . . . uh." She said, "It's like a shout or a scream that wants to come out, but it's really dangerous to express anything."

I reflected to Liana that we were learning there was a person who was frightened of something. We were also finding out that she was scared to scream. We didn't know these things before. If we tried to get her over her resistance to sharing her singing voice in public, we'd miss the scream that lives inside her. That was also part of her voice.

"Thank you for acknowledging the scream," she said. "That's very touching." Tears slid down her cheeks.

"Do you know anything about those tears? And then we're going to go back to the screaming and the terror. What kind of tears are they? Are they child tears, sad tears?"

"They are a child's tears."

"Thank you. We're going to love the scream and accept it as part of you. Can you hear the scream inside? What's it like?"

"It's a scream of fear. I can hear the shakiness in it. If I were to make this scream, it would become louder, and then it would be less fear and more anger. Interesting. So that's maybe one of the roles of the freezing, because it's really dangerous for me to feel that anger. It's a sound meant to intimidate and to make the other back off. It's pretty loud and high pitched, and it's a bit growly."

"Cool. It's growly like an animal. I guess we're animals, too. And what kind of animal would make that growly, high, intimidating sound?

"A jaguar," Liana replied.

"A jaguar. Great. When Liana comes out with her singing, it's not just going to be sweet and lovely. It's going to be a jaguar. Liana is coming out, and that's what's scary. Isn't that amazing? Some people would say, oh, you're vulnerable. You must be a weak little child. But jaguars can be scary."

She said, "It's really interesting that you're saying this, because when I started to create something and write some verses, the message is not sweet and soft and pink. It's full of power, and it kind of conveys that screaming in a different way." This is so important, because if we only treated Liana as if she needed tender care or more safety, we'd miss the flowering jaguar medicine she'd been cooking in her trauma.

"Okay," I said. "We have to take one more step if we can. Liana, you may need to sit over to the side, so to speak, because Jaguar wants to sing. We want to ask Jaguar full of power. Loud, high pitched, growling. Jaguar wants to make more space because in a funny way, that part has less space."

"That's true," Liana said. "The jaguar actually is being dominated by the sweetness. Yes. Give me some space, please."

"The powerful part of you needs more space. Can you drop into that growling, angry, full-of-power jaguar energy and see if it's in your chest or throat, or mouth and tongue? Where would the sound come from?"

"It's coming up from my pelvic area." Her hand rose up and pushed outward.

"Keep using that hand, and then let's begin making some sound. You don't have to do it loudly yet; just a little bit of the growling."

Liana growled.

"Let's do that a bunch of times," I said. "Like singing exercises. So you have a space for Jaguar."

"It wants to amplify," Liana said. "Yeah." She continued to growl, but louder. Then she began to scream, over and over. Each time she screamed, it got louder. I encouraged her to make it even louder, and her hand took on a clenched position.

"Let's do the clenched hand," I said, "and this time let's take it up to a seven or eight out of ten. Go ahead. Let it really be free. Wow. Okay, one more. All the way this time. Total freedom. Open up all the mouth, all the diaphragm, all the chest. Can you hear a song that might go with that?"

"It's actually something I created recently, and the chorus is very simple. It only consists of two words: 'No more.'"

"Teach me how to do the 'No more' song."

"It's very vulnerable and full of power." She began to sing, "No more."

"No more what?" I asked when she paused.

"No more pushing."

"I'm a pusher," I said.

"Fuck off," she said.

"I'm still pushing. I'm almost going away, but I'm not giving up yet. I'm still pushing you. You need me."

"No, I don't need you, your time is done."

"I'm feeling it. As soon as you come out all the way, I'll be gone—but not until then."

"This is so similar to my process," Liana said. "I feel the powerlessness. I really, really want to make you go away. Go away. Just respect my boundary. I don't want you here. Right?"

"Yeah. This is where your voice is growing, up against something that violates your boundary. Right now, in your experience, right next to something that would push you too hard, comes the strength of the voice. The jaguar arrives there. You're stealing back the power of some kind of an abuser. Anybody who violates a boundary is abusive. Start your singing lessons with that 'No more,' and then you can move on to other things. Consider writing on a piece of paper, 'Come out, I'm going to violate your boundaries,' and look at it before you start singing 'No more.' Because you're stepping into the full-powered, growly, high-pitched, loud jaguar. She's the singer, and she's going to sing to the world."

"That's so accurate," Liana said. "All the things I'm trying to create have this essence of power in them."

"Right! Some psychotherapists heal by working one on one like you and I are doing, and then some psychotherapists say, 'I also feel called to heal the world. How do I do that? I have to find my gift. It exists with individuals, but I want to project it into the world as a healing that comes through the medicine of my voice as the jaguar, and that's the way you do psychotherapy with the world.'"

"It's really interesting that you say that, David, because most of my clients who come to me for help have this repressed power."

"Yes, you are the perfect person because you are learning to come out with your power. That's great. Some people think, 'No, you should be way beyond everything to work with a client in that area.' But when you're right in the midst of it and it's part of your own story, it has a certain kind of power."

"I'm really resonating with everything that you're saying, and I feel more encouraged right now," Liana said. "I also feel more welcome to be with this part of me."

"I'm so glad. This process doesn't ask you to change or to grow into your voice. It's a shamanic task. Why is it shamanic? I'm asking you to shapeshift into another aspect of yourself. The sweet child part of yourself never needs to learn how to sing, but the jaguar wants and needs to be the singer."

"It's the first time in my life that I'm actually receiving an answer that makes sense," she said. "I've looked and I've read and I've worked with therapists and spiritual counselors and whatnot about this, and I haven't heard this yet until now. The shape-shifting makes so much sense. I'm already feeling like there's a whole family inside of me."

"Give them all voices. Let them make up their songs, or find songs that they like, and sing them."

If we only treat Liana as if she is wounded, in need of safety and compassion, or even as if she needs affirmation to build up her traumatized self, we will neglect the deeper medicine she's been alchemizing—the medicine from which her true voice arises.

If we don't witness the trauma as part of the healing, we lose the gift.

Family Introjection

One of the benefits of healing family-based trauma is dethroning our parents from occupying too central and dominant of a role in our psyches. Trauma locks us into seeing our parents as embodiments of power, as if we were still children, instead of as fallible individuals. And if a parent dies, what to do then? When we can't resolve issues with a parent, people often start acting out those issues through other relationships.

Psychology, with its emphasis on the childhood origins of our malaise, has locked us onto our parents. Unshaming and healing trauma help us to individuate further, which frees up energy and focus for our deepest self-actualization. I have a lot more energy to put toward my antiracism and antisexism work now that I see "father" as a system or role in the larger culture, instead of seeing my personal father as the embodiment of power.

Before you begin to heal trauma, you may need to unshame the act of acknowledging and claiming the trauma, addressing your personal, biological parents. Many people don't want to talk or even think negatively about their parents, which prevents them from going into the trauma. That dismissal or denial breeds shame, leaving the wound unwitnessed. Then all the associated symptoms look like pathologies instead of the meaningful results of an experience and a story.

This is the task that my client Alma worked on with me. "My family emigrated from Cuba when I was eight years old," she said, "and every time that I want to work on my small-t trauma, a part of me says, 'How can you not honor your parents' sacrifices, everything they did so you could be where you are today? In our family, there's so much gratefulness, respect, and reverence for our elders, but I'm at the point where I feel like I need to share about my small-t family traumas. How can I do that while also honoring my family?"

"Two things," I said. "First, there's no such thing as a small trauma. I don't care if I blew my nose while you were talking, and that triggered a traumatic response. That's yours. It belongs to you. Any time a person compares their trauma with someone else's and finds their own to be less, it's a shaming view. When I'm working with a person, I don't care if a person says, 'I don't know. My parents looked away from me a lot. I don't think they saw me.' Or if they refer to more obvious physical or sexual violence. The seemingly little things are carried through generations, through the immigrant story and how your family survived. The small thing is entwined with epic issues like grief, dispossession, war, and regime change."

"That's so validating," she said. "Thank you. Because I always feel like, 'Who am I to complain about something so trivial?'" How many of us have been forbidden from exploring parental violence guided by the dictum, "Honor thy father and thy mother"?

"What year did your family emigrate?" I asked.

"They escaped Castro and communism in 1973. And they were in survival mode, but they still sacrificed to ensure that my sister and I lived a successful life here."

"So to unshame the story and its bigness, it's not just your small-t trauma," I said. "It's being an immigrant. It's Cuba. It's escaping to survive. It's communism, and the oppressiveness that took away the lives and freedoms of hundreds of thousands of people. It's huge. And lots of people need help with those stories."

Taking a moment to amplify the bigness of her story unshames her current viewpoint, interrupting the tendency to pathologize and to think that her experience didn't matter.

"Alma, let's continue learning about this shaming belief system—the one that prevents you from exploring your trauma. How would you not be honoring your parents by working on your trauma?"

"I witnessed how they sacrificed their lives," she said. "They were accomplished people in their country who came here and then had to do odd jobs. They no longer had the same identities and passions. They had to give them up to give us a better life."

"You're saying that you shouldn't work on your trauma because that would be not honoring the sacrifices that they went through?"

"Right," she said.

"Tell me more. I still don't understand."

"They worked harder than I'm working," Alma said. "Physically they struggled, worked with their hands, and they experienced discrimination."

"You're sharing two messages," I said. "One is, 'Please be empathetic and care for and appreciate their experiences.' I can do that. But you're also saying, 'Another way to do that is by not working on my trauma.' That's the part that I don't understand yet."

"Why isn't it okay to work on my trauma?" she asked. "Because their life is so much bigger than mine." Alma is still dismissing her experience.

"So speaking as you, I shouldn't do anything for my own life?" I asked. "What are you saying to me?" I begin to use a role-playing dialogue to deepen her experience.

"It's almost like I have my parents' voice then," she said. "It's like, 'Why are you so ungrateful for everything that we did? How can you not honor us? We sacrificed everything for your success. Your life is happy. You should not complain.'"

"Stay with being your parent," I said. "'Dear Parent: I thought you sacrificed all that so that I can be myself and I could grow and heal and become more me than we ever could under a communist regime.' But you're saying, 'You sacrificed, so I should be a grateful child who doesn't push against things.'"

"That's such a good point," Alma said.

"I thought honoring your sacrifice is to put every ounce of my being into becoming the very best I could possibly be, because you gave me a good start," I continued, still speaking as her.

"But the person that I want you to be is the American dream," she said. "We came here for the American dream, and we bought into the whole American culture dream."

"You're starting to sound like a communist country," I said. "You're starting to become an oppressive regime that you haven't dealt with enough. And now that you've escaped it, you want to put me in a tyrannical regime of how I should think and feel and what I should and shouldn't say and do. You're telling me I have to survive instead of being free to make other choices that help me thrive."

"Oh, wow," she said. "Yikes, David. That really hit home."

"That's how you honor the sacrifice," I said. "The honoring of the deep parent, not the surface parent. The surface parent is resentful and jealous and wants faithfulness. I'm not putting them down for that. They get to be human. But the deep honoring of their sacrifice is for you to become every damn ounce of yourself that you can."

"I came across a Maya Angelou quote that said, 'You've been paid for,'" Alma said. "And I feel like that. I felt shame. I'm like, 'Oh, she's right.' To me it brought up the 'I have been paid for.' I don't have autonomy."

"I don't think you understand what she was saying," I said. "She says, 'You've been paid for, and therefore you should become the self that is deepest and most important in you.' And in the poem 'The Phenomenal Woman,' she adds, 'I am the hope and the dream of the slave. The slave person dreamt of me. Six foot tall, bare arms, high heels, Black woman, black skin, in front of hundreds of thousands of people talking. They dreamt of this. They paid for me to be this. Not to be shrinking somewhere and acting like, "Oh, thank you. Thank you." That's what they paid for, for me to be this way in the world.'"

"Wow," Alma said. "I took it the other way."

"That's the communist culture inside of you," I said. "It turns everything into that kind of regime." Healing the trauma would take a lot more than addressing the violence her parents perpetrated against her; we would also need to address a ubiquitous dynamic of systemic oppression and silencing.

"I love that," she said. "What a different perspective."

"Alma, I invite you to take everything you're calling a complaint and make it so big that the whole earth shakes from hearing it, because complaints are the beginning of a need and a story. *Complaint* is a shaming word. When a need is called a complaint, the need is denied, dismissed, suppressed, and turned into something small. Small-t trauma, when in fact it's a cry for my freedom from tyranny. That's your job. That's not an easy job."

"No, it isn't," she said. "It's just the beginning."

"The deep parent will be honored," I said. "The earth will be honored. The spirit of the ancestors will be honored, even though the personal parent gets caught up in the jealousies. 'I'm resentful. Now, you're doing something that I couldn't do. And it's hard and painful to me.' That's human stuff. No blame. But they shouldn't stop you. That's not a definition of honoring a sacrifice." Here the unshaming process is unfreezing her relationship with her personal parents, widening and deepening her understanding, while lifting and amplifying what she calls her "small" trauma.

"I love it," she said. "That was huge. Thank you so much."

"Your story is touching, beautiful, so important," I said. "Your internalized critic has been stopping you by proclaiming your parents' viewpoint from inside your mind, like an implanted operative. My teacher Arny Mindell calls it a 'ghost.' It's hanging around, putting you in certain places, and it needs to be identified and outed. And then we can see it and go beyond it by seeing the background human conditions that imprison and shrink us."

I used to closely watch the purchases my wife made, scrutinizing the costs while trying to be open. I didn't like that about myself; I didn't like that about my father, who did the same thing. Over time, as I worked on that issue—the impulse to want to know how much everything costs (beyond reasonable budgetary concerns)—I noticed that the impulse softened and eased, but it didn't go away entirely. One day I said to Lisa, "Marty needs to know the cost of everything" (Marty was my father's name), and we laughed about it. Now when we talk about using things up or not making wasteful purchases, we call it "Martinizing." Some symptoms have relieved, but even more healing is the ability to play and laugh. The personal father is no longer the oppressive figure he once was.

While trauma freezes abusers into one particular person (and they may be one particular person or parent who can't be dismissed), as we work on the longer-term trauma healing, that person becomes a representative of social beliefs, internalized figures, or oppressive systems that many in the world must deal with. In this way, rather than shrinking into our personal story, our childhood wound, it enlarges us, connects us to others, and gives us a path to be healers for the larger world.

Conclusion

Perhaps we are all traumatized. Perhaps we have all experienced abuses in our lifetimes that we have not sufficiently processed, or that we have never even spoken of or known about. Perhaps we all have crafted personalities, family traits, and cultures that are, in part, responses to trauma. As Resmaa Menakem says, "Trauma decontextualized in a person looks like personality. Trauma decontextualized in a family looks like family traits. Trauma decontextualized in people looks like culture." In that case, we all have a sacred task: to understand our symptoms and relieve them, and to unfold the flower of our lives and live the powers and gifts that are enfolded, residing right next to our deepest wounds—our traumas. And by doing that, we change ourselves, our families, and our culture, helping to create a truly deep democracy.

EXERCISE

Allowing Your Traumatic Wound to Draw Out the Wounded Healer That You Are

1. Take a moment to ask your body, "Dear body, where does my trauma live in you?" Wait a moment until your body answers by drawing your attention to a specific area. This could be obvious because you have had regular physical symptoms in that area. You also might just have an intuition, or body sensations may draw you to that area.

2. Breathe into that area of your body, as if each inhale guides your awareness into that area.

3. Slowly, with great mindfulness, allow one of your hands to touch or be placed on that area of your body.

4. Imagine that your hand belongs to a great healer. Perhaps it is someone you know or have heard about. Now allow your hand to slowly explore that area of your body: touch it gently or firmly; stroke or stay stationary; tap, press, or embrace. Your hand will know what to do. Take a few minutes to explore what it is like to have this healing hand—a hand that is guided to heal your wound.

5. Once you have the feel of your hand being a healing hand, turn your hand outward toward people you love or the world at large. Imagine you are sending them the healing energy you have been

exploring. As you do that, begin to speak words to those people, to our world, allowing your words to be congruent with the touch your hand had. Keep talking, sending healing outward.

6. Ask this healer: "What kind of healer are you? What is your medicine like? Why have you come here at this time in my life? What do you want from me? What is my life purpose?"

CHAPTER 11

Patterns, Dependencies, and Codependencies

I once worked with a man who came to me because he felt he was smoking too much cannabis. He and his friends liked to listen to live music, and at some point during the night they'd go outside and smoke.

"What's it like to smoke?" I asked.

He replied, "It's good, but I shouldn't do it."

The statement "I shouldn't do it" almost always shows a person coming from a shamed place. I began to explore that statement on a somatic level by handing him a pen. "Imagine this is cannabis," I said. When he took the pen, his body came alive. Before, during his self-shaming comment, his body had been slumped over. He put the pen in his mouth, and his eyes lit up.

"I see your face, it's lighting up. What's happening?"

"I'm seeing the glow of the match, and my friends around me, in the dark, at night. We light this match, and I see their faces. Those are the deepest friendships I have." His eyes filled with tears. He thought he wanted an experience of cannabis, but his body was saying, "The experience I want is the glow of the people I love around me." It's that match-strike moment he's looking for, more than actually smoking. That's very intimate; that's what he's hungry for.

I have had similar conversations with many smokers. They are all surprised I would ask them to take a pen and act as if it is a cigarette because none of them have ever tried to describe their experience of smoking: what they do and how it makes them feel somatically. They're all trying to get over something without knowing what they're actually experiencing. Many had enrolled in stop-smoking programs that neglected to inquire about the person's fundamental experience, other than the negative consequences. None of the programs treated the person as if their system, even within the addictive behavior and impulse, was meaningful.

Some people take deep, long inhales when smoking cigarettes. I ask them to take more of those deep, long inhales consciously in the moment with me. Some say they feel relaxed, as you would expect, but others say they feel filled up, proud as their chest expands, or even energized. And when I ask cigarette smokers to imagine smoking with a pen as a substitute for the cigarette, and to feel what it's like in their body (which everyone can do, even without the actual cigarette), some say it's like a pause from life or a mini vacation; some say they feel lighter, or freer with others; and some say they become reflective. These experiences, however idiosyncratic they might seem, are meaningful. The topic of addictive patterns and dependences is yet another example of how the powerful, even harmful patterns of our lives contain intelligences that are partly unconscious, veiled by shame's conclusion that something is wrong with us. We sacrifice our wellness and often risk our lives for reasons yet unknown. We do it because we're hungry for something; we need or desire something. This chapter will help you uncover that need or desire via unshaming, so you can find fulfillment without putting yourself and your loved ones at risk.

Unshaming Addictive Tendencies

As far as I know, everyone has addictive tendencies. An addictive tendency is a powerful hunger that is not being satisfied in the course of normal life and that, when partaken in, provides a sense of fulfillment through a set of ritualized behaviors or the use of a substance. I call it a "tendency" because while everyone appears to have these tendencies, not everyone develops a harmful addiction. Why do I say a *sense* of fulfillment? Because the actual hunger is very rarely satisfied through the addictive process; the person is only engaging in an experience that resembles the fulfillment. My teacher Max Schupbach said it this way: "When individuals can't find their way home, they may find a hotel that reminds them of home." And sometimes they will even forget they're not at home, or they'll be too scared to stray from a place that feels like home for fear that their lives will get lost and they'll stray from what truly enlivens them. Addictions can remind us of home so powerfully that we won't easily abandon them without knowing where our real home is and how to get there. Getting there requires unshaming—treating our impulses as if they're intelligent, not pathological.

Our society predominantly approaches addiction from a shaming model. Not surprisingly, our society also doesn't have effective solutions for people who are trying to stop being addicted to various substances. In an article about addiction treatment in the *New York Times*, journalist Jane Brody writes that treatment programs often fail, put their faith in unproven methods, and neglect to address the deeper issues that underlie addiction and relapse rates. Her message to those who have spent thousands of dollars on rehab efforts is this: "You're not alone. And chances are, it's not your fault." Many programs can temporarily help people stop using a substance or behaving in a particular way, but it is actually quite rare for people to sustain their abstinence.

Before treatment or after an unsustainable treatment, people are judged as having insufficient willpower or some kind of aberrant expression of pain that they medicate through patterns of behavior or substances. They may be told that they're powerless or that they're trying to escape reality. This pathologizes people's unfulfilled needs and desires. Additionally, there's a lot to shame related to substance abuse: failing out of school, losing a job, saying things we didn't mean, embarrassing ourselves and others, or making decisions we regret once the substance wears off, not to mention the humbling experience of engaging with something that is more powerful than we believe we are.

All too often, ideas and opinions about addictions prevent the inquiry and wisdom of the unshaming process. A person who says "When I use heroin, I'm self-medicating" is replacing experience with a received idea. It's part of the dominant allopathic paradigm that sees the issue as a pathology instead of an intelligent message from your system. "I don't have to think or get to know myself. The answer is, I'm self-medicating."

And then I ask, "What's it like to use heroin? What's it like to be you in that moment?" It seems like such a simple question, but it's so rarely asked that it blows people away. Try it. Otherwise, the loudest information about who you are will come not from your own experience but from the projections, judgments, and opinions of the people and the cultures around you, which is not to say these ideas are never useful. When people set aside these opinions to explore their experience, they can witness that aspect of themselves: the authenticity, depths, and needs; the intelligent message nested within the substance use. They can become intimate enough with themselves to learn how to care for that hunger outside of the substance experience. In the story above, my client learned that he needed social companionship and connection. He could now foster opportunities to access it regularly and consciously without the involvement of smoking.

What does unshaming add to our understanding of the deeper issues entangled with addictive tendencies? There are three issues revealed when we unshame the addictive experience: the experience of fulfilling the hunger, need, or desire; the experience of the harmful effects; and the experience of the power behind the addictive tendency that can move a person to do something regardless of the consequences. These revelations arise from the unshaming process as a consequence of focusing uniquely on witnessing a person's actual experience of the addictive pattern, whether that experience is accessed through alcohol, methamphetamines, watching pornography, scrolling the internet, cigarettes, coffee, or even carrot juice, if it's done to achieve an unfulfilled state of being or feeling. The goal of unshaming addictive actions and tendencies is to stop using the substance to try to get our profound needs met, and to recraft our lives to live a life more aligned with satisfying our natural hungers in sustaining, edifying ways.

Need, Desire, or Hunger

For several years in the early 2000s, I taught a course at the University of Phoenix called Addictions and Dependencies. The first page of the text we used showed a picture of a child on a swing looking ecstatic. The text indicated that people crave all kinds of feeling experiences, from euphoria, pleasure, freedom, and excitement to grief, rage, and deep pains. But from the first page of chapter 1 until the end of the book, this fundamental clarity was abandoned in favor of theories and models that suggested addiction was caused by self-medicating, escaping, peer pressure, or even boredom. What happened to that first self-evident understanding?

As we've already noted, every addictive impulse or tendency is moved by a hunger. It's not very difficult to identify that hunger if we make an unshaming inquiry. People are almost never fully conscious of these hungers, because consciousness comes from having an inner unshaming witness. We rarely stop, even for a few minutes, to feel and describe the state of mind or feeling that the substance or behavior helps us achieve. When a person won't give up a substance, they're saying, "Something about using this substance is more important to me than all the costs." They may even be saying, "Something about using this substance is worth dying for." We can think this is crazy or pathological, but that won't help us understand the hunger. Further, trying to convince people that their behavior is not rational, or asking a Dr. Phil–type question like "How's that working for you?" will have far less power than the mostly unconscious hunger. Instead, we need to identify the craving behind the craving.

One obstacle to fruitful inquiry is that we tend to see addictions as monolithic. For instance, alcohol reliably creates disinhibition in the human prefrontal cortex. However, alcohol use isn't driven by one single state or need. People are varied, and so are their states; inhibitions are unique to the individual. When they drink alcohol and become uninhibited, what are they actually like? One person sings and dances. Another weeps uncontrollably. Another reads poetry. Others get belligerent and go looking for a fight. Someone else might talk to strangers, say what they really think without a filter, or have sex with someone they just met.

When you inquire about how a person experiences a substance, the unfulfilled need, desire, or hunger becomes clear. How can the person who only dances when they're drunk find ways to feel comfortable dancing at home, at a wedding reception, or in an exercise class? Does the weeping person need permission to grieve, to express their feelings freely without a shamed belief that it makes them weak, whiny, or needy? What stops the poetry reader from enjoying a poem with their morning coffee? In a culture that says it's not okay to be angry, people will access suppressed anger when alcohol softens their artificial boundaries. A person's soul may be thirsting to step into a more outgoing role, or to stop appeasing people around them who shame the telling of difficult but vital truths. A person who thinks alcohol is causing them to have indiscriminate sexual encounters might have been commanded as a teenager to only have sex within the bounds of marriage; alcohol drowns out their parent' voices. The problem with using substances in all these ways is that the true hunger never gets consciously met; and, as we will see, there is collateral damage as a result. The true hunger can only be fed when we unshame it and find a direct path to its conscious fulfillment.

Unshaming in Action

Radha came to me seeking help with her use and abuse of alcohol. "It's part of my family culture," she said. "I've had a relationship with it, on and off, all my life. I stop, but inevitably something will pull me back in. I can drink a bottle of wine each night." She became particularly emotional when she said, "One of my children is also struggling with addiction. It's really important for me to resolve this."

When a child is suffering in some way, many parents feel two kinds of responsibility. One kind is generated by the love of their child and themselves; they want to bring healing to the suffering. The other kind is more like criticism: "You're causing difficulties in your child. You're a bad parent." This criticism, at best, can get a parent to seek help, but once the decision to get help has been made, it's no longer helpful. Instead, it creates more shame.

With regard to the wounds parents inflict or pass on, psychology has done some good, but I think it's been misguided in this area, too. It has opened the door to those of us seeking healing from having been hurt by our parents, but it also lays too much responsibility on the parent, ignoring cultural and generational factors and turning a blind eye to the shame heaped upon parents.

"Tell me more about drinking," I said to Radha. "What do you know?"

"Drinking seems like the only thing to do to have fun—to see how drunk I can get. I like who I am when I'm drunk. I'm really fun, easier to connect with. It helps me in my relationship with my partner. I started really young, junior high school, high school. I didn't realize how much anxiety I had. I would quit for a few months and then start back up. It's been with me ever since."

"It's always been with you," I said. "You become somebody you like to be: open, fun, and connecting. Those are already interesting ideas, important ideas. There's someone who is anxious, and there's someone who is fun and connecting. Alcohol is the ally of the fun one. I'm not supporting the literal use of alcohol; I'm saying it serves a function, and I want to know what that function is. I don't want to see your impulse to drink as only pathological, without intelligence."

Radha had already offered some insight into the hunger behind her addictive impulse, but we needed to go deeper by accessing her body intelligence.

"Radha, can you settle into your body? Just relax a little bit. No pressure, gentle and easy. You can even move a little bit, sway a little bit, so your body is being invited in. This could be fun, not difficult."

Because Radha said she became open and fun with alcohol, I wanted to create an atmosphere that matched the experience she had when she was drinking. I wanted to begin creating within our relationship the ally she found with drinking.

To connect to her experience, I asked Radha to recall a time when she'd been drunk. "When was the last time you remember having a fair amount to drink, enough to inebriate you? Do you remember that?"

"Yes, New Year's Eve, just days ago"

"Go back to that night and remember what it was like. Allow your body to become a little 'drunk.'"

"I can feel it in my arms," she said, making the direct bodily experience that would promote the discoveries of unshaming. It is also worth noting that almost everyone can connect with the feeling of a substance without the substance. This is essential if the person has abstinence as their goal.

"Put your attention on your arms. Let your arms be drunk."

She smiled and began to move. I said, "Dear arms, please be free to do what you're doing. Please do that even a little bit more, as if you're exaggerating it."

Her arms moved up a bit. Her hands begin making a dance as she giggled, and her arms became more free. I said, "Ah, we're getting a bit 'drunk' together. Let go even further. Have another 'glass' and see what your arms are doing."

She made a whooping sound. Her hands flowed and moved up above her head, and then to the side, and then her hands moved as if they were pounding on a door.

I continued to help her amplify her body intelligence. "Let those arms go. They've been waiting generations to do this." She punches the air some more. Stronger, bigger feelings rose up in her face and tears.

"I'm trying to break out of something, a box," she said. "A box of expectations to be sweet and kind and quiet and fearful. I want to get past the outward appearance. I want to come out."

"You live in a box, and someone inside you says, 'Give me a drink so I can break us out.' We need to learn about the breaking-out energy and the one who is broken out. What is she free to do, to be?"

So far I had noted two intelligences that flowed from her body: a free, fluid dance, and the pounding. I wanted to give her access to both without the alcohol.

"Let's go back to the hands, the breaking out. Believe that this is important, expressing this energy. We are not supporting alcohol, but the energy. If we don't help you integrate the intelligence behind your drinking, you will get pulled back in, as you said earlier. We don't want you to be victim of the alcohol. We want you to break out on your own volition."

Unshaming and then integrating the intelligence makes the pattern conscious, allowing the person to make an intention to not only abstain, but live the energies and intelligence in what they love and need.

Her hands started pounding again and again.

"You want to break out," I said. "Even when you do it in an unhealthy way, you still do it. What keeps you inside?"

"Fear."

"Fear of what?"

"Fear of being wrong, of being a burden, of needing too much, taking too much, being selfish, drawing attention to myself, being too provocative, being too loud." I especially heard the emotion emphasizing the words "too much."

I said, "I see a person, a woman, who takes attention, who is provocative. She looks to alcohol to help her with that; taking more attention, more space, being loud, being provocative." We were now seeing the internally oppressive space that she lived in that she asked alcohol to help her with. She would have to learn to use her pounding force to break free. But that was not all. As I said, we also wanted to know what she was like when she was free, when she had broken out, so she could know herself more deeply, love herself more truly.

"Let's do one more thing," I said. "Before you went into the breaking out, your hands did something free and fluid. Let's go back to that, because that may be what you're like when you're broken out. It's not just fight for fight sake; it's to be used to free you."

Her hands went up, and they started a fluid dance.

"Yes, your hands are doing something important. Let them keep going. Become this person—the one who moves this way. Forget about your normal identity, as if this is who you are meant to be. Break out of boxes so you can be this way. How is this different from normal Radha?"

"Free, big. I'm a painter, and I feel like I'm painting a loud, giant canvas."

Radha was telling me, and herself, who she was. This kind of self-knowledge can cause tectonic shifts in a person's life.

"You are an artist, a painter," I said. "It's literal art but also a painter of life. The painter is in the box. She creates life as if it's a painting . . . mothers as a painter. Lives as a painter."

I recalled her love for her child and how they share an addictive tendency, so I made a suggestion: "If you were at the end of your life and I were your child, and I said, 'Teach me your life lesson, dear giant loud painter, give me some guidance,' what would you say?"

"Allow creativity to flow. Express what's inside out in the world." Her hand went to her heart, and she wept. "Don't waste your life; get out there and express."

"But I'm frightened of expectations. How do I deal with that?" I asked, bringing her normal identity and usual feelings forward in order to help her stay close to the loud, giant painter. In a real way, she was now channeling the "spirit" of alcohol for herself. She was now the ally, teaching herself the lesson of being drunk. "How do you get to be free?" I continued. "I use a bottle of wine to get there. Don't leave me there with the wine. I need you; I need other options to access you."

"Get out of your head," she replied. "Get into your body and being. Trust that what comes out is beautiful. Open the curtain." She sighed deeply. "Get outside of yourself, your home, your isolation, and connect to other artists. Engage in life. Connect, connect."

"You can paint and express punching, flow, dancing," I replied as me again. "Life is a creative expression. Connect with people who get you a little 'drunk,' not on literal alcohol, but people who make you care less about what people think. Express yourself—all of it, let it out. Less time trying to heal and more time being the painter, expressing all of what happens. You are a creative spirit with a large, loud canvas. That's your life."

"That's truth," she said. "I can feel that. That's really exciting. I've been trying to figure it out for forty-seven years. Now I get it. This is so powerful for me. Express, *yes*. Thank you so much."

Radha and I later spoke about learning to be "alcohol" for people, to become that kind of ally. That intelligence is in her. In some cultures it would have been seen as her medicine—not the alcohol, but the capacity to help people break out of boxes and artistically express what is in them in big, loud strokes. Unshaming teaches us how to access the intelligence behind addictive tendencies for ourselves, as well as how to become that ally for others.

Although alcohol is a shape-shifter, other substances can alter our state of feeling. For example, cocaine often provides energy and empowerment. One client of mine found that cocaine helped her feel confident about writing. It showed her what it felt like to have zero doubts about whether she should share her experience, thoughts, or opinions. Even though the drug and its effects wore off, she said doing it felt like getting an important puzzle piece back—one that she had lost after being told by clergy, her parents, and even boyfriends that her point of view wasn't valid, that she as a woman should be quiet and subordinate her voice within patriarchal structures.

Heroin can be seen as a mode of escape, but the question is: escape from what, and to where? If we don't ask these questions, we dismiss the intelligence behind the addictive impulse and pathologize the person by believing they're choosing the substance to shirk life's difficulties. Close, but not close enough. It's common for people who take heroin to want to leave this world. Many of my clients have said, "I don't want to be in the world."

If you've seen someone on heroin, you'll agree that they appear to be temporarily gone. It's a highly detached "I'm not in this world" state. We could say "That's dangerous" or "It's suicidality." Both statements are true. We don't want to support people in taking heroin or taking their lives, that's clear. But asking "Why don't you want to be in this world or your life?" also supports the individual.

One of my clients said, "I was in the Iraq war. Now that I'm back, I can't go into the grocery store because I can't bear it if anyone is walking behind me. It makes me panic." He chose to address this problem by taking heroin. He wanted out of a world in which he couldn't handle anyone walking behind him, which occurred in most places. That's a deeply restricted world. Wouldn't you want out of that situation? Not everyone with his challenges would use heroin, but he used it that way.

I asked this client to imagine, to actually *feel*, what it would be like to not be here. "What's it like for you to leave? Where do you go?"

The unshaming process says, "What's the specific state of consciousness that heroin is putting you in that you're using to address your need?"

I asked my client this question, and he replied, "It's like, let's float for a while. I'm just in the clouds."

"What's it like being in the clouds?"

"The stuff of this world doesn't mean anything to me."

"Let's talk about making the stuff of this world less important."

Over the course of this discussion, we were able to identify the qualities of where the substance took him, and we found ways for him to access that relief without endangering his health and well-being.

Perhaps people who want to escape this world are looking for a spiritual center in their being; perhaps they're looking for a safe place to heal their trauma. Perhaps they're looking for their mother who has passed on, like the many who reach out with the word "Mama" when they pass. If we can discover these kinds of desires within the substance user, they can help us to understand the person and give us direction in helping them. If we simply walk away, saying, "You're self-medicating," they feel further away from themselves, as shame continues to hide their deeper intelligence.

Our curiosity about the person's experience serves as a key that can release the need and allow it to flower in the warmth of new suns. The hunger behind the substance is intelligent, human, and valid.

Unshaming Suffering and Pain

Along with unshaming the hunger to reveal the intelligence, there's a second intelligence to be revealed. We need to unshame the suffering and pain one is experiencing as a result of using the substance. "It's really bad for me," users often say. What's the bad thing? Let's make contact with it by asking questions about it, as in the examples below:

"I'm hurting people."	What is your inner critic saying? What does your guilt feel like in your body?
"It's bad for my health."	How does your body tell you this?
"I'm embarrassed."	How does that feel in your body?
"I don't show up."	What's it like to be somewhere else?
"I don't go to work."	What's it like to not be able to support yourself?

When I taught an addiction class, I had everyone express their pain through sound. Each of us thought about the way our addictive tendencies and patterns cause us suffering. Then instead of just thinking about them and listing them, I led people into feeling, in their body, what that suffering was like. Lastly, I asked each person to make the sound of that suffering—moans, screams, sounds of anguish. They made pure, unshamed sounds. They shed tears. It was profoundly moving. People felt seen for their suffering without criticism.

The unshaming process reveals the pain and suffering entangled in the addictive process. (This pain largely abates when a person learns to more directly fulfill the hunger, unlike when it's fulfilled indirectly and incompletely via a substance or ritualized behavior.) Why does the pain and suffering need to be revealed? Isn't it obvious that people are simply in denial? Yes, denial is a significant factor, but the truth is that most of us never directly feel our painful experiences. For example, many people can say they worry because of their addictive tendencies and substance use; many people have theories about themselves; and many people can describe some of the outer costs of substance misuse (making relationships less stable, impairing health, threatening financial stability). Those factors are important, but they are very rarely potent enough to make a difference. Not only is there an unaddressed deeper need in the background, but the person is not in touch with the experience of suffering. Perhaps these concerns have been part of their lives for so long that they feel habituated to them. Perhaps the substance softens the drive to improve health, relationships, and financial stability. Essentially, people are rarely in touch with their actual experience of suffering. Instead, we are in touch with ideas and opinions about it. That level of contact is not sufficient to really impact the person or move others to compassion.

The goal of this part of the unshaming process is to compassionately increase a person's awareness of their ongoing suffering. We do this by inquiring about their somatic experience: "Can you feel the physical symptoms that you suffer from? What are they like? Let's get to know them." Or, "Let's talk about the financial costs of your substance use. Now, take a moment and feel, in your body, what it's like to have those costs." Once a person makes that direct contact, they can then express those feelings in a way that moves one or more people around them to feel compassion, to become a compassionate witness.

Reclaiming the Lost Ally

The third intelligence revealed by the unshaming process is power. When my clients and I get in touch with the experiences of addiction, we see that in every addictive tendency, there's a part of the person that says, "I don't give a fuck, I'll do it anyway."

This insistence is powered by extraordinary strength. The sentiment "I can't help it, I stuff myself," is not about power. It relates to the unmet need or hunger. The statement "I don't give a shit, I'm going to have a second donut even if I have diabetes," represents power and commitment, a potential ally. "I want this so bad I don't care if it kills me. I will do it. Nobody and no repercussion will stop me."

These strong viewpoints, however, are usually veiled by shame. The person holding them doesn't own them. They need to be unshamed so the person can claim that power in themselves and use it for other things. If a person is going to stop an addictive pattern, they'll need contact with that kind of power. It's an ally, waiting to be transformed.

I invite you to try it yourself. Imagine the addictive substance or object right in front of you, but don't touch it. Tell yourself, "You can't have it."

Feel into the part of you that would take it anyway. And then lift your hand and begin reaching for that pill, the drink, that phone to scroll through. Feel the part of you that would do it anyway. Get to know the one who thinks, "I keep telling myself not to do it, but I do it anyway." Stay in touch with the part of you that won't heed the warning, "You shouldn't do that. Stop doing it. It's hurting your life. You need to be more disciplined. You're an idiot. How many times will you make the same mistake?"

Stay with the energy that would do it anyway. Now make the face of the persistence, the one who would do it anyway regardless of what I say. Use your body—your face, your hand—the reach, the grab. Be the voice of this energy. What would you say? Be fierce; these addictive hungers are fierce. Speak a word or phrase. Get to know that one.

Now forget about the substance, but keep saying the words and feeling the energy. "No way, you won't stop me. Fuck you. I'll do whatever I want." It's a power that is unstoppable. "Criticize me all day long, I'll still do it. Threaten my health and relationships, I'll still do it." Who is that one in you? Where do you need that energy?

When I work in groups, I have them get in touch with that energy and choose a phrase to represent it, like "I want what I want."

Then I say, "What if you had access to that strength in your life? Where do you need that life force? Where would you use it?" People come up with answers very quickly.

Then if a person wants to plan a strategy, it will be built on this foundational knowing: "This is how much it hurts me, and I know it. I'm not a bad person; I'm in a lot of pain, there are things I really want, and there are parts of me that go after things I want with an incredible amount of power."

That all sounds great, right? It *is* great. But if someone you love is in an addictive pattern, you may be asking, "Will it work, David, and will they stop?"

Not necessarily. It has a timing, and there are moments in a person's life when not a single intervention will make a change. Unshaming is sometimes a slow intervention. In the meantime, I hope the addiction doesn't kill them. It might. You can sometimes modulate that process for others, but you may not be able to stop that flowing river.

If you study addictions, you'll see that there's no approach that works a high percentage of the time. The people who are able to change are mostly ready, and many different strategies, not just unshaming, may help them. It has a lot to do with the timing that empowers that moment.

To summarize: the unshaming process reveals information about the addictive process that is rarely brought to light—the valid and intelligent need or desire the person is trying to fulfill, the actual pain and suffering that is talked about but not truly felt, and the raw power to reach for what you want regardless of oppressive and suppressive voices and consequences. These three energies are all bound up in the addictive process; we need to unshame them. The unshaming question is, "How will I live those hungers, be informed by the pain and suffering associated with the addiction, and unleash the energy to live the life that is mine?"

Unshaming Codependency

Almost every person living their addiction has loved ones who are suffering and shamed. Parents, kids, partners, exes, siblings, friends, grandparents, grandchildren, cousins, aunts, uncles—the web extends. Often addictions thread through generations. Does someone in a codependent role also have an addictive pattern? Of course they do. From an unshaming point of view, they have a deep hunger they believe they can fulfill—not through a substance, but through a relationship. And although that relationship doesn't often truly offer that fulfillment (just like the substance doesn't offer actual fulfillment), the person keeps hoping for it, keeps denying the fact that they are not fulfilled. In other words, the relationship is a hotel, not home.

As with any addiction, unshaming codependency proceeds by exploring that hunger first and inquiring what it would be like if the person did achieve that fulfillment or their hope did come true. That hunger is real and cannot be bypassed, even if it is pathologized. What is called "codependency" is fueled by deep hungers, needs, and desires that are neither met nor fully conscious; by pain that is not deeply experienced and is mostly denied; and by the power to persist regardless of the consequences, as with any addictive process.

When we unshame the codependent addictive tendency or behavior, we must validate the need rather than pathologizing it. This rarely happens because when healers see the person's harmfulness, unconsciousness, and denial they try to talk the person out of their pattern without inquiring about the hunger in the background, which keeps the shame alive. However, if we ask people questions like "What would it be like if your partner became what you really want? What if they could consistently be what you hope they will be, or who they are at certain moments?" this inquiry would allow the person to begin making the need conscious. When we know what the person hopes their loved one will be—such as reliable, devoted, romantic, safe, boundaried, or thoughtful—they can begin to own what they need and find ways to meet their own needs instead of chasing the hotel version.

The voice of denial sounds like this: "They'll change. It's really not that bad." My teacher Max Schupbach called denial "being drunk." A drunk person's judgment is not sound. If a spouse of a person in an addictive pattern believes against all evidence that their spouse will change, that's a kind of drunkenness, too. Being judgmental or trying to convince a person does not wake them up out of their denial. Unshaming their suffering wakes them up, because they make direct contact with their suffering. They relearn their own needs, learn to trust their needs, and notice how these needs are not currently being met. Schupbach called this "a sobering."

The next step of unshaming is to unshame the person's suffering. The person is regularly experiencing the severe pain of their need's unfulfillment. Lastly, the unshaming process invites the person to make contact with that part of them that would never give up the relationship, never give up hoping, always sacrifice themselves at the altar of their hope. As I pointed out earlier in the chapter, this is a great power. In fact, it is a power the person will need if they are going to wake up, see things clearly, and turn toward a direction where their need can be truly and directly met. It bears saying that this change is often magnificently difficult.

I once worked with a married couple who were in this situation. In a session that included both of them, the husband said, "My wife says I have an alcohol problem."

She said, "You need to stop drinking."

I asked, "What is he like when he's drinking?"

"He's never available for me. He spends money out at the bars, and when he's drunk, he gets violent."

We were starting to see her needs show up: availability, safety. If we focus only on changing his alcohol consumption, which is the most common tactic in these circumstances, her needs will be totally bypassed. She'll never have to know herself and free herself from her own addictive tendency.

It's easy to be "drunk" on hope that someone will change when you're compartmentalizing experiences, from the unpleasant to the deeply traumatic. The person needs to be connected to what is happening for them. The labels "codependent" and "addict" labels don't go deep enough for them to connect to their experience.

My next questions went deeper into the wife's experience. "What's it like when he's unavailable, or when you're scared or hurt?" This question invites her to experience the pain of the need not being fulfilled.

When she told me that her spouse hits her, I asked, "Where did you get hit? Put your hand on that place." I helped her to connect with the actual body experience. Being hit by someone who is supposed to love you is deeply shaming if it's not truly witnessed. Someone has to see the act and the injury, even if it happens days, months, or years later. In the larger world, being hit by your spouse takes your personhood and identity and collapses them into the cliché of a battered spouse.

Once a person is supported in feeling the suffering, their body will have natural reactions, as we saw with other types of abuse, including expressions of pain (crying, moaning, screaming) and expressions of resistance (pushing away, punching, yelling, turning or moving away) The person undergoing this process is almost never fully in touch with this experience. From an unshaming point of view, that is part of their codependent process.

The statement "The substance is the problem" ignores the specificity of the way each person experiences that substance, the need it's meeting for them, how the user acts when under its influence, and how that affects their loved ones.

Then, going further, I asked the wife, "What do you need?"

"I need to be safe, and to not worry that we will go bankrupt."

"What would it be like to feel this safety and lack of worry?"

Taking a person to this depth of the experience of their need is foundational in unshaming the codependent process. This need is valid. It is not a pathology; it is sacred. Guiding the person to holding it as sacred empowers the person with a truth of their personhood. This person doesn't just need their partner to stop drinking; they need a kind of safety. Here's where the soberness of the person in a codependent role needs to come in. And so I lead my clients through the following steps:

"Very soberly, as clearly as you can, imagine you are looking into your partner's eyes. Ask yourself, 'Will that person be able to take care of my need?' Don't fool yourself. Do you see that changing? Not your theory about how and why they should change, or your dream for what they would be like if they changed." In a real way, they are looking at their own "substance" to see if it can ever be truly fulfilling.

When I ask some people this question, they say no, and they do so in a context where their needs are valid, their injuries are acknowledged.

If that person leaves that relationship, they need to leave knowing that their need is precious and important to them. If they conclude, "I have this fucked-up need and it gets me all screwed up in relationships. When am I going to get over it?" then that pattern will continue. You can't change by saying, "I won't have that need anymore." The need will arise unconsciously, veiled in shame, and the dilemma will likely resurface in another relationship.

Some people answer by saying, "I'm not sure, I don't know."

At that point I say, "Do you want to try one more time in that relationship?" Maybe they're not done.

If they say, "I do want to try one more time," then I support that. But I also say, "If you believe that experience, what now?" We are speaking from a place of acknowledgment of their unshamed, unmet needs. We are doing it from a place of emotional sobriety. Instead of calling them a "codependent," I'm waking the person up to their experience. They have dignity in their needs. They're not a cliché of a sad spouse. They're a full-fledged, robust, complex, intelligent human being.

Labeling Can Shame

The following session I had with a client named Miriam will allow us to go deeper into learning about honoring our gifts.

"I need to work on my codependency," Miriam said. "I care for and listen to so many people in my life, and I'm exhausted. It's been my pattern since childhood." She told me she grew up in an emotionally and physically abusive family. Although her parents didn't abuse her, she watched them abuse her siblings.

As part of the unshaming process, I asked her to tell me more about her exhaustion. I expressed curiosity about it, not disapproval or the need to "fix" it. Her exhaustion might be overcome by doing less, and that approach could be helpful. That said, what is her system's intelligence trying to tell her? Her exhaustion is the doorway to this intelligence.

I also affirmed to Miriam that witnessing abuse and violence is an abusive, traumatic experience for the viewer. Sometimes people think,

"I watched my brother get hurt. He had it so bad. Luckily it didn't happen to me." That can be a dismissal of the person's own experience, which has a shaming effect. "People will think I don't have a right to these feelings because my brother was really hurt and I wasn't." It's still an injury.

Miriam had a gift for holding space for others, even though she saw it through a shamed, pathologized lens. It remains a strength to be trustworthy and caring in ways that help others. Being a witness may be a very important part of Miriam's life. It's not just an abuse pattern she feels she needs to get over; it may be the story of how she lives. Maybe it will become her path. I don't want to take that seed and turn it into something wrong with her. Right now, Miriam sees it as codependency. Labels like that one can be useful in the moment, as they can provide focus and useful reflection; but they're rarely useful over the long term. Within the conceptual framework of codependency, it's believed that people need to erect boundaries to stop being codependent. I'm a big believer in boundaries; I dedicated a whole chapter of this book to the topic. However, they're not always a solution.

Caring labeled as codependent can eliminate nuance. When I was a child, there were times when I took care of my mother. Should I do that in every relationship? No. But I can care about the world and do activist work. That kid's response was loving. It's not evidence of a psychological problem.

"You might need boundaries," I said to Miriam, "and that might be right for you, but it may not be the medicine you need."

"That is such an important thing for me to hear!" Miriam exclaimed. "I've never been able to do the boundary thing. It's too hard on my sensitive nature." She was clearly signaling here that her ideas of codependency had indeed been shaming.

"Yes," I replied, "if you're just putting up boundaries because you're trying to follow a rule, it can be so painful for you, as well as for others in your life."

The unshaming approach frees Miriam from the idea that she's terrible at boundaries. I began to unshame her actual experience, her exhaustion, by asking her about it. "Miriam, let's go into the exhaustion. You care for people, you witness people. I want to know more."

"My back hurts, I'm fuzzy in the head so I can't think properly, and I have a lot of feelings. Sadness, loneliness . . . there's a heavy weight on my shoulders."

What was great about all of that is that we were getting her experience without pathologizing. *Sadness, weight, fuzzy.* There was a possibility of self-intimacy not mediated by labels, e.g., "I'm a screwed-up person," "I'm codependent."

I said, "You said you can't think properly, and you're fuzzy in the head. Some people are being pulled away from their thinking capacity to be more in the body. 'I can't think straight.' And you talked about a weight on your shoulders. Feel the weight on your shoulders; imagine it's heavier. Give in to the weight on your shoulders. If your body was moved by that weight, how would it move?"

Miriam's shoulders and hands dropped. Her head tipped downward.

"Let the weight be there," I said. "What's it like?"

"I'm melting into the soil."

What a delicious statement. The intelligent message was coming through. Not all tiredness is melting into the soil. Someone else might feel it like floating on the ocean, burrowing into a sleeping bag, or wanting to dream, rather than becoming one with the world by melting into the soil.

I said, "Please continue to melt into the soil, and tell me what it's like."

"I'm feeling calm. It's pleasant, there's grass all around me. I can taste the grass."

"Let's follow that! This is your authentic, unique experience, your connection." I was in her world, and it felt good. I wasn't diagnosing or psychoanalyzing. I wanted to know Miriam's world, and I wanted *Miriam* to know her world.

We stayed with tasting the grass for a bit. Then she said, "Now as I'm there in my calmness, I feel like I'm beginning to wake up differently." She lifted her arms. "I'm stretching like when I first get up in the morning."

She was showing her healing path. *I feel heavy, I get tired, go down, taste grass, feel the calm, and wake up anew. Stretching out!* She was not one state, one problem. She was a flow, an unfolding process. Unshaming means witnessing the whole process with her, going further than she has gone before, finding the medicine and intelligence in it, and giving it back to her.

I said, "How high do your arms go?"

"All the way to the sky."

The unshaming process now took her to feeling the earth and sky, flowing energy into her. It was like a death and a rebirth.

I asked, "Are there any sounds that go with that?"

Miriam started singing a beautiful, wordless tune. We just hung out there. That was her song. I didn't have to know what that meant yet. I compassionately witnessed, which unshamed.

"That's your song," I said. "That's the sound of your voice, the tune you would live to when not in your old pattern. How amazing; that's you! Can you imagine that your path and purpose in life was to sing that song?"

"How do I live this?" Miriam asked. "That would be so great. What would that look like?"

"How would your life be different if you lived from that song?" I asked.

"I wouldn't be online for three hours a day."

First we connected with the essence of the soul of Miriam's life: the thread. It reminds me of William Stafford's poem "The Way It Is," which begins with the line "There's a thread you follow." This lifelong thread can be interpreted as your purpose or path, and "it is hard for others to see./While you hold it you can't get lost." The poem concludes with "You don't ever let go of the thread." Miriam never let go of her thread, but she did lose awareness of it due to the shaming response to her gift, and her belief that witnessing her siblings' abuse was not a harm worthy of compassionate acknowledgement. Miriam's song was her thread. It wasn't verbal. It was somatic. It resonated, moved the body, made her dance and vibrate in a certain way.

Miriam also said, "I would take more time to be alone." This is the path, the deepest self, which is far better than saying "I should do this, that, and the other thing." Instead she said, "I get to be something that's really precious to me." That's better than a rule to follow, especially a shaming one: "I need to carve out space to be alone and recharge." She did need to recharge, but the mind goes back to a shaming paradigm so quickly. Recharging is good, yet she needed something deeper than recharging. She needed herself: to feel the weight, melt and taste the grass, let the calmness enter, hear the song, and remember who she was. It wasn't a reframe; it was *her* frame. The language that defined her to herself came from her inner wisdom, not from a received set of limiting notions.

"When you're singing your song to the people who need your help, what does that look like?" I asked.

"Being there for people, dropping down, remembering my song."

Miriam will find her new pattern, a sustainable one. The initial pattern was set by the pathologizing viewpoint of how children respond to early trauma and abuse: they grow up to be codependent. This new pattern is about melting into the earth to rest and be restored. Early abuse and trauma stories have a mythic patterning that transcends the "You're screwed up" story. People respond in different ways. The mythic element holds a seed for the person's way of life that's precious. It's so important to refrain from pathologizing. Maya Angelou responded to her trauma by being silent. I responded by caring for my mother and fighting with my father, which gave me the courage to speak up against oppression. Someone else might become a filmmaker who tells complex family stories. The person's nature is responding. When we assign a diagnosis to the person, we miss the seed of their nature.

Unshaming Relationship Patterns

Substances don't need to be involved for people to find themselves in a pattern of painful relationships that don't meet their needs, such as feeling safe and nurtured. I once worked with a woman who said, "I'm getting into relationships with people who are manipulative and dishonest. They also involve me in complicated relationships with other people."

To work on this, we went back to her history. The relationships she was talking about echoed her abusive family relationships, which she had not fully processed. There's nothing shocking in that. No pathology, either. Everybody does that. Still, to learn more about her specific situation, I asked, "Why did you not confront the last person you had a relationship with? Go into your deepest feelings. Who is she, this person who didn't say anything in her last relationship?"

She replied, "I loved that person so much. I could never say something that could hurt them."

At this point, a practitioner in a conventional model might say, "That's not love. That's an abuse scene." But I took an unshaming approach and said, "A part of you loves so deeply and unconditionally. That's amazing, that you can love like that. Even at the cost of your own harm. What kind of love lives in you? That love is so precious, you need someone to protect it. Is there anything inside you that can protect and care for it?"

"This is the first time in years I haven't felt policed about the issue."

She no longer had to be at war with herself, thinking *I feel love for this person, but my therapist said it's not love; it's an abuse scene. What is wrong with me? Why does it feel like love? I would do anything for this person. What a sicko I am.* Instead, now she felt valued. Feeling valued can lead to her valuing her love and meeting the world with the viewpoint, "This is my love. I don't give it away very easily."

One of the reasons I learned this experience of love so deeply is that when I was a child, my older brother tied me up and injured me regularly. When he came to me with rope in his hands and said, "David, give me your hands," I gave him my hands, even though I knew he would hurt me. It took me a long time to realize that I wasn't stupid and it wasn't my fault. I just loved him so much. It took somebody seeing that and hearing me talk about the kind of love I had for my brother for me to realize that. I would have done anything for him. That capacity lives in me still. I'd do anything, although not necessarily for my brother. Because I went through this process, I'm a lot more empowered to love, but not to give myself to a scene that would injure me.

This capacity for love is a gift. Creating a context for that love that keeps one safe is a gift of the unshaming process.

Addiction and Social and Internalized Oppression

An examination of addictive patterns would be markedly incomplete without considering its intersections with social issues and internalized oppression. Many people look at someone in a pattern of addiction and ask, "Why doesn't the person just get their needs met without the substance?" Addiction is not just an individual problem. Humans need to feel powerful, capable, and effective, but systemic oppression in the form of widespread and often internalized bias blocks off the typical ways of accessing those feelings. For a person in that position—who will likely face heavier burdens and greater obstacles, and the resultant stress—a substance that gives them the feeling of power, detachment, intimacy, or even happiness will be much more attractive.

War veterans are one such group. They are part of a culture that doesn't know what to do with them or how to respond to the seriousness of their trauma. They're called heroes, and yet they often feel like anything but. I learned about this when I was consulted by a group of venture capitalists who wanted to do something about unhomed war veterans who were using drugs. They wanted to create a temporary housing complex that included a rehab clinic, and they asked me to help them determine how best to get people to come into this complex and off the streets.

As I was interviewing the veterans whom my consulting clients were trying to help, I found out that many of them were going to a fellow veteran's house to seek shelter and companionship. I was invited to visit, so I went over there. It was a modest home, and people were sleeping everywhere—on the floors, on the furniture.

I asked the host, "Why do people come to your house?"

"I'll show you," he answered. He took me to a room covered in war paraphernalia: maps on the walls, unloaded grenades. "This is where we come to talk," he said.

"What do you talk about?"

"They all want to talk about one thing: 'I need to retrieve myself. I'm still in this other world. What were we doing there, and why were we there?'"

This room and house provided them with community and a place to decompress and process with other people who had been there, who would not shame them or "other" them.

I went back to the funders and excitedly said, "I think this guy should be part of the understanding of how to help people.

They said, "He's not healed enough. He's still a mess. He's still living in the past. I wouldn't trust him to offer care to people."

"That's why you want him!" I said. "They're attracted to someone who's in the mess, who *knows* the mess. He takes them back to where they got lost."

"Thank you for your information," they said, and that was the end of my consultancy. They didn't follow my advice.

I had asked this: what's the experience of these people who are using substances? We know the prevalent opinions and theories: *They're self-medicating. They're escaping from reality.* But they were very much in the reality of people who went to another country, killed innocent people, almost died, saw friends die, were damaged, and came back to a newly unfamiliar home country that didn't know what to do with them. The intelligence is in the answer to "What are they escaping from? And where are they trying to escape to?" Then we need to honor that intelligence, not help people overcome it.

After the Vietnam war, people came home much more quickly than soldiers in previous wars, without any decompression. Many weren't ready to be around civilians. For example, I once worked with someone who had just come home from Iraq. He wasn't using drugs, but he was afraid to fall asleep in the house with his little kids. He said, "If they come wake me up, I might hurt them, because I'm not in control of my response." That's a heartbreaking situation to be in. Artists and film-makers tell stories of the horrors people went through, but most Americans don't integrate those narratives into everyday awareness. They don't witness it. In the final chapter, we'll lean into something really exciting and transformational: becoming witnesses not just to ourselves and our loved ones, but to the world.

Any time we work with addictive tendencies and impulses, we must inquire into the user's social identity as part of their story. If we don't bear witness to how their social story affects their needs and their difficulty in meeting those needs, we're inappropriately individualizing them, pathologizing them, and shaming them.

Addictive impulses, like all behavior, arise out of a person's deep experience. Jumping in with fixes and theories that pathologize people neglects to respect and care for those experiences. What are we really hungry for? What is our suffering really like? What kind of powers actually live in us? How does the dominant culture make it difficult for people to feed those hungers? These questions humanize us as individuals and as members of our communities.

Why is it so rare that someone says, "Oh, you're a smoker. What's it like when you inhale from your cigarette?" "What's it like when you have four glasses of wine?" "What's it like when you put that needle in your arm?" "What's it like when your partner gives you those things you want so badly?" These are fundamental questions; in a way, they're not even psychological questions. They're human questions. In fact, if we observed a plant or animal, we would bring that same mindset: "I wonder what makes that animal do that." We can treat each other with the awareness that we too are a part of nature; we too are naturally moved to feed ourselves the best way we know how. And when we do that, we uncover the depth of the person, the beauty of the person, the real blocks to their fulfillment. When we do that, we invite them into the sisterhood and brotherhood of community instead of marginalizing them. We unshame.

Connecting to the Hunger behind Your Addictive Tendency

1. Bring to mind a substance that you regularly reach for. If there is a substance that you want but don't reach for it, or no longer reach for it, use that substance for this exercise. It could be a relatively nonaddictive substance, like coffee or chocolate, or even a food that you really like to snack on.

2. Imagine that the substance is in front of you. Don't ingest it; feel, somatically, the desire to reach for it. Take a moment to connect with the sensory-grounded experience of your desire. This will help you get closer to your body experience.

3. Now imagine slowly taking the substance (e.g., drinking the wine, inhaling from the cigarette, eating the chips). As you do that, feel how satisfying it is. Stay with that part of your experience.

4. Keep imagining taking a bit of the substance and feeling the sensations of satisfaction. Enjoy the feeling and begin to make the sound of the pleasure you feel. This could be an *ahhh*, or *wowwww, yumm, mmmm, wooo*.

5. Now let's amplify that sound. Make the sound bigger, more exaggerated, extreme. Like a child playing, keep amplifying the sound. If there is any aspect or nuance of the sound that is unusual, make just that part of the sound by itself, and amplify it.

6. As you make the sound, see an image in your mind that goes with that sound. For example, you could see a choo-choo train, a raft on an ocean, a rocket lifting off.

7. In your regular life, how are you *not* like that image? Why not? What if the purpose of your life was to live like that image? How would you start your day? How would you relate to people? What activities would you stop or start?

8. How can you live even a little bit closer to that image?

CHAPTER 12

Becoming a Witness to the World

Readers, we've gone on quite a journey together. Thank you for reading along this far. You learned about the fundamentals of shame and unshaming and the steps of unshaming yourself. You've come to understand the importance of being attentive to inner and outer boundaries. We've taken on inner criticism, unshaming it by outing its messages to redefine the relationship as conscious and subjective. We've also addressed the intimate relationship between internalized criticism and societal systems of oppression. We've spent time examining how privileged people and institutions shame people who are from minoritized groups, and we've discussed how to use our own privilege to unshame in accordance with our values.

We've applied unshaming practices to the physical body, addressing how our bodies are often shamed due to appearance, incompatibility with systemic medical norms, and the symptoms of physical illness. And just as we live in a culture that prizes physical health and perceives illness as a moral failing, this same culture prizes happiness and equanimity, and it shames feelings that disturb that imperative, such as anger, depression, jealousy, and anxiety. We've unshamed those "disturbing" feelings to find the wisdom and medicine hidden within them. We've explored how unshaming experiences of abuse and trauma can redefine our relationships with ourselves and others, and it can create freedom where we've felt trapped and victimized—often for our whole lives, until now—while also shifting our expectations of healing within a short time frame. In the previous chapter, we used an unshaming lens to interrogate attitudes about addictive patterns of dependency and codependency.

Throughout this process, we've seen time and time again the interweaving of these topics on shame and unshaming with regard to bodies, minds, and society. To name just a few examples, trauma can manifest as physical symptoms and anger; internalized criticism is almost always connected to social issues; holding inner boundaries involves a reckoning with the voice of inner criticism; and body shame is exacerbated, if not entirely generated, by social issues like sexism. The good news is that tugging on one string in a shame tapestry changes the whole tableau. Unshaming a body issue or physical symptom will transform your internalized shaming witness and your perspective on oppressive belief systems and social issues. Considering the difference between abuse and trauma will arm you with the knowledge to unshame abuse before it becomes a source of trauma. This skill also bestows the wisdom to identify and engage with the trauma that almost always propels addictive patterns.

Just as engaging with one unshaming topic reconstitutes the tableau of your life, unshaming oneself is interwoven with becoming an unshaming witness to the world. When you're in unshaming mode, it's like a toggle switch: all on or all off. Maintaining your personal unshaming process is incompatible with shaming others or being indifferent to shaming going on around you. The unshaming process brings on an invitation to eldership. Everything in this book connects and leads up to becoming a witness for the world. That doesn't mean you need to turn into an unshaming superhero, complete with a cape emblazoned with the letter *U*. That might lead to being intrusive or getting caught up in a savior persona, not to mention that it would be unsustainable. You simply need to look at the world through unshaming eyes.

How do we do this? Whenever a "problem" or conflict presents itself, a person with an unshaming perspective holds space for and is curious about bringing forward and noticing something good, intelligent, and useful. It means that we look at our difficulties and sufferings not by asking "What's wrong? What happened?" but rather "What's my experience? What's right about it? What intelligence lives in me?"

This can apply to what we call mistakes and errors, as well as what we call illness, difficult feelings, ongoing conflicts, and more.

"What intelligence is moving me? What am I trying to express through this experience?" Not "What's wrong with me?" or "How do I make this go away?" but "What lives in me that isn't free to live fully in the world?" Through unshaming, people build a deeper, more self-loving relationship with themselves despite their imperfections. *Imperfect* almost always means "I don't fit well enough in a certain category." Almost all the time, those categories are artificial, stemming from oppressive, limiting belief systems.

As someone who has developed a nuanced, blossoming proficiency in unshaming, you now have the metaconsciousness to intercede, or at the very least to recognize when someone makes a shaming comment in your presence, whether at home, online, at work, or at social gatherings. You'll notice shaming happening on news channels, on TV shows, in books, and in movies; you'll hear it on the radio and perhaps from the pulpit, and you'll see it on someone's face in the form of a disapproving look. You'll see it in geopolitics, local school board meetings, legal proceedings, stump speeches, and bills proposed by Congress. You can't unsee through unshaming, unshamed eyes.

Being an unshaming witness to the world doesn't take anything away from you. It deepens your investment in your own unshaming process. It reminds you to continue to unshame yourself. It's an ongoing awareness that not making judgments and forming opinions about challenges and problems *is* a powerful intervention.

What does the world mean? It can be as intimate as your inner circle, as vast as the globe.

Expanding the Scope of Unshaming

How can we be unshamers in more local ways? One way is by telling unshaming stories, just as Michelle Obama shared about the micro-aggression of a white woman who didn't register her and her daughters' presence cutting in line in front of them. Although it happened in Washington, DC, and she shared about it on her podcast, it resonated throughout American culture because this culture is permeated by an unconscious racial caste system. She used her position of privilege as the former First Lady to help others in a context of power differences. She spoke truth to power as someone who is simultaneously powerful and a member of a disenfranchised group.

Another kind of unshaming storytelling is to tell our own abuse and trauma stories. I have tried to do this throughout the book, in part to unshame your experience if you had an abusive older sibling like I did, or if you repeatedly gave someone more chances to hurt you, as I did with my brother, because I loved him. My intention was to help readers unshame their own loyalty and love, to honor that love while unshaming its constancy, and to find other avenues for your love and constancy to express themselves safely.

It's important not to confuse this kind of storytelling with "trauma dumping": unsolicited sharing of traumatizing experiences without asking permission, in search of the release that a therapy session might provide with people who have not signed up for this kind of listening and may be triggered by these revelations. Another type of storytelling that's contrary to unshaming is trauma one-upmanship: "You think your brother tying you up and shocking you was bad? Wait until you hear about what *I* went through." Stay present to what the person is sharing, instead of thinking ahead to how you will demonstrate knowledge and experience by responding with a story of your own.

Now is an apt time to revisit the three foundational unshaming principles I shared in chapter 1: **respect**, **relating**, and **radical belief**. My hope is that these principles will land differently now that you have a different vantage point as someone who is deeply informed about unshaming.

Respect means inquiring further and more deeply into a person's actual experience. When we do this, the person finds themself in the role of a subject, not an object, a pathology, or something to fix, which undermines shame's impact and increases their sense of authentic selfhood.

Relating is when we respond compassionately and with empathy to what a person shares about their experience: how they reacted to being hurt, neglected, or disrespected, which can lead to a sense of themself as *not mattering*. The feeling of mattering can be restored when a person, like you, inquires with compassion and empathy about the impact of the injury.

Radical belief is when we believe a person and believe *in* them. As you've seen in the sessions and stories throughout the previous eleven chapters, when we make our inquiry with this belief, people arrive at insights and enlightenments. Not only does this tell us which direction their healing will take, but it restores their inner authority and their trust in themselves, so they can stop projecting their authority outward on others, as shame has led them to do in the past.

When another person tells us who they are, we're not the experts at healing that person. It's a phenomenal gift to give: "I'm going to believe in who you are until we both get to know you, until the seed of your difficulties flowers and ignites us with the wisdom that only you carry for yourself and the world, until the genie hidden in the bottle of your troubles is released, fulfilling your greatest wish—to live the life that is meant for you."

Witnessing Someone Else's Inner Critic

You might be wondering, "How do I begin? And isn't this a lot to take on?" These are very good questions. Unshaming actions can be very small, yet impactful. And it's fine to let opportunities go by instead of forcing anything. A starting place could be witnessing people around you when they put themselves down: "I'm such a loser." "I look like I got dressed with the lights off." "I'm the king of misplacing my keys." "My hair looks stupid." "I'm always procrastinating." "I'm kryptonite to men." "I'm such a chicken." These are glimpses of their inner critics. When we don't witness those voices of self-annihilation, that can foster shame.

In a situation like that, I might say something like, "Ouch. That seems harsh."

"Well, I clearly suck at keeping track of things."

"What's it like to not keep track of things? How does it feel?"

Opening up this conversation shows that the other person matters to you and that you're curious about what it's like to be them. This is unshaming. It also outs their inner critic so they can fully notice it, because inner critics usually go unnoticed or come across as less harsh on the inside. When this happens, they become aware of themselves as subjects taking the measure of inner criticism, rather than as objects of that criticism, and they begin to know their own responses to being put down.

Unshaming in Relationships

Relationships are a good place to practice unshaming, because relationships bring up inner experiences that might not otherwise surface. Some of those experiences will be hard, but the good news is that you can apply compassionate curiosity to these experiences and be attentive to what's it like to be in that relationship.

As you know by now, unshaming always needs a compassionate witness. When an argument is happening in an unshaming context, that situation needs a witness, too. If I'm working as a counselor with a couple, I'm that witness. When two people are navigating a conflict on their own, at least one of them needs to have the capacity to witness the conflict and care about the relationship and both people. If and when neither has capacity to witness the conflict, the conflict almost never goes well, leaving an aftermath of injury instead of healing and intimacy.

There was a period when Lisa and I were having a hard time in our marriage, and we would go to our marriage counselor to work on our relationship. In session, we'd argue without Lisa or I playing a witnessing role. After observing us, Salome, our therapist, said, "Don't continue to have conflict on your own, outside of session. Nobody's home; you won't get anywhere." By *nobody* she meant that neither of our inner witnesses was present. Nobody was there to provide a protective, caring presence. "If you start to argue when I'm not around, you should both walk away until someone's at home, because right now, no one's there to witness what's going on."

If I can't pay attention to you and me both, and neither can you, it's not going to go anywhere. Conflicts need a witness. Certain kinds of healing could result if both people can be witnessed. Otherwise, indications of the wisdom and the medicine will not be noticed or recognized with curiosity and welcome. Listening is the other side of being direct.

It can be hard to bring up an issue, but sitting on it can lead to the issue coming out sideways in unconscious and often hurtful manifestations. A statement like "I want to share something that's bothering me because I care about our relationship" shows protectiveness of the relationship, and advocacy and responsibility for it. Awareness is perhaps the best way to protect both people. Relatedly, another powerful step is to own your feelings while bringing yourself into relationship with your inner compassionate witness. When my wife and I are having a tense conversation, I say to Lisa, "I'm aware that I'm angry." This takes some pressure off that feeling for me. She knows that I'm witnessing myself. I'm not unconscious about my emotional state. That's a safer situation than waiting for someone to boil over.

Sometimes the same issue comes up over and over for you in different relationships, as a pattern. Perhaps it's jealousy or feeling like you're not a priority. That's when life is saying, "Take some time with that experience." It's a kind of mirror. That's something that you are most likely carrying around with you, and it wants to be witnessed and to release its medicine or wise message. It'll keep coming up until it's expressed.

How does shame operate in relationship conflicts? When a person shames their disturbing feelings about an issue, or even their position on an issue, they cannot be direct about what's bothering them because they don't have a direct connection to it themselves. As we grew up we learned to put away our feelings, sharpness, and intelligence when our parents and other adults shamed our truth by saying things like: "If you don't have something nice to say, don't say anything at all." "Stop whining." "That's not polite." "Don't contradict me." This leads us to be out of touch with our truth and what's happening for us.

Anger and hurt need to be unshamed to unshame conflicts. Many of us grew up being shamed for feeling anger with statements like "Calm down," "Don't raise your voice," "That's disrespectful," and being shamed for feeling hurt with statements like "Don't be so sensitive," "Don't be a sissy," "You're too thin-skinned," and "Sticks and stones . . ."

As a man, I'm told by the dominant culture that I'm not supposed to say I'm hurt. To show hurt is a vulnerable thing. It's also a powerful and valuable thing. I'm also not supposed to be angry, because male anger is so often thought of as animalistic, unsophisticated, or dangerous—which it often is, given the statistics on intimate partner violence. Yet I know that every human gets hurt, and being a man doesn't make me immune. Shamed hurt and shamed anger often lead to depression, alienation, assault, addictive patterns, breakups, and other unwanted outcomes. They can also foster a communication style comprising mixed messages, patronizing statements, passive-aggressive comments, and sarcasm. These are modes of communication that have more than one message in their statements: a surface message, and something else coming through. That "something else" is not being clearly witnessed because it's veiled in shame.

Usually, when I bring up an issue to Lisa, I say, "I need x," or "I got hurt when . . ." But if I make quips or barbed comments, or I start to lay a guilt trip on her, that's a big sign that something is bothering me that I'm not fully witnessing. I need to engage, with curiosity, in a compassionate inquiry about that aspect of my statement that doesn't feel free to be expressed or show up.

Here's an example that you'll see bears some resemblance to my previous mention of "Martinizing." I used to inquire about Lisa's purchases, often orienting toward the costs. "Ah, another box from Amazon," I would say with a little elbow in my teasing.

She felt it. "Are you going to take me on a guilt trip?" she would respond, alerting me to my communication. Making an unshaming inquiry led me to share my insecurity around money and my own need to be more generous with myself.

Unshaming in Families

As we've established, shame is most often internalized during childhood. Statements like "What's wrong with you?" "Just get over it." "Why can't you be more like your sister?" "I've told you a million times . . ." "Don't be angry/hurt/upset." "They didn't mean it." "You should know better," and most explicitly, "Shame on you," are common. Although many parents go to great lengths to become more conscious of how to raise their children sensitively and compassionately, there are still many parents out there—including mindful parents, in exasperated moments—telling their children not to talk back (which carries the message "Your voice doesn't count"), not to contradict (which carries the message "The fact that you're right is not as important as protecting our power imbalance"), not to make excuses (which carries the message "Your inner and outer experiences, your subjectivity, your story are not valid or pertinent"), and so on.

There are also hierarchies in many families that disadvantage people with different or othered qualities. A queer or trans sibling may not be treated with as much approval as a gender-conforming, straight-identified sibling. Daughters are expected to do a larger share of house chores and emotional labor than sons, and often to be more responsible.

Another kind of shaming occurs when someone in the family is labeled "the problem child" or the scapegoat. This person becomes the family repository of blame, while others are judged far less harshly for doing similar or even worse things. A person in this role often has an especially strong internalized critic, because it reflects their collective family's beliefs.

This scapegoat overlaps with the figure of a family member who is physically or mentally ill. That person can become the "identified patient," described in family systems theory as the person who brings a family to the point of needing therapy. The premise here is "He's the problem, and we are the victims. He's the one that needs help; we're all okay." However, family systems theory claims that that person's problem or behavior disguises other problematic patterns and dynamics within the family. It's important to unshame the identified patient by not pathologizing them and to see the whole family as playing roles in the presenting unrest.

As we've discussed, perhaps the greatest contributor to creating generations of shame is not witnessing when various forms of abuse occur, denying their occurrence, telling victims they're making things up, or blaming them for provoking abusive treatment. When abuse of any kind is not witnessed, or is overtly denied or gaslit, shame is the result. When people come out with their stories, family members need to take it seriously, even if the stories are generations old.

Punishment that is intended or designed to inflict pain carries the message "You should hurt. You should be suffering," and it always shames. A younger person getting this message from an early age will believe, "I deserve to be in pain. I deserve to suffer. I deserve to get in a car accident, to fall ill, to be beaten up." Those ideas lead people to think they don't matter and that something is wrong with them as people. They believe, "I deserve pain and suffering for what I've done."

Many parents believe punishment is necessary to raise a child who is community-minded, responsible, and law-abiding. Tragically, it is not. It leads people to be out of touch with themselves—and being out of touch with themselves doesn't help them or their communities. As a person parenting unshamingly, cultivate and express curiosity about why your child is doing things that bring up ideas of punishment. What is the unnoticed, concealed medicine and wisdom in their actions? As I mentioned earlier, be authentic and honest about their actions' impact on you.

Evidence is all around us of people who think they deserve to suffer because they've done something that they view as bad or unethical. I've heard so many clients say, "I know I'm sick because I've committed this misdeed." A mentality inside people that causes them to feel like they deserve to have bad things happen to them is vicious and self-annihilating. Lots of people treat their physical symptoms that way; they feel like karma has led them to have a painful, difficult life.

Governments also promote this shaming idea. In the 1980s, the government's response to AIDS and HIV was to ignore the ongoing tragedy of illness and death, framing it as a "gay plague" visited upon people whom the culture at large deemed to be deviant and immoral: "They had it coming."

Sometimes public figures make statements that reveal the depth of disconnection and dehumanization they take for granted. During Hurricane Katrina, President George W. Bush's mother Barbara Bush said, "so many of the people in the [Astrodome] arena here, you know, were underprivileged anyway, so this is working very well for them." They had lost their homes and all of their belongings: photo albums, prized mementoes, clothes, documentation, everything. She was not a compassionate witness; she was shaming, not unshaming. Unshaming requires becoming more sensitive to what people are going through. People living in poverty are shamed by attitudes claiming that they're poor because they're lazy, unmotivated, or irresponsible. Immigrant success stories are often weaponized to blame and shame immigrant folks who are contending with more difficult circumstances.

That mindset and culture that believe pain should be inflicted as punishment are rather insidious. Punishment to inflict pain teaches people that they don't matter, and when this happens, they lose touch with their own empathy and goals, and what they care about in life. How does this benefit a culture? It disincentivizes civic involvement, voting, and advocating for ourselves and our communities. A person out of touch with their own empathy and goals will not be motivated or energized to change an unjust status quo, to organize, to notice their own privilege and identify ways to be an ally. Inflicting pain as punishment benefits a capitalistic culture by making people feel like they need to buy things and programs to fix themselves and chase acceptability.

Unshaming Parents' Feelings

I imagine parent readers are extra attentive right now about how to stop shaming their children and also to unshame them if necessary. I support that! But first, parents need to make sure they're unshaming their own reactions to their children.

If you're ashamed of feeling anger as a parent, go someplace where you can feel and move the anger freely so you aren't making the act of feeling angry a foe to you, or making your anger a reason to devalue yourself: "I'm bad for getting angry." Once you get to know your anger and the unexpressed needs behind it, you can reengage with it more powerfully, with this intention: "I know what that anger is like. I know what it's asking me to change in my life, to feed in myself. I won't let it loose on my kid, but I might need a dose of it to build an authentic relationship."

If you're ashamed of feeling ill, leading you to feel like a bad parent, share that with someone who can unshame your symptoms so you can find the meaning and message in them and learn what kind of unique parent you are so that inner criticism doesn't dominate your sense of self.

It's also vital to unshame your forbidden thoughts. Maybe you sometimes think, "I hate being a parent. Why did I want this? I wish I'd made a different decision." These are taboo thoughts in American culture, but they are also understandable thoughts that, unshamed, would reveal their wisdom and medicine. What do you miss about not being a parent? Freedom, simplicity, predictability, being spontaneous, being seen as an individual, having a stronger sense of identity, more flexibility to pursue your personal goals . . . there are so many possibilities. What do you miss the most? How can you bring those qualities into your life in ways that don't negatively impact your child? Once you've done this rewarding work, you'll be ready to reengage with parenting your children while guided by unshaming principles.

I've learned through working with parents that a parent's genuine reactions in relationship to their children are almost always more useful than a rote punishment like "This is the consequence you'll have to suffer for what you've done."

I once worked with parents who had a child who was hitting them. And it hurt! They didn't want to say anything to their child about it because they didn't want the child to feel bad. Sharing your real experience of how they're hurting you is better for the relationship: "That hurts me. Ouch. That makes me angry." Kids do really well when there's some level of authenticity in the relationship. It builds trust. When a parent takes on the persona of playing a "parent role" it doesn't land, because it feels performative and false.

For example, instead of saying, "You've been bad," "You'll have to be punished," "Say you're sorry," "Only dogs stay mad," you can say, "That's not okay with me," "I don't want to be around you when you treat me that way," "Stop; I won't put up with that," "You hurt me/someone." If there's time and space, you can ask questions like, "Let's learn about your anger," "What happens when you hurt people?" or simply "What's been going on lately?"

Unshaming in Community Groups

What does unshaming look like in action in your local community? I once attended a Portland town hall meeting planned in response to a police officer's killing of an unarmed Black woman. Black community members and police officers agreed to meet. I was there to support the Black community and to protest the systemic murder of Black people by police. As I listened to the police officers talk about their jobs, I learned a great deal about how difficult their jobs are, having to make momentary decisions, often under duress. This is not an excuse or an explanation about "why" they abuse their power; it simply opens the door to a dialogue where people's experiences can be shared. Of course, as highlighted in the chapter on abuse, we must always witness power differences, in this case the greater power held by police officers.

One of the things that came out of that meeting is that the police should not be the most prominent group that is engaged in witnessing community members. I'm not a police officer, but if I think you're drunk, I shouldn't let you drive. If I decide not to step up and make sure you get home safely and don't hurt anyone else along the way, that job will then be left to a person with a gun who has permission to shoot to kill. And if police officers know that someone holds racial bias and animus, they should bear witness to that rather than leaving it to victims of abuse to make that declaration. Unshaming often highlights how we can all be witnesses who have a responsibility to do what is best for the community as well as for our friends and family members. In a real way, the deepest resolutions involve all of us, beyond the blame and accountability of the polarized sides.

Unshaming from Afar

Social media, for all its ills, allows us, under the right circumstances, to compassionately witness things happening on the other side of the globe. I'm not talking about falling for divisive, fake content, but seeking out accurate sources. The awareness you gain fights the human impulse to gray out, disbelieve, or dismiss distant situations as irrelevant. For instance, when something happens in Gaza, the people affected directly can share their experiences with me. Dialoguing in real time with people from another part of the world is an incredible thing. I'm not just reading the *New York Times* or watching the news. Subjects are sharing their experiences—not theories and opinions—in a specific place and time.

I recently met with a Palestinian woman activist on Zoom after making her acquaintance on Instagram. She held up her arm to show how she had written her name in ink on her arm, in solidarity with the children who write their names on their limbs so their bodies can be identified if they die in a bombing. What she shared by raising her arm was grounded in an experience that I witnessed. It broke my heart; I wept as she explained it to me. That's not an opinion; it's a real experience. My body has now integrated a compassionate feeling, and she feels that she matters to me, taking us both beyond a polarized debate and the dehumanizing attitudes that people have for others that only represent an idea.

Usually, when any world disturbance occurs, it is difficult to witness, because people's understanding and experience become polarized almost instantly. There are different levels of being a witness to the world. A lot of people express their witnessing by taking sides: "I'm standing with *these* people and against *those* people." That's super important, especially when there are great power differences, as we have seen. But the world also needs people who can witness conflict.

Witnessing conflict is different from being on a side. It's not about being on *both* sides; it's about being on *neither* side. It has the intention, "I'm going to help make space for a conflict." Sometimes a conflict can find resolutions that are unexpected.

After Hamas attacked Israel on October 7, 2023, killing over a thousand people and taking hundreds of hostages, Israel started bombing Gaza, which prompted a woman from Spain to write to me. She wrote about how Spain had persecuted, tortured, banished, stolen from, and killed Jews during the Spanish Inquisition. This pained her, and she wanted to share it with me. She clearly saw that the current event was a moment in a longer history—she knew in her heart that even her own Spanish history had played a role in creating the horror we were experiencing now—and that trauma begets trauma over years and centuries. This wasn't about Spain apologizing to Jewish people, but I felt a little medicine come in as I read her words. In a way, she bore witness to the legitimacy and validity of Jewish experience while also not using it as the basis for a stance against Palestinians. Her deep empathy and vision created a wider context, allowing me too to feel part of this larger story, beyond the horror of this moment in history.

On social media, I witness injustice, violence, and polarization through a diverse group of connections with people of all ages from all around the world. It's an amazing education, kind of like being at a university. Yes, unshaming the world requires ongoing learning, and social media is not necessary for that. You can educate yourself by expanding beyond what is familiar to you. Reading books and essays, watching documentaries and films that are foreign to you, listening to music from all over the world, writing, telling stories—all of these practices make space for people who feel and think differently from you and your dominant culture.

Years ago, a woman who attended one of my talks confronted me in front of the audience about how I was talking about body shame. She, an expert due to her lived experience, was asking me to witness how I, a thin white man, was having a hurtful impact on her and likely others.

"It's hard for me to hear you talk about this," she said.

I encouraged her to tell me more, expressing curiosity about her experience.

"You spoke about research and obesity. The word 'obesity' is a painful word for me to hear. You connected it to addictions, but I'm not an addict. You talked about gaining weight after a sexual assault. Not every fat woman has been raped." She continued with more examples.

I was honored that she had chosen to share her experience with me. "You brought up a lot of good issues," I said, and I read back to her the notes I'd taken on what she'd said.

She started weeping, in a good way. It moved her so much to be compassionately witnessed. And yet even though I had affirmed her right to share her wisdom with me, doing what she had done had almost always led to hurtful retribution, so she expressed regret afterward. "I said too much," she said. "I shouldn't have done that."

I said, "What you said had force, but that's okay! Now I want to say something to you that's strong. It's not okay with me that you take it all back and say you shouldn't have said those things. By speaking up the way you did, you educated me and the whole group. I call that a level of enlightenment; don't shame that."

New Eyes

What does it mean to stop shaming oneself? We stop seeing our lack of sleep as only something to fix; we stop treating our feelings as problems; we stop seeing our symptoms as only indicators of illness; we stop correcting, fixing, trying to heal away all that disturbs us. Instead we listen for the deep intelligence embedded in our experience, the seed waiting to flower. We form a relationship with ourselves based on love, not self-annihilation, and as such we engage with the world knowing that something is very right about who we are, from a place where our true selves are necessary to the unfolding of life around us.

Someone once asked the Vietnamese Buddhist monk and peace activist Thích Nhất Hạnh this question: "Do countries have karma like people?"

He answered that they do.

The questioner asked, "What was Vietnam's karma?"

"The Vietnam War didn't happen to Vietnam," the monk replied. "It happened to everyone."

Thích Nhất Hạnh's spiritual genius rendered a powerful unshaming. First, he unshamed a distorted view of karma by distinguishing it from the notion that people deserve to be punished. Second, he witnessed our interconnection, what he called our "interbeing," sending the message that we all matter and that no person or group should be looked at as if something is wrong with them. That's a different kind of witness, one who understands what a myth separation is; one who doesn't pathologize, who notices potential criticism and social bigotry, who treats us all as important. We're interwoven. Don't leave yourself out. If you do, you'll hurt everybody, including yourself. No one was shamed. All present were healed. That is my wish for you, me, and our world.

Index

U

T

About the Author

David Bedrick, JD, PW Dipl, grew up in a family marked by violence. While his father's brutality was physical and verbal, his mother's denial and gaslighting had its own covert power. This formative context introduced David early to the etiology of shame and instilled an urge to unshame.

David pursued his passion by studying family and social dynamics at the University of Minnesota's program in organizational psychology. For twelve years, he consulted with dozens of organizations before pursuing clinical training at the Process Work Institute (PWI), an offshoot of the Jung Institute. He was on the faculty of PWI, and its sister school in Warsaw, Poland, where he taught about the link between the body, psyche, and shame.

David spent thirty years studying Jungian psychology, nighttime dreams, and conflict resolution focused on social justice. He continued that pursuit in law school, graduating at the top of his class and helping women and children navigate domestic conflict. He was recognized for offering the highest level of pro bono service in Oregon.

David also spent eight years on the faculty of the University of Phoenix, teaching a range of courses in psychology (from Clinical Interviewing to Addictions and Diversity) and philosophy (Critical Thinking and Ethics). David began his research there on gender and body shame—his findings revealed that shame and self-hatred not only motivated many women to diet, but also prevented them from succeeding. His research led to his 2020 book, *You Can't Judge a Body by Its Cover,* about which *Publishers Weekly* wrote, "Bedrick celebrates the deep wisdom held in . . . hearts, minds, and bodies of women in this powerful collection of profiles."

He also wrote the book *Talking Back to Dr. Phil*, which addressed body shame, family violence, and issues of addiction and power, in 2013, and in 2017 *Revisioning Activism*, a collection of essays that examined psychology's role in social activism.

To learn more about David, visit his website at www.davidbedrick.com, where you can get access to his free TV episodes on unshaming, links to eighty essays published by *Psychology Today,* or purchase programs on addictions, chronic symptoms, abuse and trauma, or unshaming.

About
North Atlantic Books

North Atlantic Books (NAB) is an independent, nonprofit publisher committed to a bold exploration of the relationships between mind, body, spirit, and nature. Founded in 1974, NAB aims to nurture a holistic view of the arts, sciences, humanities, and healing. To make a donation or to learn more about our books, authors, events, and newsletter, please visit www.northatlanticbooks.com.